Rules of Evidence: A Practical Approach

Doug Cochran

Michael Gulycz

Mary Ann Kelly

2008
EMOND MONTGOMERY PUBLICATIONS
TORONTO, CANADA

Emond Montgomery Publications Limited
60 Shaftesbury Avenue
Toronto ON M4T 1A3
http://www.emp.ca/highered

Printed in Canada.
Reprinted September 2013.

We acknowledge the financial support of the Government of Canada through the Canada Book Fund for our publishing activities.

The events and characters depicted in this book are fictitious. Any similarity to actual persons, living or dead, is purely coincidental.

Acquisitions and developmental editor: Peggy Buchan
Marketing manager: Christine Davidson
Director, sales and marketing, higher education: Kevin Smulan
Copy editors: Jim Lyons and David Handelsman
Proofreader: Debbie Gervais
Typesetter: Nancy Ennis
Indexer: Paula Pike
Cover designer: John Vegter

Library and Archives Canada Cataloguing in Publication

Cochran, Doug, 1950-
    Rules of evidence : a practical approach / Doug Cochran, Mary Ann Kelly, Michael Gulycz.

Includes index.
ISBN 978-1-55239-163-1

    1. Evidence (Law)—Canada.   I. Kelly, Mary Ann, 1948-
II. Gulycz, Michael, 1958-   III. Title.

KE8440.C62 2008   347.71'06   C2007-904005-5
KF8935.ZA2C62 2008

To Liz, who always gives me the benefit of a reasonable doubt.
—Doug Cochran

For Veronica, who has always encouraged and supported me.
—Mike Gulycz

To my students at Seneca College, who remind me that teaching
is also a learning experience.

—Mary Ann Kelly

Contents

PART I

The Basic Concepts and Fundamental Principles

CHAPTER 1

Who's Who in the Courtroom

CHAPTER OBJECTIVES

After completing this chapter you should be able to:

- Understand the adversarial system and how evidence fits into it.
- Understand the roles of the judge and jury and the division of their responsibilities.
- Understand the function of the voir dire and the charge to the jury in the trial process.
- Identify the evidentiary issues that may arise on appeals.
- Distinguish the use of evidence in criminal and civil cases from the use of evidence in alternative dispute resolution mechanisms and military justice proceedings.

OVERVIEW OF THE CRIMINAL AND CIVIL LITIGATION PROCESSES

The criminal and civil litigation processes are similar in a number of respects. Each starts with a specific court document commencing the action. In a criminal trial, the Crown prosecutor lays an information, which outlines the offences the person charged has allegedly committed. In a civil process, the person starting the case, usually called the plaintiff, issues a document required by the rules of court. (The name of this document may differ from province to province, from court level to court level, or from type of civil proceeding to type of civil proceeding. It is often called a writ or a statement of claim.) In this document, the plaintiff outlines the wrong that she feels was done to her by the opposite party, usually called the defendant, and sets out how she is asking the court to correct that wrong. In both criminal and civil matters, there are various pre-trial steps that are taken. Most often these steps are designed to ensure that there will be a fair hearing of the issues and that parties have an opportunity to discover the evidence that is available both for and against their position, as well as to explore alternatives to a full trial on the issues.

On television and in the movies, court cases are often won when one side surprises the other with a major witness or a major piece of documentary or physical evidence right in the courtroom. While this might make for good drama, it does not reflect the real-life litigation process in Canadian courts. In both criminal and civil cases, the parties are required to share evidence before the trial begins. The sharing of evidence—called disclosure in the criminal process and discovery in the civil—is designed to ensure fairness, particularly in relation to a person accused of a crime. In a criminal case, the defendant need not disclose evidence to the Crown but the Crown must disclose its evidence to the accused. In a civil case, both sides must produce their evidence to the opposing party before a trial can even be scheduled.

The sharing of evidence is also designed to streamline the trial process and, where possible, avoid trial entirely by permitting all parties to evaluate what their chances might be in a trial. By being able to assess the case the opposing side will present in court, each party can weigh the advantages and disadvantages of continuing on a litigious path. In a criminal matter, after reviewing all of the Crown's evidence against him, an accused may want to offer a guilty plea if the Crown is willing to reduce the charge or agree to a lesser sentence in exchange. This is commonly referred to as a plea bargain or a plea arrangement and is a central process in the criminal justice system. In a civil matter, settlement may be a safer and more economical route than the very expensive and uncertain road of litigation.

The following chart compares and contrasts all of the steps involved in the criminal and civil litigation processes.

Litigation Process Chart

Criminal	Civil
Process commenced by an information.	Process commenced by a specified court document, often called a writ or statement of claim.
Pre-trial process to ensure full disclosure to the accused of the Crown's case.	Pre-trial process to ensure that each side has full opportunity to discover the evidence that the other side has at its disposal.
Selection of mode of trial. (For most serious offences, the accused can choose trial by judge alone or trial by judge and jury.)	Selection of mode of trial. (In the superior civil court in the provinces, either party usually can choose trial by judge or trial by judge and jury.)
Trial commences with the Crown presenting evidence first, usually by having its first witness testify. The Crown's questioning of its witnesses is known as direct examination or examination-in-chief. The defendant then has an opportunity to ask questions or "cross-examine" the witnesses.	Trial commences with the plaintiff presenting evidence first, usually by having its first witness testify. The plaintiff's questioning of its witnesses is known as direct examination or as examination-in-chief. The defendant then has an opportunity to ask questions or "cross-examine" the witnesses.

Criminal	Civil
Evidentiary issues that arise before or during the trial may be dealt with in a voir dire.	Evidentiary issues that arise before the trial may be dealt with in pre-trial motions, but evidentiary issues may arise during the course of the trial as well and are dealt with as they arise.
The Crown continues to call evidence until it has presented all of its evidence. The Crown then closes its case.	The plaintiff continues to call evidence until she has presented all of her evidence. The plaintiff then closes her case.
If the accused believes that the Crown has not met its burden of proof (that is, proof beyond a reasonable doubt), the accused may decide not to call any evidence but to make an application to the judge for a directed verdict of acquittal. If the application is successful, the accused will be formally acquitted of the charges against him.	If the defendant believes that the plaintiff has not met her burden of proof (that is, proof on the balance of probabilities), he may decide not to call any evidence but to bring a motion for non-suit and argue that the case against him has not been made out and there is nothing to answer or defend against. If the motion is successful, the case will be dismissed.
The defendant who chooses to present evidence then calls his first witness and so on until he has presented all of his evidence.	The defendant calls his first witness and so on until he has presented all of his evidence.
Once the Crown and the defendant have presented their evidence, the Crown may be entitled to call reply or rebuttal evidence.	Once the plaintiff and the defendant have presented their evidence, the plaintiff may have an opportunity to call reply or rebuttal evidence.
Both the Crown and the defendant now have a chance to argue their case or to state to the trier of fact (judge or jury, if there is one) why they should "find" in their favour (that is, give them what they are asking for). It is at this stage that counsel argue that the evidence that has been presented supports the outcome they are seeking. This stage of the proceedings is called submissions.	Both the plaintiff and the defendant now have a chance to argue their case to the trier of fact (judge or jury, if there is one) showing why they should "find" in their favour (that is, give them what they are asking for). It is at this stage that counsel argue that the evidence that has been presented supports the outcome they are seeking. This stage of the proceedings is called submissions.
The trier of fact (judge or jury, if there is one) then considers the evidence and submissions and makes a decision (renders a verdict). This involves a finding that the accused is guilty or not guilty of the offence he is charged with. If the accused is found not guilty, the judge discharges the accused, who is then free to go on with his life. If the accused is found guilty, the judge initiates the sentencing process.	The trier of fact (judge or jury, if there is one) then considers the evidence and submissions and makes a decision. This involves a determination of liability (is the plaintiff right that the defendant has wronged her?). If the defendant is found liable, the trier of fact awards compensation to the plaintiff in a set amount of dollars.

ADVERSARIAL SYSTEM

In Canada, as in most other countries whose legal system is based on the British common-law system, the judicial process is adversarial. In theory, each party in the **adversarial system** is represented by a skilled advocate (known as counsel), knowledgeable in the law, who presents the party's case in the best possible light, within the permitted ethical rules. The case is presented before an impartial, unbiased judge who remains relatively passive during the proceedings.

The premise of the adversarial system is that when each party presents his case in the most favourable light, and has an opportunity to vigorously challenge the opposing party's case through cross-examination before an impartial judge, the truth can be approached or reached more often than not.

While the adversarial system has profoundly shaped common-law legal thinking, other fact-finding systems exist. The one we may be most familiar with is the inquisitorial system, also known as the scientific process, used in most civil-law jurisdictions such as Quebec and France. This system involves an investigation directed at finding the truth. The fact-finder may use various avenues to resolve the problem she faces, whether the problem is the spread of HIV infection or who caused an automobile accident. She is an active participant who seeks out the truth by investigating and questioning the facts as they are presented.

Passive Decision-Makers in the Adversarial System

Judges in the adversarial system do not take an active part in the search for truth. In the Canadian system, the judge does not question witnesses or make other investigations into finding the "truth." In fact, too much comment or active questioning of witnesses by a judge can be the basis for a successful appeal and a new trial.

A passive decision-maker has less opportunity than an active decision-maker to influence the outcome of the judicial process through any bias she may hold. This is especially evident in a trial by judge and jury. If the judge does not express any opinions, either directly or through hints picked up by the jury, then there is no mixing up of the roles of the judge, who controls the process, and the jury, who determines what facts they adopt as proven. As noted above, judges have been criticized for engaging in "excessive" questioning of witnesses; it is said that a judge who "descends into the arena ... is liable to have his vision clouded by the dust of conflict" (*Yuill v. Yuill*, at 189, per Lord Green). That is, a judge who takes too active a role risks losing the objectivity we so prize in a decision-maker. Even where the judge decides a case without a jury, every word uttered by the court may be scrutinized because of the potential of a judge to misdirect herself.

On the other hand, the passivity of the decision-maker can also be reviewed by a higher court if the trial judge acted in a manner that favoured, or appeared to favour, one party over another ("raised a reasonable apprehension of bias"). In cases where a witness has some frailty due to age or limited knowledge of English, a judge often must take a role in ensuring that the witness can effectively communicate her evidence. In fact, a judge who does not intervene to facilitate testimony in such circumstances may be subject to criticism. The main concern is that the judge

IN THE NEWS

Provincial Court Judge Removed from Case for Acting Like Counsel

An Ontario Provincial Court judge was prohibited from hearing an impaired driving case when it came up for trial again because he appeared to be wearing two hats, Crown and judge, in the matter. On reviewing his conduct, the Court of Appeal noted that the judge had "become an advocate in his own cause in the forum reserved for disputes he is to decide impartially in a process of calm and detached deliberation." The judge did not disguise his distaste for those who represent impaired drivers and for the law that the court must apply in these cases. The judge's descent into the arena was particularly strongly demonstrated when he sent a series of emails to Crown counsel who would deal with any appeal of his decision, inquiring whether an appeal had been commenced and whether they would like his "thoughts on it" to assist them. The judge also crossed the line with some comments in *obiter dicta* which were critical of an appeal court judge. In prohibiting the judge from hearing the case, the Court of Appeal stated that "an atmosphere has been created where it appears that the trial judge has matters of his own reputation and integrity in mind when approaching these cases, rather than the dispassionate adjudication of the underlying cases."

Source: *R v. Musselman* (2004), 25 CR (6th) 295 (Ont. SCJ).

not engage in behaviour that actually aids one side to the disadvantage of the other or prevents an accused from mounting a proper defence to the charges he faces.

By opting for the adversarial system, we have chosen to temper the quest for truth with other values, such as limiting the power of the state to prosecute individuals and emphasizing the appearance of fairness and impartiality. Some would argue that the latter maintains the high regard in which the system of justice is held, an essential ingredient in any system of justice in a democracy.

However, there are criticisms of the adversarial system. The nature of the adversarial system implies that only one party can be a winner. If each side is partially right, then a process that only affords a win–lose resolution contains, by definition, some injustice. Trials are not the only system for resolution of legal disputes in our society, but they remain the main vehicle of last resort. Some parties will opt or even contract to resolve disputes through arbitration but this process looks very much like litigation by trial. Its main advantage is speedier decision making, thus allowing the parties to go on with their lives. With the speedier decisions can also come monetary savings, but since the arbitration system is largely private, the savings are not assured.

HOW EVIDENCE FITS INTO THE ADVERSARIAL SYSTEM

The rules of evidence that we apply today were developed over a considerable period of time in an effort to ensure that there was a fair and equitable process in place for resolving legal disputes. In the early stages of development, fairness and equity were not always prime considerations; the original process was more about protecting royalty and other highly placed persons from having their power (property and ability to tax) eroded. But as the concept of democracy took root, fairness and equity became more important goals of the judicial process, and the principles of natural justice evolved in keeping with the political evolution under way. Philosophically, the Age of Reason contributed the thinking that a system of justice should be rational.

It used to be that disputes were settled by trial by ordeal and trial by battle. That is, the legality of a claim (say, to ownership of land) was determined by how strong or skilled in fighting a claimant was. But these approaches to justice gave way to more rational concepts such as relevance and materiality, which were developed to ensure that the decision-maker would consider valid or useful information in coming to its conclusions in a dispute. Think of the expression "garbage in–garbage out": essentially, a decision-maker cannot make a good decision when considering unhelpful, confusing, or useless information. And the parties to the dispute cannot be relied upon to present only valid information that will help the decision-maker come to a just conclusion, because at least one of the parties would prefer simply that the conclusion was favourable to him, whether or not it was just.

Just as the adversarial system of justice has evolved to its present form over a thousand or more years, the use and abuse of evidence law has likewise evolved over time, and we should not assume that there is nothing to improve upon. We should also keep in mind that an evidentiary system that works well at one point in our history may become outmoded, awkward, and unsatisfactory at a later point in time.

The primary function of evidence law is to ensure that useful or valuable information is placed before decision-makers. It is a vehicle for transmission of information to the decision-makers, and, as with any vehicle, we must ensure that it provides a safe and reliable conveyance.

DIVISION OF RESPONSIBILITIES IN THE ADVERSARIAL SYSTEM

trier of fact
person in a trial who assesses the evidence and renders a verdict; in a jury trial, the jury

trier of law
person in a trial who controls the trial process, determines the admissibility of evidence, and instructs the trier of fact on the applicable law; in a jury trial, the judge

In a trial, two types of decisions must be made. The facts must be decided and the law that applies must be determined. The decision-maker may be a judge sitting alone or it may be a judge and jury hearing the case. A very important aspect of this latter situation is the division of their responsibilities.

When a judge sits alone, without a jury, he fulfills both decision-making roles. In other words, he is both the **trier of fact** and the **trier of law**. When there is a judge and jury, the judge is the trier of law and the jury is the trier of fact. The responsibility of the judge in a jury trial is to make all the decisions that require legal training. She controls the process to ensure that all parties are treated fairly and that the

PERSPECTIVE AND RELEVANCY

One particularly egregious example of how perspective can cloud a determination of relevancy is the case of Frank Joseph Paul. He was a New Brunswick Mi'kmaq who froze to death on the streets of Vancouver after having been taken from police custody and dumped drunk and wet in an alleyway in freezing weather. Paul's treatment was in fact consistent with the common police practice in some parts of Canada of taking intoxicated people, particularly intoxicated Natives, and dumping them in areas where the police won't have to deal with them.

In reviewing the matter, Crown counsel determined that no charges should be laid against the police, saying, "Given the available evidence, the Crown is unable to establish that any police officer failed to perform a duty upon them in such a manner that demonstrated a marked departure from the conduct of a reasonably prudent person *or that it was objectively foreseeable that the conduct of the officers in failing to provide a more adequate shelter for Mr. Paul endangered his life or was likely to cause permanent damage to his health.*" How it is not foreseeable that dumping a severely intoxicated person in an alley in freezing weather would at the very least endanger his health is unclear. There were police records and a police surveillance video showing the police dragging Mr. Paul into the elevator, dripping wet, a short time before depositing him into the alley.

Paul's death led to calls for a public inquiry. Those advocating for an inquiry questioned whether the Crown's assessment of available evidence or application of the standard of objective foreseeability and reasonable prudence is impartial, or whether it reflects the Crown's close relationship to the police.

In 2007, as a result of revelations that jail guard Greg Firlotte, who was present the night Paul was dumped in the alleyway, was not even spoken to in the police investigation of the incident, the BC attorney general announced that an inquiry would be held.

rules, including the rules of evidence, are complied with. Thus, the judge determines whether information that one side wishes to present to the jury in the form of evidence will be admitted before the jury. This means the judge can control whether the jury gets to see or hear this information. This role is like that of a gatekeeper, someone who protects a group from harmful intrusions. In this instance, the harmful intrusion is the admission of information that will potentially damage the fact-finding process, that will make it harder or impossible for the jury to do its job properly.

The gatekeeper lets in the desirable information and keeps out the mischief-making information. Desirable evidence is information that will assist the trier of fact in coming to a fair determination of the issues on the basis of the facts before them. As we will see when examining the other roles of evidence law, the gatekeeper may keep information from the trier of fact that might be helpful in terms of fact finding but is undesirable for other reasons. These reasons include the maintenance of societal values that are considered more important than the proper resolution of one particular dispute.

The jury, where there is one, has the duty of determining what information they accept and what weight they assign to that information. As the trier of fact, the jury has exclusive authority over issues involving credibility and reliability of the evidence, once it has been admitted. The jury is also responsible for rendering a verdict on the issues—guilty or not guilty in a criminal matter, and whether the plaintiff or defendant has proven her claims in a civil matter. In a jury trial, the roles of judge and jury must be carefully segregated to ensure that the process is fair. If a judge erodes the jury's independence by directing their conclusions on the facts, the decision in the case may be appealed by the losing party.

Where a judge is sitting without a jury, the judge must play a dual role of trier of law and trier of fact. Thus, the judge will consider certain evidence as required by law and will not consider information he has heard but not admitted into evidence. An example can illustrate the judge's position. Say an accused person has confessed to an offence. The defence lawyer argues that the confession should not be admitted into evidence for a number of alleged violations of the Charter. The defence asks the judge to rule the confession inadmissible. Obviously, the judge must hear that there was a confession before he can rule on whether or not it is admissible as evidence. If the judge determines that the confession is not admissible, then he will not consider the confession in any way in determining the guilt of the accused.

However, when there is a jury, it is the responsibility of the judge, in his gate-keeper role, to ensure that jurors hear only admissible evidence so that they are not swayed by information that they are not permitted to consider. The thinking is that a judge, because of his legal training, can more easily separate admissible evidence from inadmissible information.

The following chart summarizes the division of responsibilities in the courtroom.

Roles in the Courtroom

Trier of Law (always the judge)

- Controls the process in the courtroom.

- Determines the admissibility of individual pieces of proposed evidence.

- Instructs the trier of fact on the law that applies.

Trier of Fact (judge or jury)

- Weighs all admissible evidence.

- Assesses the credibility and reliability of witnesses and evidence.

- Renders a verdict.

VOIR DIRE

voir dire
a mini trial, or trial within a trial, that is designed to determine the admissibility of evidence in the absence of the trier of fact

A **voir dire** is an examination that is designed to determine the admissibility of a proposed piece of evidence. The expression, which found its way into the English common-law system through the Norman influence, literally means "to speak the truth." It is a process that can be used with information such as a confession where the Crown is obliged to prove that the statement is voluntary, or with any other evidence where the two parties are in disagreement about its admissibility. It is sometimes said that a voir dire is a trial within a trial.

The process used to keep information from being wrongly considered by a jury is to exclude the jury from hearing information in dispute until the judge determines whether the information is admissible as evidence. The judge declares a voir dire and the jury is sent out of the room while the parties argue the issue. Counsel then present arguments to the judge as to whether the disputed information should be admissible. If the judge determines that it is not admissible, the jury returns and never hears any of it. If the judge determines that it is admissible, the jury returns and the information is repeated in front of the jury, as evidence. Where the judge is sitting alone and has heard the proposed evidence on a voir dire but excluded it, she must forget what she has heard, or "disabuse herself of the evidence," and not consider it in her decision. If a judge does consider information that did not properly become evidence, the decision may be appealed for this error.

We have seen that the admission and consideration of evidence are roles that are handled by two separate bodies, the trier of law and trier of fact. This is so, even where the two groups are contained within one physical body, the judge. We also know that it is an error for the trier of fact to consider information that is not properly before it. Since the legally trained trier of law determines what information is seen and therefore can be considered by the trier of fact, the system has a built-in protection from improper or dangerous assumptions or conclusions that can result when the trier of fact considers prejudicial information in reaching his decision in a case.

THE CHARGE TO THE JURY

In a jury trial, once all the evidence has been presented by all parties, counsel for each side will make submissions and attempt to persuade the jury to accept their version of the facts. The judge then gives the jury very precise instructions about the law that must be applied to the facts of the case. In a criminal trial, the judge gives a summary of the facts the Crown must prove in order to establish the guilt of the accused. The judge must also explain all defences that are reasonably available to the accused, even if the defence was not raised by the accused during the trial. In a civil trial, the judge outlines the issues the plaintiff must establish and the defences available to the defendant. Jury charges may be very lengthy in some cases, taking several days or longer. The jurors are then instructed on their duties once they begin deliberations. This process is called the **charge to the jury**.

Many US jurisdictions have standardized jury instructions and have "refined" the instructions so that they are much simpler and shorter than Canadian jury instructions. Many provinces are also looking at standardization of jury instructions and other processes that will make the task of juries more manageable, particularly where lengthy trials are involved.

The Supreme Court of Canada has summarized the role of the charge to the jury as follows (in *R v. Osolin*, at 683):

> The jury system has in general functioned exceptionally well. Its importance has been recognized in s. 11(f) of the Charter. One of the reasons it has functioned so very well is that trial judges have been able to direct the minds of jurors to the essential elements of the offence and to those defences which are applicable. That process should be maintained. The charge to the jury must be directed to the

charge to the jury
judge's instructions to the jury, before the jury begins deliberations, regarding the applicable law, the standard of proof, and the available defences

essential elements of the crime with which the accused is charged and defences to it. Speculative defences that are unfounded should not be presented to the jury. To do so would be wrong, confusing, and unnecessarily lengthen jury trials.

Due to the importance of the charge to the jury, it is often the subject of an appeal. One party or the other may take the view that the jury has come to an improper conclusion due to errors in the judge's charge.

JUST NOT GETTING THE POINT

A jury in British Columbia was hearing the case of a man charged with stealing a horse. After hearing all the evidence and the judge's instructions, the jury went off to deliberate. The jurors returned with their verdict: not guilty, but the accused had to return the horse. When the judge patiently explained that they couldn't come up with such a verdict, the jurors dutifully returned to the jury room for further deliberations. They returned with their new verdict: guilty, but the accused could keep the horse.

Source: Peter V. MacDonald, *Court Jesters: Canada's Lawyers and Judges Take the Stand to Relate Their Funniest Stories*. Don Mills, ON: Stoddart.

COMMENTARY ON THE JURY SYSTEM

The jury system developed in England under Henry II in 1166 with the appointment of twelve knights who would resolve civil disputes over land and taxes. Criminal matters were still dealt with by way of trial by ordeal or trial by battle at this time. In the 13th century, the jury system began to be applied to criminal matters. Initially, the jury was an "informed jury," meaning that they either had knowledge of the parties and the facts beyond what they heard in court, or were charged with conducting an investigation of the facts on their own. Oath helpers, or witnesses who comment on how reliable or believable other witnesses are, were commonly called upon to bolster the credibility of the parties themselves. By the 16th century, the concept of an informed jury was replaced by the principle that the jury should be independent and impartial, and thus not "informed" in the sense of having any foreknowledge of the parties. Decisions were to be based solely on the information that was legitimately placed before them. This established the importance of evidence law, which attempted to ensure that reliable evidence made its way into the courtroom and prejudicial and unreliable evidence was excluded. Witnesses testified under oath. These rules were all positive influences in the search for truth and justice.

The separation of the roles of judge and jury was solidified in 1670 in the trial of the Quaker William Penn. (Penn later left England for the United States, where he was so influential that the state of Pennsylvania was named after him.) Penn was charged with unlawful assembly under the *Conventicle Act*, which had been passed by the Catholic Parliament to suppress religious dissent. Thousands of Quakers were imprisoned for their beliefs. Penn challenged this oppression by organizing a public meeting on August 14, 1670. The Lord Mayor had him arrested, and at his trial Penn made an eloquent defence of liberty:

[I]f these ancient and fundamental laws, which relate to liberty and property, and which are not limited to particular persuasions in matters of religion, must not be indispensably maintained and observed, who then can say that he has a right to the coat on his back? Certainly our liberties are to be openly invaded, our wives to be ravished, our children slaved, our families ruined, and our estates led away in triumph by every sturdy beggar and malicious informer—as their trophies but our forfeits for conscience's sake.

Penn and his co-defendants were acquitted by the jury, but this displeased the Lord Mayor, who fined the jurors and imprisoned them in Newgate to encourage them to alter their verdict. They seemed to have listened to Penn's comments about liberty, for they declined to change the verdict. After two months in the terrible conditions of the prison, they were set free by the Court of Common Pleas. The outcome of this episode was that the highest court in England affirmed that juries must not be coerced to come to a particular verdict or punished if they disagreed with the court. Thus was born one of the more important features of our democratic system, the concept of jury independence.

In most serious criminal matters and many civil trials in courts of superior jurisdiction, a litigant can choose a trial by jury. Most criminal matters empanel a twelve-member jury, just like the knights of yore. In civil matters, depending on the province, the jury may consist of fewer than twelve jurors; eight is not uncommon. Failure to reach a unanimous decision results in a hung jury and the accused must be tried again by a new jury.

Suggestions for Reforming the Jury System

It has been suggested that the jury system should be reformed and that jury sizes could be reduced and majority verdicts be allowed. A majority verdict would eliminate the need for a unanimous verdict. However, a disadvantage of this reform is that it could result in more wrongful convictions. Academics suggest that a more cautious and reasoned approach be taken to the problem presented by jury trials and jury instructions. It would certainly be easier to obtain convictions without unanimity, but Canada already has a scandalous level of wrongful convictions. If we reduced the size of a criminal jury to ten and required only a majority for a verdict, then six jurors in favour of conviction and four against could send a person to jail for life. Contrast that with the scenario of *Twelve Angry Men*, where one obstinate juror forces the jury to weigh the evidence and test its credibility and reliability, thus avoiding wrongfully convicting a teenaged boy. If prosecutors can obtain "quick and dirty" verdicts from juries, then the dangers of a miscarriage of justice skyrocket.

Still, one can appreciate the frustration of professionals in the criminal justice system, who see so much time and energy go in to prosecuting a case only to have a jury not resolve the issue and a mistrial result. Consideration could be given to implementing, on at least a test basis, some of the following modifications:

- require pre-trial training of jurors in a workshop setting to prepare them for the task

- allow juries to include "professional jurors" who are trained in the legal aspects and who could assist the jury-room process of dissecting the evidence and understanding the instructions from the judge

- shorten and simplify standard jury instructions

- give judges more freedom to set aside an unreasonable verdict from a jury (subject to appeal of the judge's decision).

EVIDENCE IN APPELLATE COURTS

In the adversarial system of justice, decisions of trial courts may be appealed to a higher court, and many are. For the sake of certainty, there are time limits within which a party who does not like the outcome of a case must commence an appeal. It may even be possible to appeal the appeal, so to speak, and take the issue to "the highest court in the land." Although many litigants would like to go "all the way" with their appeal, few cases fit the condition of being of national importance that is required for an appeal to the Supreme Court of Canada. There is no right to appeal to the Supreme Court. The court determines what cases it will hear on appeal and usually only chooses cases that involve a major point of law, a legal issue that will affect a large number of people, or some other matter of significance.

The judge or judges hearing an appeal are generally restricted to considering whether the decision-maker in the initial case ("the first instance") applied the law correctly or whether a reasonable decision-maker *could* have come to that decision on the basis of the admissible evidence. Thus, it is vital for litigants to have the necessary evidence admitted at the trial level; otherwise, they may be stuck with an unfortunate outcome simply because the appeal court cannot say the decision-maker got it wrong on the basis of the evidence admitted at trial. In addition, appeal courts claim that they will not second-guess the decision-maker in the trial, partly out of respect for the other decision-maker, but largely for fear of opening the floodgates if they send a message that a litigant can get a "second kick at the can" through an appeal. On rare occasions, an appeal court will admit new evidence, but not when the evidence was available to a litigant who neglected to present it at trial. Appeals are not opportunities to second-guess trial strategies and relitigate the issues.

As a rule of law, lower courts are bound to follow the decisions of higher courts, including their rulings on matters regarding the admissibility of evidence.

ALTERNATIVE DISPUTE RESOLUTION MECHANISMS

Not all civil matters are resolved through the court process. There are alternative dispute resolution mechanisms available to litigants, including arbitration and mediation. Criminal matters are always tried through the courts, but there are alternative sentencing mechanisms. There has been an increase in the use of the process of "diversion" and, in youth matters, "extrajudicial sanctions." Both of these measures circumvent the court process and are advantageous for the accused because they allow the accused to avoid a criminal record.

Arbitration

Arbitration is not bound by the rules of evidence under which courts operate, but because it is an adversarial system, it tends to take a somewhat formal approach to litigation, including its approach to admissibility of evidence. While evidence that would not be admissible in some courts may get before an arbitrator, individuals who are legally trained are less likely to give such evidence any weight, thus defeating any advantage of relaxed rules of evidence.

Mediation

Mediation is also an alternative to litigation through the courts. Although it is growing in popularity, it remains a fringe approach. The main advantage of mediation is that no result is imposed on the parties; instead, a resolution is facilitated by a neutral, experienced, third-party moderator. This means, however, that there may not be a resolution at the end of a mediation. An additional drawback is that the mediation process cannot even get started without the cooperation of both parties.

In some instances, one party can require a mediation, for example, by serving the other party with a notice to mediate. In practical terms, however, because it requires agreement, the process cannot be successful without genuine participation. Mediation can also be an "extra" cost if the two sides cannot resolve their dispute. This may be hard to accept when a party willing to mediate feels that the other side is not genuinely trying to reach agreement. In addition, mediation does not work well where there is a power imbalance. When one side, who may be entirely wrong in its position, has enormous funds to spend on litigation, mediation will often result in the well-heeled litigant taking baby steps in compromise and expecting or demanding that the financially strapped opponent take giant steps to bridge the gap in their positions.

Mediations tend to be very relaxed in their evidentiary requirements. They often feel more like informal discussions than legal proceedings. Mediations are almost always "without prejudice," which means that information disclosed in mediation cannot be used in any subsequent trials. This encourages each party to be freer in its comments and to acknowledge the strong points in its adversary's position. When a party acknowledges some weaknesses in its own position and some strengths in its opponent's, a resolution prior to trial often appears much more appealing. Both plaintiffs and defendants can use the mediation process to "test-drive" their positions and to assess how well the other side will stand up to litigation in the courts. While statements in mediation cannot be disclosed ("attract privilege from disclosure") in court proceedings, parties are not prevented from exploiting new information to shore up their case prior to trial by exploring avenues they had not thought of and by revising their questioning approach and other evidentiary strategies.

An interesting twist on mediation privilege arose recently in Ontario. In this matter there was a mediated settlement with a number of defendants which included a costs award. Defendant "K" was inadvertently left off of the order regarding costs and thus was unable to enforce costs against the plaintiff. In breaking the cloak of mediation, the judge noted that the purpose of confidentiality in mediation is to encourage parties to be candid by assuring them that anything said in the mediation will not be used in court. However, once settlement is reached and an is-sue arises involving a disagreement about the exact terms of the settlement, media-tion privilege must be overridden to ensure substantive justice. The mediator could certainly help clarify or resolve this issue and it would not undermine the media-tion process to shed light on the terms of the resolution.

MILITARY JUSTICE

Military justice in Canada is unique and separate from the civilian criminal justice system. The Supreme Court of Canada has endorsed a separate system that would not meet the standards required of civilian courts. There are systemic obstacles to the application of civilian principles of fairness in a military context. Social organi-zation in the military is built on unquestioned adherence to commands from supe-riors. Thus, a higher-ranking officer's word by definition carries greater weight than a lower-ranking officer's.

The rules of evidence are very relaxed in the summary trial process used by the Canadian military. A commanding officer is free to accept any evidence he thinks is appropriate. In this process, the accused has no right to counsel and unsworn hear-say statements can be admitted as evidence. In the much more formal **court martial** process, which can be chosen by an accused and is sometimes mandated, the same rules of evidence used for civilians apply. The election of the court martial process comes with considerable risk because the penalties are much harsher than in civil-ian courts. For example, a sentence of five years is served in its entirety, no time off for good behaviour.

court martial
formal military justice
process in which civilian
rules of evidence apply

Some offences, such as murder and crimes against children, must be tried in civilian courts, not military courts.

CHAPTER SUMMARY

In the adversarial system, there are similarities and differences between the crimi-nal and the civil litigation processes. The adversarial system is the approach to fact finding that is used in the Canadian judicial system and in the other systems with their roots in the British common-law tradition. The adversarial process has evolved to temper the quest for truth with other values, including limiting the power of the state to prosecute individuals and emphasizing the appearance of fair-ness and impartiality. The rules of evidence that are applied today developed over a considerable period of time in an effort to ensure that the process for resolving legal disputes is fair and equitable.

There are two primary decisions to be made at trial. The first is what the facts of a particular case are and the second is how the law applies to those facts. The role of the jury is to determine the facts and the role of the judge is to apply the law. When the judge sits alone, without a jury, he fulfills both decision-making roles.

The judge also acts as a gatekeeper to ensure that only the evidence that will as-sist in a fair determination of the issues is admitted. The voir dire is the process of "a trial within a trial" to determine what information may be properly admitted into evidence. At the end of the trial, the judge gives a charge to the jury, instructing them on the application of the law to the facts of the case.

Suggestions for reforming the jury system in Canada have been proposed, but they are not without their problems.

In alternative dispute resolution systems, such as mediation, and in the military justice system, the results for admitting and considering evidence are different from those in the usual adversarial system.

KEY TERMS

adversarial system

trier of fact

trier of law

voir dire

charge to the jury

court martial

REFERENCES

Canadian Charter of Rights and Freedoms, part I of the *Constitution Act, 1982*, RSC 1985, app. II, no. 44.

Osolin, R v., [1993] 4 SCR 595.

Yuill v. Yuill, [1945] 1 All ER 183 (CA).

Rudd v. Trossacs Investments Inc., [2004] OJ no. 2918 (SCJ).

REVIEW QUESTIONS

1. What are the major differences between the civil and the criminal justice systems? What are the similarities?

2. Describe the major features of the adversarial system.

3. Describe the differences between the role of the judge and the role of the jury in the trial process.

4. What is meant by the term "trier of fact"? Who performs this function in a trial?

5. What do we mean when we say that the judge is the "gatekeeper" for the admission of evidence?

6. What is the role of a voir dire in the trial process?

7. What is the purpose of the charge to the jury?

DISCUSSION QUESTIONS

1. Do you think the adversarial approach to court proceedings is one that tends to render a just determination of the case? What other approaches might be considered?

2. The following suggestions have been made for improving the jury system:

   a. require pre-trial training of jurors in a workshop setting to prepare them for the task

   b. allow juries to include "professional jurors" who are trained in the legal aspects of trials and who could assist the jury-room process of dissecting the evidence and understanding the instructions from the judge

   c. shorten and simplify standard jury instructions

   d. give judges more freedom to set aside an unreasonable verdict from a jury (subject to appeal of the judge's decision)

   What effect do you think each of these suggestions might have if implemented? Can you think of any other suggestions?

CHAPTER 2

Evidence in the Decision-Making Process

CHAPTER OBJECTIVES

After completing this chapter you should be able to:

- Explain the role of evidence in the court process.
- Understand the part that judicial discretion plays in the application of evidence law in a proceeding.
- Explain the effect that the admission or exclusion of evidence has on a proceeding.
- Identify the source of evidence law.
- Understand how evidence is dealt with in administrative tribunals.

THE ROLE OF EVIDENCE LAW

The primary purpose of a legal proceeding is to resolve the dispute between the parties according to the law. Legal disputes involve both issues of fact and issues of law. Whether the matter involves a court case or an administrative hearing, or some other comparable proceeding, a decision must be made as to which version of the facts is the most credible and how the law applies to those facts. In most cases, the decision-maker who determines the facts then also applies the law. However, as we saw in chapter 1, in court proceedings involving a jury, it is the jury that decides on the facts and the judge who decides on the applicable law. The jury is the "trier of fact" and the judge is the "trier of law." If there is no jury, the judge or other adjudicator is both the trier of fact and the trier of law.

The role of evidence law in a proceeding is twofold. First, it establishes a set of principles that operate to exclude facts that may not be helpful to the trier of fact as well as facts that may be downright harmful in the fair determination of the case.

Second, the rules of evidence function to limit the sheer volume of information put before the trier of fact so that legal proceedings are kept to a reasonable length and therefore manageable within our system of justice. For example, consider the case of a car buyer suing a vendor who sold her a used car in poor condition. In his defence, the vendor might want to ask all his friends to testify that he is an upstanding, honest person. The vendor has a lot of friends, so calling them all as witnesses would take a couple of days. No court would permit all this evidence to be called. In fact, even one witness of this sort may be irrelevant, because the issue is the condition of the car and the contractual terms relating to its sale.

In other words, the rules of evidence are meant to provide an orderly method of determining what facts may actually be considered by the trier of fact in deciding the case, keeping in mind the fundamental principle of fairness. However, in any discussion of what is fair, there may be competing interests and concerns. As a result, the application of evidence law is a balancing act, and in order to understand how the law is applied, this struggle for balance must be kept in mind. For example, in a criminal trial, if the police have gathered evidence in a manner that contravenes the Charter rights of the accused, the evidence may not be admissible. The evidence might be very helpful to the trier of fact in deciding the guilt of the accused, but there is a higher consideration to be taken into account by the court and that is the right of all persons to be protected from illegal interference by police.

JUDICIAL DISCRETION

Although we refer to the "rules of evidence," in practice these so-called rules are often more flexible than other rules one encounters in the law. Because the legal dispute-hearing process is an attempt to find the truth, or as close an approximation of the truth as possible, and at the same time must be fair and efficient, judges have a considerable amount of discretion when applying the rules. This discretion allows judges to balance competing considerations.

judicial discretion
a judge's freedom to apply rules or decide issues in the context of a case

Recent developments in evidence law have widened the scope of **judicial discretion**. Now, each case is examined on its own basis to determine the best application of the evidentiary principles within the context of that case. This approach involves an examination of the policy that gave rise to the rule in the first place to determine whether that policy is achieved by the application of the rule in the case at hand. In this way, the rules of evidence support the finding of truth, the concept of fairness, and the promotion of efficiency in the judicial system, rather than directing or driving the proceedings by stringent and automatic application. This

principled approach
method of applying rules of evidence by reference to the policy underlying the rules

method of applying the rules is often referred to as the **principled approach** and it has changed the face of evidence law over the last several decades. It is crucial in the principled approach to have a solid understanding of the policy behind an evidentiary rule to determine whether application of the rule will actually promote that policy in a particular case.

The bottom line is that although we have "rules" in evidence law, they may be applied differently in different cases in order to achieve the underlying principle of justice for which the rules were developed. In this way, judicial discretion plays a major role in the application of evidence law.

ADMISSION AND EXCLUSION OF EVIDENCE

Evidence that is **admissible** is evidence that may be considered by the trier of fact in determining the issue that she has been asked to decide. Evidence that is **excluded** is evidence that cannot be considered by the trier of fact. It is important to remember that just because evidence is excluded does not mean that it is not heard by the trier of fact.

If a judge is hearing the case without a jury, she must actually hear the evidence before she can rule whether or not it is admissible. For example, in a murder trial, if the defence wants to call evidence that the deceased victim told his mother that he was a drug dealer, it must first establish that the evidence is relevant. Because this information involves a statement made by one person to another, it is, on the face of it, **hearsay**. It will not be admitted into evidence unless it fits within one of the exceptions to the rule that makes hearsay generally inadmissible. But how can the judge possibly determine these issues if she does not hear the statement itself? She can't. Therefore, she will hear the statement and the legal arguments the parties want to make about the admission or exclusion of the statement, and then decide on its admissibility. If she rules that the statement is admissible, she may consider it in deciding whether or not the accused is guilty of the charge against him. However, if the judge rules that the evidence is inadmissible, she must not consider it in deciding the case.

Things get more complicated when the trial involves a jury. Judges, with their legal training and experience, are considered to have the ability to ignore or disregard information they have already heard, but jurors are not expected to possess such a skill. Therefore, every effort is made to keep the jury from hearing any evidence until a judge has determined whether it is admissible. If the evidence is ruled inadmissible, the jury does not hear it. In fact, if the jury inadvertently hears a piece of excluded evidence, the result can be a mistrial. In the event of a mistrial, the trial has to be started all over again from the beginning with a new judge and jury, or with a judge alone.

The process of determining the admissibility of evidence usually starts with one of the parties objecting to the admission of a particular piece of evidence that the other side wants to introduce. Whenever possible, the judge sends the jury out of the courtroom and then conducts a voir dire. A voir dire is a little trial within a trial. The issue on the voir dire is the admissibility of the evidence in dispute. All parties make their legal arguments before the judge and she renders her decision. If the judge rules that the evidence is admissible, the trial resumes and the evidence is introduced. If the judge rules that the evidence should be excluded, the trial resumes and the jury is not aware that there is information that they have not been permitted to hear. Even when there is no jury, the portion of the trial in which the judge rules on the admissibility of evidence is still referred to as a voir dire, and the same rules apply to admissibility even though the judge has heard or seen the evidence.

Despite a judge's best efforts to keep inadmissible evidence away from the jury through voir dire, sometimes a witness will just blurt out evidence that the jury cannot help but hear. If that happens, and the evidence is ruled inadmissible, the judge will instruct the jurors that they must disregard the witness's remark and not consider it in any way during their deliberations.

admissible evidence
evidence that may be considered by the trier of fact

excluded evidence
evidence that cannot be considered by the trier of fact

hearsay evidence
evidence given by a witness that is based on information received from others rather than personal knowledge; generally considered inadmissible

The expression "voir dire" found its way into the English common-law system following the Norman invasion and conquest of England in 1066. For a period of time, the language of the courts in England was Norman French. Many of the expressions of that time remain part of the legal language in court systems that are based on English common law.

A voir dire is designed to determine the admissibility of a proposed piece of evidence. It can be used with information such as a confession where the Crown is obliged to prove that the statement is voluntary, or with any other evidence where the two parties are in disagreement about its admissibility. It is important to remember that the judge does not determine the truth of the evidence, only its admissibility. Determining the truth of the evidence is the exclusive domain of the trier of fact.

SOURCES OF EVIDENCE LAW

1. Common Law

Most evidence law is common law. The vast majority of the rules of evidence used today in Canadian courtrooms have their roots in judge-made law, some of which dates back centuries to the earliest courts in England. But that does not mean that the rules have not been updated. In fact, over the last 25 years or so, the Supreme Court of Canada has made major changes in the common law of evidence. As discussed earlier, the court has moved away from a rigid application of the rules of evidence to an approach that examines the policy behind the rule and considers how best to apply the rule to achieve that policy in the case at hand. This principled approach has had a profound effect on many of the long-standing common-law rules of evidence, most notably hearsay (as in *Ares v. Venner*). We will look at these changes as we go along.

2. Statute Law

Statute law also plays an important role in evidence law. The federal government and each of the common-law provinces and territories in Canada have an evidence act. (Note that Quebec is a civil-law province and does not have an evidence act, though it does have rules and regulations regarding the use of evidence in court and tribunal hearings. See the appendix to this chapter for a complete list of evidence acts in Canada.) The federal act applies to court proceedings conducted in relation to federal legislation—for example, the *Criminal Code* and the *Divorce Act*. The provincial/territorial statutes apply to proceedings conducted under provincial/territorial legislation.

All the evidence acts are very similar in approach. In some instances, they codify various aspects of the common law of evidence. In other instances, they alter or add to common-law rules. For example, the common law has established that business records that meet a court-established test are excepted from the hearsay rule. Most of the evidence acts in Canada also deal with business records as a hearsay exception but they have added variations to the common-law rule.[1]

In addition to the various evidence acts, there are individual statutes that have specific evidentiary requirements for particular proceedings under that statute, as well as rules of procedure in each province that dictate the process for civil cases at various court levels.

EVIDENCE IN ADMINISTRATIVE TRIBUNALS

Over the last number of decades, governments in Canada at both the federal and the provincial/territorial levels have enacted numerous pieces of legislation regulating the interaction between individuals and the government and governmental bodies. This area of government regulation is administered by an array of agencies, boards, and commissions that have their own decision-making bodies, collectively referred to as tribunals. Among the more well-known tribunals are the Labour Relations Board, the Workers' Compensation Appeal Board, and the Canadian Radio-television and Telecommunications Commission. **Administrative tribunals** are like courts in the sense that they are established to pass judgment in circumstances where there is a dispute. One of their major purposes is to ensure a fair and just determination of a regulatory dispute in a timely and cost-efficient manner. Tribunals are often referred to as "quasi-judicial" bodies. They tend to be adversarial and individuals who appear before them often have lawyers to assist them in presenting their case. Tribunals deal with a wide variety of issues including labour relations, workers' compensation, immigration and refugee claims, and property zoning. In fact, Canada has embraced administrative tribunals as a way of resolving disputes more than have most democracies in the world.

administrative tribunals
decision-making bodies, similar to courts, that rule on regulatory disputes

Take the example of a person whose social assistance benefits have been cut off. The statute that governs social assistance payments typically allows a decision to deny benefits to be appealed. The person who has been cut off would file a notice of appeal with the appeal board, which would then arrange a hearing. The person appearing before the appeal board ("the appellant") would present her evidence and arguments as to why she is entitled to benefits. The appeal board would then "exercise its discretion" and either agree with the appellant, allowing the appeal and restoring the benefits, or disagree with the appellant, denying the appeal and thus upholding the decision of the social assistance agency to cut off benefits.

Over the last half-century, there has developed a body of law, known as administrative law, that deals with the rules and procedures for proper decision making in the tribunal hearing process. Although tribunals themselves are created by statute, most of the main principles of administrative law are common law. The principles were made by judges in courts that were reviewing tribunal decisions.

Relaxation of Rules of Evidence in Administrative Tribunal Hearings

The rules of evidence in administrative hearings are much more relaxed than they are in civil or criminal court cases. There are a number of reasons for this difference in approach.

First, there is less danger in administrative tribunals of "faulty" evidence misleading the decision-maker. Administrative tribunals are run by people who have distinguished themselves as experts in their field—workers' compensation, labour relations, property tax levies, or whatever the specific area the tribunal is set up to administer. Of course, judges are also experts in areas of law, but in both civil and criminal matters the parties often have a right to choose trial by jury. In a jury trial, the decision-makers are lay people, who are much less sophisticated than judges in their knowledge of the law and in their ability to discount or "forget" evidence that should not be considered in their decision. Strict rules of evidence are enforced to ensure that a jury hear only the evidence that the expert judge decides is admissible.

A second reason that the rules of evidence for administrative tribunals are more relaxed than they are for courts is that tribunal hearings are meant to deal with issues more expeditiously and less formally than court proceedings. In addition, while administrative tribunals deal with important matters such as whether a worker can retain his job or whether a person will succeed with her refugee claim, they do not deal with matters where the personal liberty of an individual is at stake.

Another reason for the relaxed approach to the admission of evidence before administrative tribunals is that while their decisions may be reviewed by a court, courts have generally taken a "hands-off" approach to tribunal decisions. Therefore, the admission or rejection of evidence by tribunals is not closely scrutinized. Given the specialized nature of administrative tribunals, courts often defer to their findings on the basis that it is better to have such decisions made and enforced close to the source of the issue, by the tribunals themselves.

Judicial Review of Administrative Tribunal Decisions

There are two circumstances where a court will overrule an administrative tribunal: where the tribunal exceeds its legislated jurisdiction, and where it denies the applicant natural justice.

JURISDICTION

Tribunals are creatures of statutes; their powers derive from that legislation. A tribunal may only make a decision permitted by the statute that created it. Any other decision is not within its jurisdiction. So a tribunal's jurisdiction is the scope or limit of its authority. For example, a human rights tribunal could not order Air Canada to improve its meal service. Such an order is not within the power of a human rights tribunal and would certainly not be upheld by a court because it would be a clear breach of the tribunal's decision-making authority.

NATURAL JUSTICE

Natural justice is one of the fundamental legal principles applied in administrative law. Basically, natural justice entitles a person who may be affected by a decision of government or a governmental agency to a hearing conducted in a fair and unbiased manner. This includes the right to call witnesses and present evidence. It would not be fair if a person was denied representation, was denied the right to cross-examine the opponent's witnesses, was presented with evidence and not permitted to respond to it, or had "secret" evidence used against him. At the end of the day, a person who has been dealt with by an administrative tribunal should be able to determine the factual basis of the tribunal's determination and to know that the process was a fair one.

Natural justice balances two aims: to provide flexibility in the admission of evidence, and to carefully consider the weight to be given the evidence that is admitted. The search for truth in the administrative hearing process is balanced against fairness to the parties. As a society, we reject a situation where a person can be treated unfairly by government or be denied rights that any person should be able to count on from a quasi-judicial body.

Although courts generally defer to the decisions of administrative tribunals, a court will intervene when a party has been denied natural justice, including in the admission or rejection of evidence. Some enabling legislation attempts to limit or eliminate the ability of the courts to overturn the decisions of administrative tribunals. These provisions are known as "privative clauses," implying that what goes on in the tribunal is "private" and not to be interfered with. Courts do tend to respect tribunals, if only to protect themselves from a flood of litigation if they do not, but they will review and modify or overturn a tribunal's decision if the tribunal acted in a particularly cavalier or outlandish way. A decision can be so unreasonable as to exceed the tribunal's jurisdiction and such decisions may be interfered with if they are "patently unreasonable." In appealing a tribunal decision, the appellant can complain that the tribunal made an error of law or simply an error of fact. Errors of fact are much less likely to be interfered with because even if the judge hearing the appeal would have had a different view of the evidence, the discretion of the tribunal is still to be respected.

Questions of law that would require intervention by a reviewing court include:

- where the tribunal exceeds its legislated jurisdiction
- where an adjudicator exceeds his discretion.

Questions of fact, which are less likely to be overturned on appeal, include:

- the weight given to certain pieces of evidence
- assessments of credibility of witnesses
- the balancing of competing interests in complying with the tribunal's mandate.

While the formal rules of evidence do not constrain administrative tribunals from admitting evidence, they do assist tribunal members in determining the weight to give particular kinds of evidence on the basis of the reliability of the evidence. Even where an appeal court determines that evidence was wrongly admitted, the court will not interfere with the outcome of the tribunal hearing unless it can be shown that admission of the evidence affected the outcome from the tribunal.

Like courts, tribunals are responsible for managing the evidence that is before them. In that respect, tribunals can limit the number of witnesses or determine that certain kinds of witnesses are not necessary. Because tribunal members have the expertise to understand the central issues between the parties, they are in the best position to determine what evidence will be relevant to their determination. A tribunal cannot refuse to permit a party to cross-examine a witness, although it has the same powers as a judge to limit the cross-examination if it is irrelevant or argumentative. If a tribunal were to deny a party the right to cross-examine, then any assessments of credibility by the tribunal would be suspect because the party did not have the opportunity to test the credibility of the witness. Tribunal members can also play a part in questioning a witness, particularly where a party presenting evidence is not represented by counsel and may not have a clear grasp of the subtleties involved in proving her case. If a tribunal member does partake in the questioning process, she must be careful not to "descend into the arena" and take an adversarial position in relation to one of the parties. Tribunal members must be careful to show favour to no one. The point is to be fair to all and show no bias.

One danger that is particularly problematic for tribunal members is their familiarity with the issues, the parties, and counsel. Knowing too much can cause tribunal members to base their decisions on information that is "known" to them but not in evidence. Tribunals often have access to legal opinions, can review the "record" or pleadings in the matter, and will hear submissions in the course of their handling of the application. None of this is evidence as such and their decision must clearly be based on the admissible evidence in the proceeding, not on these other sources of information. Tribunal members can also become biased in favour of or against parties who frequently appear before them, and they may be inclined to discount approaches or submissions from counsel whom they have learned to distrust. However, even if a particular counsel may have attempted to "pull one over on" tribunal members in the past, it is the client of counsel who is before the tribunal, and he or she deserves to start with a clean slate.

Standard of Proof in Administrative Tribunal Hearings

Administrative tribunals are civil processes and thus apply a civil standard of proof on the balance of probabilities in assessing the evidence before them. In some rare instances, that standard is raised, requiring proof on "clear and convincing evidence." This higher standard is typically used in circumstances where professional misconduct is alleged, which could result in the loss of a person's capacity to practise their chosen profession or where there are penalties that make the proceedings quasi-criminal. (The civil standard of proof is discussed in more detail in chapter 3.)

The burden of proof usually lies with the party who initiates the proceeding in the tribunal. Typically, an individual applicant is seeking to overturn a decision of a government body, and therefore the applicant is required to establish her case in order to succeed. In some instances, the legislation governing a tribunal reverses the burden of proof. For example, under ss. 30 to 33 of the *Employment Insurance*

Act, the government body (the Canada Employment Insurance Commission) must establish that an employee who is denied benefits was terminated for misconduct. Where a tribunal finds that the evidence is equally balanced, the benefit of the doubt goes to the applicant (*Canada Evidence Act*, ss. 29, 30, and 31).

CHAPTER SUMMARY

Evidence law has two purposes. The first is to eliminate information that would not be helpful to the trier of fact in coming to a fair and just determination of the facts, and the second is to reduce the sheer volume of information, thereby keeping trial times within reason. The judge has significant discretion to determine what information is admissible as evidence and what is to be excluded.

There are two sources of evidence law: common law and statute law. Most evidence law is based on common-law principles, but federal and provincial/territorial statutes may alter or add to common-law evidence rules.

Administrative tribunals generally adhere to the same general principle of evidence law, but the rules of evidence are not applied as strictly as they are in courts.

KEY TERMS

judicial discretion	hearsay evidence
principled approach	administrative tribunals
admissible evidence	natural justice
excluded evidence	

NOTE

1. Only Alberta and Newfoundland and Labrador do not provide a provincial statutory hearsay exception for business records. See the following for the business records provisions: *Canada Evidence Act*, RSC 1980, c. C-5, s. 30 and RSBC 1996, c. 154, s. 23; CCSM, c. E150, s. 49; RSNB 1973, c. E-11, ss. 49 and 51; RSNS 1989, c. 154, s. 23; RSO 1990, c. E.23, s. 35; RSPEI 1974, c. E-10, s. 32; and RSS 1978, c. S-16, s. 32.

REFERENCES

Ares v. Venner, [1970] SCR 608, 14 DLR (2d) 4.

Canadian Charter of Rights and Freedoms, part I of the *Constitution Act, 1982*, RSC 1985, app. II, no. 44.

Employment Insurance Act, SC 1996, c. 23.

APPENDIX: EVIDENCE ACTS IN CANADA

Canada, *Canada Evidence Act*, RSC 1985, c. C-5.

Alberta, *Alberta Evidence Act*, RSA 2000, c. A-16.

British Columbia, *Evidence Act*, RSBC 1979, c. 116.

Manitoba, *Manitoba Evidence Act*, RSM 1987, c. E150.

New Brunswick, *Evidence Act*, RSNB 1973, c. E-11.

Newfoundland and Labrador, *Evidence Act*, RSNL 1990, c. E-16.

Northwest Territories, *Evidence Act*, RSNWT 1988, c. E-8.

Nova Scotia, *Evidence Act*, RSNS 1989, c. 154.

Nunavut, *Evidence Act*, RSNWT 1988, c. E-8.

Ontario, *Evidence Act*, RSO 1990, c. E.23.

Prince Edward Island, *Evidence Act*, RSPEI 1988, c. E-11.

Saskatchewan, *Saskatchewan Evidence Act*, RSS 1978, c. S-16.

Yukon, *Evidence Act*, RSYT 1986, c. 57.

REVIEW QUESTIONS

1. What are the primary reasons why information may be excluded from evidence?

2. What do we mean when we say that the rules of evidence are flexible?

3. What role does the judge play in the admission and exclusion of evidence?

4. What is the primary source of evidence law? What is the secondary source?

5. In what circumstances will the courts overturn decisions on admission or exclusion of evidence made by administrative tribunals?

DISCUSSION QUESTIONS

1. Do you think the wide discretion afforded to judges in the application of evidence law is justified? Should the rules should be more flexible? Less flexible?

2. Compare the treatment of evidence in administrative tribunals and in courts. Do you think there should be any difference in the rules of evidence between these settings? Why or why not?

CHAPTER 3

Burden of Proof and Standard of Proof

CHAPTER OBJECTIVES

After completing this chapter you should be able to:

- Explain the issues of burden of proof.
- Define the different kinds of standard of proof.
- Understand *prima facie* cases and motions for dismissal for failure to meet a *prima facie* case.
- Identify presumptions and the different kinds of judicial notice and explain how they assist parties and courts in establishing facts that might be otherwise elusive and next to impossible to prove.

BURDEN OF PROOF

If a burden is thought of as a weight on someone's shoulders, then **burden of proof** implies that a party has an obligation to prove certain facts or matters in issue. We say that the burden falls on the Crown to prove that an accused committed an offence. The accused has no obligation to prove anything but is presumed innocent until the Crown has met the onus or obligation of proving the accused's guilt. In a civil matter, the plaintiff has the burden of establishing the claim against the defendant. Like a defendant in a criminal matter, the defendant in a civil matter has no obligation to call evidence to refute the plaintiff's claim. If the plaintiff fails to establish her claim, the defendant is entitled to judgment in his favour.

It is for this reason that in a criminal or civil matter the judge will inquire of the defendant if he has evidence to call. If the Crown or plaintiff's evidence is not sufficient to prove the charge or claim against the defendant, there may be no need to respond to it. The trick is that the trier of fact, whether judge alone or jury, will not deliberate on the issue whether the "burden has been satisfied" until the defendant chooses whether to call evidence. If the defendant assesses the circumstances incorrectly and decides not to call evidence, he cannot change his mind when the judge finds him guilty or finds in favour of the plaintiff in a civil matter.

burden of proof
a party's obligation to prove certain facts or matters in issue

There is one complication to this relatively neat analysis. The burden of proof may shift from one party to the other at certain points in a trial, usually over the issue of admissibility of evidence. For example, if the accused wishes to argue that a particular piece of evidence was obtained through a breach of the Charter and should therefore be excluded, he has the burden of satisfying the judge that a Charter breach occurred. In fact, in most instances the party seeking to challenge the admissibility of evidence is obliged to prove that the evidence is *not* admissible. The burden of proof shifts to the party who seeks to exclude evidence because the primary objective of the rules of evidence is to ensure that all relevant and material evidence is put before the trier of fact. (One exception to this thinking pertains to statements to persons in authority or confessions. The Crown must prove the voluntariness of a confession and, as we shall see in chapter 11 on self-incrimination, there are extensive criteria for proof of voluntariness.)

rebut
to present opposing
evidence or arguments

The need to prove a fact or matter is generally a legal burden, but it can also be a tactical burden. Sometimes, a party faces a strategic choice whether to present further evidence. For example, where the Crown has presented a case against the accused that will likely result in a conviction if the accused does not try **rebut** it, then the tactical burden has shifted to the accused, even though the accused is still not required to call evidence. No one can make the accused call evidence, but if he does not, he will almost certainly be convicted. The same applies to civil matters. The defendant is not required to present any evidence, but if he thinks the plaintiff is likely to win on the basis of the evidence she has presented, the defendant will usually want to present his own evidence in support of his position. In making a tactical decision whether to call evidence or not, the defendant must always keep in mind that the other party can also gain some advantage from any witnesses called. The trier of fact is not restricted to considering only Crown evidence against the accused or, in a civil matter, only the plaintiff's evidence against the defendant. Indeed, the trier of fact must consider all the evidence in reaching its conclusion, so the decision to be made is whether the defendant's chances are likely to be improved by calling additional evidence. In short, a tactical burden is a matter of strategy, and counsel must try to read the trier of fact to determine whether it is necessary or, more properly, whether it is advisable to call evidence to counter the opponent's case.

THE AIR OF REALITY TEST

air of reality test
a test of whether the
defence to a charge is
reasonable in light of the
evidence

Not all evidentiary situations are created equal. In some circumstances, an accused faces a hurdle in presenting certain defences to the trier of fact. In the past, some pretty ludicrous defences were actually successful in front of juries. In an effort to curtail such potential abuses of justice, judges required that certain defences pass a test, now known as the **air of reality test**. Where an accused seeks to rely on the defence of provocation, necessity, drunkenness, mistaken belief in consent (in sexual assault matters), self-defence, or duress, he must first convince the trial judge that there is an air of reality to that defence. The question for the judge is whether the evidence before the court reasonably lends itself to such a defence. For example, where there has been a violent sexual assault that leaves the victim in hospital for two weeks, the suggestion by the defendant that the defence of mistaken belief in consent ought to be put to the jury would likely fail because there is no air of reality to that defence. The test is imposed between the hearing of the evidence and the instructions to the jury. If the judge decides that a defence does not pass the test, she will instruct the jury to disregard it. The goal is to ensure that jurors do not consider ridiculous defences that might confuse their deliberations and potentially lead to miscarriages of justice.

Interestingly, a judge is required to put to the jury any defence that would meet the air of reality test whether or not the accused specifically raised that defence. This issue can be raised on appeal for the first time and permit the accused to succeed in a bid for a new trial. The Supreme Court of Canada reviewed the air of reality test recently in *R v. Cinous*. In this case, the accused was a career criminal who thought two of his accomplices intended to kill him. He agreed to go with the accomplices to steal some computers. He was very nervous because he was driving the van the three of them were in and one of the accomplices was behind him. The two accomplices were also wearing gloves, one of them surgical gloves, which the accused associated with situations where a person expects there to be a lot of blood. He pulled into a gas station and went to buy something. Upon returning to the van, he opened the back door, pulled out his gun, and shot one of the men in the back of the head, killing him. He sought to have the judge instruct the jury on self-defence. In considering whether this defence should have been put to the jury, the Supreme Court stated (at paras. 50-51):

> The principle that a defence should be put to a jury if and only if there is an evidential foundation for it has long been recognized by the common law. This venerable rule reflects the practical concern that allowing a defence to go to the jury in the absence of an evidential foundation would invite verdicts not supported by the evidence, serving only to confuse the jury and get in the way of a fair trial and true verdict. ...
>
> The basic requirement of an evidential foundation for defences gives rise to two well-established principles. First, a trial judge must put to the jury all defences that arise on the facts, whether or not they have been specifically raised by an accused. Where there is an air of reality to a defence, it should go to the jury. Second, a trial judge has a positive duty to keep from the jury defences lacking an evidential foundation. A defence that lacks an air of reality should be kept from the jury. ... This is so even when the defence lacking an air of reality represents the accused's only chance for an acquittal.

On the issue whether the air of reality test usurps the jury's role as the sole determiner of the facts, the Supreme Court stated:

> Indeed, the air of reality inquiry has been found not only to be consistent with the traditional division of labour as between judge and jury, but actually to *enhance* the jury's ability to carry out its task. Again, Cory J's statement in *Osolin* ... is apposite:
>
> > The jury system has in general functioned exceptionally well. Its importance has been recognized in s. 11(f) of the Charter. *One of the reasons it has functioned so very well is that trial judges have been able to direct the minds of jurors* to the essential elements of the offence and *to those defences which are applicable.* That process should be maintained. The charge to the jury must be directed to the essential elements of the crime with which the accused is charged and defences to it. *Speculative defences that are unfounded should not be presented to the jury. To do so*

would be wrong, confusing, and unnecessarily lengthen jury trials. [Emphasis added.]

Clearly, the determining factor is that the jury deserves to be protected from mischievous defences that serve to complicate and confuse its task and have no merit other than to mislead jurors into acquitting where the evidence does not support such a defence.

STANDARD OF PROOF

In both criminal and civil matters, the party who carries the burden of proving its case must meet a standard of proof. In criminal matters, that standard is proof beyond a reasonable doubt; in civil matters, that standard is proof on a balance of probabilities.

The Criminal Standard: Beyond a Reasonable Doubt

beyond a reasonable doubt
very high standard of proof in criminal matters

In a criminal matter, the Crown must prove its case against the accused **beyond a reasonable doubt.** Judges often say that triers of fact instinctively know what this term means, but when a person's freedom is at stake, judges and juries alike are not comfortable in leaving it that loose. In defining "reasonable doubt" for juries, judges have described it as being "not an imaginary or frivolous doubt," but one based on reason and common sense. However, because the way this term is used in legal proceedings is not just "common sense," the Supreme Court of Canada has given very clear directions about how trial judges should explain the term, as well as very clear warnings of the dangers. In *R v. Lifchus*, the court stated (at para. 36):

> It should be explained that:
>
> - the standard of proof beyond a reasonable doubt is inextricably intertwined with that principle fundamental to all criminal trials, the presumption of innocence;
> - the burden of proof rests on the prosecution throughout the trial and never shifts to the accused;
> - a reasonable doubt is not a doubt based upon sympathy or prejudice;
> - rather, it is based upon reason and common sense;
> - it is logically connected to the evidence or absence of evidence;
> - it does not involve proof to an absolute certainty; it is not proof beyond *any* doubt nor is it an imaginary or frivolous doubt; and
> - more is required than proof that the accused is probably guilty—a jury which concludes only that the accused is probably guilty must acquit.

On the issue of what the definition of reasonable doubt should *not* contain, the Supreme Court stated the following references should be avoided (at para. 37):

> - describing the term "reasonable doubt" as an ordinary expression which has no special meaning in the criminal law context;
> - inviting jurors to apply to the task before them the same standard of proof that they apply to important, or even the most important, decisions in their own lives;

- equating proof "beyond a reasonable doubt" to proof "to a moral certainty";
- qualifying the word "doubt" with adjectives other than "reasonable," such as "serious," "substantial" or "haunting," which may mislead the jury; and
- instructing jurors that they may convict if they are "sure" that the accused is guilty, before providing them with a proper definition as to the meaning of the words "beyond a reasonable doubt."

Finally, the Supreme Court attempted to set out a "model charge" to overcome the challenge facing all trial judges instructing juries in criminal trials (at para. 39):

> The accused enters these proceedings presumed to be innocent. That presumption of innocence remains throughout the case until such time as the Crown has on the evidence put before you satisfied you beyond a reasonable doubt that the accused is guilty.
>
> What does the expression "beyond a reasonable doubt" mean?
>
> The term "beyond a reasonable doubt" has been used for a very long time and is a part of our history and traditions of justice. It is so engrained in our criminal law that some think it needs no explanation, yet something must be said regarding its meaning.
>
> A reasonable doubt is not an imaginary or frivolous doubt. It must not be based upon sympathy or prejudice. Rather, it is based on reason and common sense. It is logically derived from the evidence or absence of evidence.
>
> Even if you believe the accused is probably guilty or likely guilty, that is not sufficient. In those circumstances you must give the benefit of the doubt to the accused and acquit because the Crown has failed to satisfy you of the guilt of the accused beyond a reasonable doubt.
>
> On the other hand you must remember that it is virtually impossible to prove anything to an absolute certainty and the Crown is not required to do so. Such a standard of proof is impossibly high.
>
> In short if, based upon the evidence before the court, you are sure that the accused committed the offence you should convict since this demonstrates that you are satisfied of his guilt beyond a reasonable doubt.

Perhaps an example will help. In a murder case, one of the elements of the offence that the Crown must prove beyond a reasonable doubt is that the alleged victim is in fact dead, not just missing or in hiding. Usually, this element is not at all difficult to prove because there is a dead body that can be identified and then sent to a pathologist, who can usually determine the cause of death—strangulation, drowning, blow by a blunt instrument, etc. Where there is a body, there is no doubt at all that the victim is dead. But what happens if there is no body?

The absence of a body does not automatically mean that the Crown cannot prove beyond a reasonable doubt that the victim is deceased. It certainly presents a challenge for the prosecution but not an insurmountable one. For example, say that the victim is a young female college student who is extremely close to her family. She also has some close, long-time friends with whom she is in almost daily contact. One day, she disappears under mysterious circumstances and is never seen again. Her car is found with her blood inside. Her bank accounts and credit cards are never touched after her disappearance. She is gone for several years. After a long investigation, the police arrest her boyfriend and charge him with murder. The theory is that she was about to jilt him and so he murdered her.

At trial, the Crown must prove that the young woman is dead, that she was the victim of a murder, and that the accused killed her. While the Crown may have trouble proving beyond a reasonable doubt that the accused murdered her, it will likely be able to pass the first step and convince the trier of fact that she is deceased. It is not an absolute certainty. However, given all the circumstances, reason and common sense would indicate that she is dead. It is beyond reasonable doubt, not beyond any doubt, that the victim is deceased. (This example is based on the facts in *R v. Baltovich*. While there is serious concern that Baltovich was wrongly convicted of murder, no question remains that the victim is deceased.)

The Civil Standard: Balance of Probabilities

balance of probabilities
standard of proof in civil matters, determined on the basis of more likely than not

The standard of proof in civil matters is not as high as it is in criminal proceedings. This is because of the less serious jeopardy that an accused faces and the fundamental principle of presumption of innocence. The civil standard is proof on the **balance of probabilities**. Other terms for it include "preponderance of the evidence," 50 percent plus one, or simply "more likely than not." It is up to the judge or the trier of fact to weigh the evidence presented by the plaintiff and the defendant. Picture the scale held aloft by the statue of blind justice. If the plaintiff's evidence is heavier—more convincing—than the defendant's, the plaintiff wins; if it is not, the defendant wins. For example, if the plaintiff claims that the defendant caused injury to him through her negligence, the trier of fact must look at the evidence and determine whether it is more likely than not that the plaintiff has established the defendant's negligence. At the end of the trial, on the basis of all the evidence before it, the trier of fact must determine whether the existence of the defendant's negligence is more likely than the non-existence of her negligence. If, at the end of the day, the trier of fact finds that the arguments for and against the plaintiff's position are equal, then the plaintiff has "failed to discharge his burden" or has lost the case. Because the plaintiff has the obligation to prove his case, a tie goes to the defendant.

PRIMA FACIE CASE

prima facie case
a case in which there is sufficient proof on its face that no further proof is required for a party to succeed

A **prima facie** case is one in which there is sufficient proof on its face that no further proof is required for a party to succeed. In a criminal matter, if the Crown has established a *prima facie* case, it has established all the elements of the offence beyond a reasonable doubt and will obtain a conviction unless the accused is able to call evidence to shake the reasonable doubt. Similarly, in a civil matter, if the plaintiff has established a *prima facie* case, she will succeed if the defendant does not call any evidence.

In some circumstances, a party must establish a *prima facie* case. For example, at the end of the Crown's case in a criminal matter, if the Crown has failed to establish a *prima facie* case, the accused may make a motion for a **directed verdict**. The Crown has failed to provide evidence on all material matters and, as a result, a jury could not find the accused guilty. If a person is accused of robbery and none of the witnesses identifies him, then he must be acquitted, identification being a matter in issue in the proceedings.

directed verdict
the judge directs that the accused be acquitted because the Crown has not made a *prima facie* case

The Crown must also establish a *prima facie* case in a preliminary inquiry. The Crown must show that there is some evidence on all material issues that a reasonably instructed jury could convict on. For the purpose of assessing whether the

Crown has made a *prima facie* case in a preliminary inquiry, the judge must assume that all the evidence presented is true, even where it was unconvincing to her. In the past, judges were not permitted to "weigh" the evidence in order to determine whether they would convict on the evidence, or even whether they would likely convict. Instead, they were restricted to assessing whether a jury could convict on the evidence. Recently, however, courts have undertaken the task known as "limited weighing." In this process, the preliminary inquiry judge assesses the evidence and considers whether a properly instructed jury could draw an inference of guilt. Only where the evidence appears so weak that a jury could not draw such an inference can the judge dismiss the charge. This same standard is applied in extradition hearings, where the court considers evidence presented by a foreign jurisdiction in order to determine whether the applicant has established that there is a case to meet in the foreign court.

In a civil case, if the plaintiff does not establish a *prima facie* case, the defendant need not call any evidence but, instead, may make a motion to have the case against him dismissed. This is sometimes referred to as a motion for **non-suit**. The basis of the motion is that since the plaintiff has not proved all the elements of her case, there is no case for the defendant to meet. For example, in a torts case, if the plaintiff is unable to establish that the defendant owed her a duty of care—one of the elements of a claim for negligence—then the defendant could move for dismissal of the case against him.

non-suit
the judge directs the dismissal of the case because the plaintiff has failed to meet a *prima facie* case

PRESUMPTIONS

A **presumption** is a thing that is taken to be true. In criminal and civil proceedings, presumptions are a way of assisting parties in proving facts that they must establish in order to succeed in their case, in circumstances where it would be unfair to make them prove the facts. By their very nature, presumptions are rebuttable. That is, the person against whom the presumption operates has an opportunity to call evidence to show that the presumption is not accurate and should be disregarded. There are presumptions that operate in both criminal and civil proceedings.

presumption
a fact that is taken to be true without the requirement of formal proof

Presumptions in Criminal Cases

In criminal matters, presumptions are primarily used by the Crown in proving the case against the accused beyond a reasonable doubt, but the most fundamental criminal presumption is the presumption of innocence. That is, the accused starts off with a clean slate and is presumed to be innocent. This presumption helps the accused person in her case because the obligation of proof is clearly laid at the Crown's feet. Another fundamental presumption is the presumption of mental competence. That is, any witness is presumed to be sane and if a party wishes to convince the judge that a person's evidence ought not to be accepted because she is insane, then it is up to the person making that allegation to prove it. Thus, any person who calls a witness is aided in that she does not have to prove that the witness is sane before the evidence can go in.

Since proof beyond a reasonable doubt in criminal matters is a very high standard to meet, and since some things are just really hard to prove because the only person who really knows is the accused, presumptions are employed to permit the trier of fact to make certain conclusions unless the accused proves otherwise. This process helps the Crown overcome its burden of proof. To understand this concept some examples may assist.

EXAMPLE ONE

A driver collides with another vehicle. She gets out of her car, quickly surveys the damage, then hops back into her car and speeds off. A passerby witnesses this, follows the driver to her home, and calls the police on his cellphone. The driver is charged with "leaving the scene of an accident in order to avoid criminal or civil liability." At trial, the Crown establishes that it was in fact the accused who was driving this vehicle and that she was involved in this accident. The Crown seeks to rely on the following presumption in s. 252(2) of the *Criminal Code*:

> In proceedings under subsection (1), evidence that an accused failed to stop his vehicle, ... offer assistance where any person has been injured or appears to require assistance and give his name and address is, in the absence of evidence to the contrary, proof of an intent to escape civil or criminal liability.

The Crown is still required to prove that the accused left the scene without leaving her name and offering assistance, but once that has been established, the Crown is entitled to rely on the presumption that the accused did this in order to avoid civil or criminal liability. Once the preliminary points have been established, the trier of fact must conclude that the accused left the scene to avoid civil or criminal liability unless there is "evidence to the contrary," likely from the accused. Because we can never know what is in a person's head, where there is one logical conclusion that arises from the proof of certain facts, the legislation provides for this presumption, which is really a logical inference.

Thus, a presumption has three important components:

1. The Crown must prove the basic fact.

2. The presumed fact follows on proof of the basic fact.

3. The accused can rebut the presumption by disproving or raising a doubt about the basic fact.

EXAMPLE TWO

A young man, upon reaching the age of majority, spends an evening drinking with his friends. As he is driving home he is stopped by the police for not signalling a lane change. The police demand a breath sample and his reading an hour and a half later is 140 milligrams of alcohol per 100 millilitres of blood. Because he is over the 80 milligram limit, he is charged with impaired driving. At trial, the Crown proves that the accused was the driver and that he "blew" 140 on the breathalyzer after a proper demand. The Crown then seeks to rely on the presumption that the reading on the machine equals his blood-alcohol level and that this was the level he had at the time of driving.

In this case, the trier of fact is required to conclude that the reading accurately reflects the blood-alcohol level at the time of driving. In fact, the reading may not be accurate. The breathalyzer machine measures the amount of alcohol in a person's breath, and the science behind the machine says that it is possible to make a

reasonably accurate extrapolation from that to conclude that if the machine measures X amount of alcohol in a person's breath then there will be, say, 140 milligrams
per 100 millilitres of the person's blood. There are many variables from person to
person, and the machine, in spite of careful standardizing and testing, can be
wrong. For example, a number of years ago, after breathalyzer machines had been
in use for many years, it was discovered that police officers' radios (the ones strapped
to their service belts) could cause the machines to give erroneous readings.

The protection afforded to the accused is that he can call "evidence to the contrary." In breathalyzer cases, evidence to the contrary would likely involve the accused's testifying about his pattern of drinking and related matters, as well as an
expert witness calculating from the pattern of drinking what the actual blood-
alcohol level would be. Faced with this evidence contradicting the machine readings, if the court did not disbelieve the accused's testimony about his drinking
pattern, the judge would have to acquit.

Problems with Reverse-Onus Presumptions in Criminal Cases

In a case where a presumption operates, as we have seen, the Crown is not required
to prove the presumed fact beyond a reasonable doubt. The trier of fact may presume that the fact is true unless the defence can effectively challenge or rebut the
presumption. In other words, if there is a presumption that the Crown may rely
upon, the only way that the defence can challenge the presumption is to call evidence. Therefore, the usual burden on the Crown to prove all the material facts has
been "reversed" so that the accused is required to disprove some of the facts. This is
called a **reverse onus**. Reverse-onus provisions are necessary in some instances but
they can dangerous because they may require the trier of fact to make conclusions
that are not logical.

In *R v. Oakes*, the Supreme Court of Canada reviewed the issue whether
reverse-onus provisions violate the Charter-protected right to be presumed innocent. The court made a number of important points in reviewing and clarifying
where and when such reverse-onus provisions would meet the standard for accept-
ability. The legislation at issue in *Oakes* was s. 8 of the *Narcotic Control Act*. It provided that when an accused person was determined to be in possession of a
narcotic, the trier of fact must conclude that the accused possessed the narcotic for
the purpose of trafficking, unless the trier of fact is satisfied by evidence to the contrary that it was "simple possession"—essentially, for personal use.

The Supreme Court made the following observations about presumptions.
They are either

- presumptions of law   *or*   - presumptions of fact
- with basic fact   *or*   - without basic fact
- mandatory   *or*   - permissive
- rebuttable   *or*   - irrebuttable

The Supreme Court concluded that the presumption contained in s. 8 of the
Narcotic Control Act was a presumption of basic fact (proof that the accused possessed

reverse onus
situation where the
obligation to prove a fact
is shifted from the Crown
to the accused

a narcotic) that was mandatory but rebuttable. It found that such a presumption violated s. 11 of the Charter:

> I am in no doubt whatsoever that [s. 8 of the *Narcotic Control Act*] violates s. 11(d) of the Charter by requiring the accused to prove on a balance of probabilities that he was not in possession of the narcotic for the purpose of trafficking. Mr. Oakes is compelled by s. 8 to prove he is not guilty of the offence of trafficking.

The court went on to consider whether the violation could be "saved" by s. 1 of the Charter as a limitation that was acceptable in a free and democratic society. We will review this test in part III of the text, dealing the Charter and adherence to a higher standard.

Most legislated presumptions are mandatory; otherwise, there would not be much point in having such a presumption. An example of a permissive presumption is the presumption that a person intends the natural consequences of his actions. This presumption *permits* a trier of fact to conclude that if a person drives his car into a crowd, the person intends to cause injury to persons there, without any other evidence of his intention. However, the trier of fact is not *required* to come to that conclusion, even where there is no evidence led by the accused to counter that presumption.

Presumptions are designed to aid the Crown in proving its case against an accused, particularly where a component of the Crown's case is elusive, inside the accused's mind. Although it may be very difficult for the Crown to obtain a conviction in some circumstances, the *Oakes* case tells us that any attempt to simplify or streamline that process must still comply with the Charter. Whether the wording of a provision violates s. 11(d) is a matter for the court's interpretation, but generally speaking, if the provision does not require the Crown to prove very much of anything before the burden shifts to the accused to prove his innocence, the provision will be seen as a Charter violation.

Presumptions in Civil Cases

There are a number of presumptions in the common law. For example, it is presumed that an adult is mentally competent. There is no need to prove that fact. In contrast, a party who wishes to challenge an adult's mental competency bears the onus of proving incompetence.

Tort law has a number of presumptions. One basic presumption is *res ipsa loquitur*, which is a Latin expression that means "the thing speaks for itself." In other words something is so obvious that it needs no further explanation. In cases of negligence, for example, the plaintiff usually has the burden of proving all the elements of negligence, including that the defendant did not meet a proper standard of care in dealing with the plaintiff. The plaintiff would be required to call evidence of what the defendant did or did not do in taking care not to cause injury. However, in many instances, the plaintiff has absolutely no knowledge of what the defendant did that was careless and has no way of reasonably finding out. In these instances, applying the principle of *res ipsa loquitur* relieves the plaintiff of the burden of proving how a defendant who owes a duty of care was negligent where it is obvious that there must have been negligence for the injury to happen.

For example, if the plaintiff drinks a bottled beverage that had been sealed until she opened it and discovers a dead snail at the bottom of the bottle, she has no reasonable way of learning how the snail came to be there. It must have occurred at the manufacturing plant because the bottle was sealed until the plaintiff opened it. But what exactly happened? Did the manufacturer have inadequate sterilization equipment? Was the storage facility improperly maintained? Perhaps an employee purposefully put the snail there to get back at the employer? All of these things are possibilities and the law says the manufacturer would be responsible in all these instances. The principle of *res ipsa loquitur* operates in circumstances like these where the thing that caused the damage was under the sole control of the defendant, the injury could not have happened without negligence, and the facts of the incident are not known to the plaintiff. Of course, the defendant is entitled to call evidence to rebut the presumption and show that he was not negligent. (See *Donoghue (or McAlister) v. Stevenson.*)

JUDICIAL NOTICE

To a layperson, it may seem that the legal process is largely about the creation of confusion through the overcomplication of matters. This may be because so many interests and considerations must be balanced in the delicate act of attempting to achieve justice. In some instances, evidence law is refreshingly logical in attempting to put reliable information before the trier of fact with the least amount of cost and frustration.

Judicial notice permits the judge to recognize or "take note of" the existence of a particular fact without requiring a party to formally prove it. If the judge is sitting alone, she will just state that she is taking judicial notice of a particular fact. If there is a jury, the judge will direct the jury that certain facts are to be taken as proven. The facts must be so commonly accepted in the community that no reasonable person could challenge them. These include some facts that can be easily ascertained by consulting sources that are acknowledged as accurate. Such facts are frequently referred to as **notorious facts**. The term simply indicates the notoriety or recognition of the facts; it does not imply anything improper in them.

> **judicial notice**
> a judge's recognition of a fact without requiring a party to prove it

> **notorious fact**
> a fact that is so generally known and accepted that it may not reasonably be disputed

In assessing whether a fact is a notorious fact, a court may ask:

1. Is this a fact that is part of society's common knowledge?

2. Is this a fact that is commonly known in this locality?

3. Is this a fact that is commonly known to a specific group within the community or locality?

If any of these questions can be answered "yes," the court may permit the fact to be proved by way of judicial notice.

One of the primary virtues of employing judicial notice as a means of proving a fact is that one or more of the litigants, as well as the court, are saved the time and expense of proving the fact. With the cost of legal proceedings today, this can be a considerable economic saving.

Examples of Judicial Notice

There is no exhaustive list of matters that judicial notice may be taken of, but some of the areas are: the hour the sun sets in a particular location at a particular time of year, the impact of a recession on real estate prices, traffic patterns (rush hour), the impact of a loss of power on perishable foods, activities that were widely publicized in the newspapers, that Christmas day is a holiday, and that certain expressions commonly used by a prostitute and a potential client constitute an offering of sexual services. Further examples of judicial notice include determining the definition of a word by consulting a dictionary, or determining a geographic location by consulting an atlas. At least part of the rationale for provisions for judicial notice is that the justice system would look silly if "indisputable" facts were ignored by the courts. Let's look at some examples.

EXAMPLE ONE

There is a motor vehicle accident and the defendant shows that it was raining at the time, implying that the plaintiff should have driven more slowly because of that. No one offers evidence that roads are more slippery when wet. Can the judge take judicial notice of the fact that wet roads are more slippery than dry ones?

EXAMPLE TWO

A landlord evicts a tenant for damage to his property. It turns out that there was a marijuana grow operation located there and that the tenant knocked down walls and ripped out the living room floor to make space for the taller plants. The landlord is suing the tenant for the damage. The tenant claims that the landlord told him he didn't mind if the tenant did some fixing up, and even offered to pay for the paint. Can the court take judicial notice of the fact that a landlord would not authorize tearing down walls and ripping out floors as "fixing up"?

EXAMPLE THREE

A witness states that an incident took place on the first Tuesday in September last year but does not recall the date. Should the court be permitted to consult a calendar to ascertain the date?

Administrative Tribunals

Administrative tribunals have considerable latitude in the exercise of judicial notice, or what is sometimes referred to as "administrative notice" (given that tribunal members are not actually judges). Most administrative tribunals are made up of persons who have considerable experience in the particular area of the tribunal's jurisdiction (for example, labour relations or environmental regulation). Tribunal members are often in possession of a multitude of facts that are commonly known in the area, and thus they may choose not to require the parties to go through the process of formally proving those facts.

Social Framework Facts

There is a very interesting area of judicial notice that has had a huge influence on recent developments in the law, particularly in the age of Charter challenges. This involves the court taking judicial notice of "social framework facts." The idea is that the court should have at its disposal scholarly studies and research in relation to social interaction because decisions made by the court have long-term impact on these areas. An example of this is the family law case, *Moge v. Moge*. The issue in *Moge* was whether Ms. Moge was entitled to ongoing maintenance many years after the marriage had come to an end. She was working as she had throughout the marriage. The amount of maintenance at stake was only $50 per month, but the case went right up to the Supreme Court of Canada.

The Supreme Court permitted numerous intervenors to present evidence regarding the impact of divorce on the incomes of former spouses. This evidence relied heavily on research that showed that, after divorce, women and children almost invariably ended up in worse economic condition while the financial fortunes of men improved. This information formed a backdrop or foundation for the judgment, which, in simple terms, held that the economic impact of divorce should be equally shared by former spouses. There later arose some controversy over the research that supported this decision, and it appeared that some of the statistics showing the disparity of economic positions of men and women may have been inflated. This, of course, raises a question about the validity of decisions if they rely on facts, even social framework facts, that are faulty.

In *R v. Zundel*, the court was asked by the Crown to take judicial notice of the Holocaust. If we are talking about something that the community in general (as opposed to a fringe community that chooses to deny the existence of the Holocaust) accepts as indisputable, then there should be no problem with the Crown's request. However, the Ontario Court of Appeal was concerned that allowing the Crown to establish an essential component of its case without formal proof would be prejudicial to the defence.

An interesting case involving judicial notice took place in the Maritimes. In *R v. S. (R.D.)*, a young person was charged with assaulting a police officer. The evidence was that the police were arresting another youth and that the accused interfered with this arrest. Both the trial judge and the accused were black and had roots in the local black community. In her reasons, the judge commented that police officers had been known to lie in court and to overreact in dealing with black youths. No evidence to support these comments had been presented in court; the judge was drawing on her life experience in making her statement. Her generalized experience of systemic racism led her to conclude that the particular officer dealing with this matter in fact overreacted. The decision was appealed and the Supreme Court of Canada was split on whether the judge was entitled to draw the conclusions that she did.

In the end, while many justices of the Supreme Court expressed concern about the wording used by the judge, the majority maintained the acquittals she imposed. It is clear that the judge took a general impression that she had of police officers and applied it to her deliberations on the specific facts of this case. We find this approach troubling. The simple way of viewing this from our perspective is to consider what would happen if the trial judge had other assumptions, perhaps more commonly shared by the public. Let's say the judge stated, "Young people usually lie in court and have no control over their emotions," and then convicted the accused. This would be scandalous and it is quite likely that the conviction would be overturned. In fact, there are instances where judges have made negative credibility findings based on race and then had their findings reversed on appeal. (For example, see *R v. W. (S.)*.)

It is essential that any conclusions of a court be grounded in facts specific to the case before the court. To clarify the distinction between proper judicial notice of facts and what took place in *R v. S. (R.D.)*, consider the example of a human rights complaint by a black person claiming he was not hired by the police force due to systemic racism. In this instance, the qualifications of the applicant would be reviewed and evidence of systemic racism could be presented. If such racism was so "notorious" as to be indisputable, then the court could (theoretically) take judicial notice of these facts. The problem with the *S. (R.D.)* case is that the court made a determination that the officers in fact acted a certain way based on a generalization. There was no link established between the stereotypical observation and the case before the court.

An interesting footnote to this discussion is that judicial notice of a fact may be taken for the first time in the process of an appeal. This is unusual since most appeals are based only on the evidence that was before the trier of fact. This approach seems to acknowledge that failure to recognize an indisputable fact would, in essence, bring the administration of justice into disrepute. While there is some division on this point, it appears that when judicial notice of a fact is taken, it becomes conclusive evidence of that fact, incapable of being disproved through other evidence. This is not to say that the parties may not debate whether a proposed fact is capable of judicial notice, or that a judge should not alert the parties that she is considering taking judicial notice of a fact. But once judicial notice of a fact is taken, evidence disputing that finding would likely not be allowed in the trial.

JUDICIAL NOTICE GONE AWRY

Judicial notice can save litigants and courts time and expense, but that saving can sometimes come at a cost. In a family law case in British Columbia, a father was seeking to obtain custody of his child from the mother. The mother had a drug and alcohol habit, and though she loved the child, she was not very interested in devoting much time to her care. The father was caring and had steady work, and he had a new wife who was devoted to the child and was a good role model. At trial, the mother and the father presented their evidence and it seemed likely that the judge would conclude that it was in the child's best interests to be with the father and his wife. The judge reserved and wrote a decision. In his decision, the judge referred to a report that he had read, which had not been discussed during the trial, that led him to conclude that girls should be with their mothers. The father had no opportunity to comment on the findings or counter them with other studies or observations. The father appealed the decision. The appeal was cut short when the mother agreed to change custody to the father. Even she must have seen how wrong it was for the judge to base his decision on "beliefs" that neither side had an opportunity to comment on or counter.

CHAPTER SUMMARY

The burden of proof in criminal and civil matters requires the Crown (in criminal cases) or the plaintiff (in civil cases) to prove certain facts or matters in issue. At certain points in a trial, however, the burden can shift to the accused or the defendant. In some special criminal cases, when certain defences are raised, the accused must also meet the air of reality test; that is, the accused must prove that the defence has the air of reality before it can be considered by the trier of fact. When the Crown or plaintiff has met the burden of proof, we say that a *prima facie* case has been made out.

The standard of proof in criminal cases is proof beyond a reasonable doubt; in civil cases, proof or a balance of probabilities. Presumptions assist parties in proving facts that they must establish in order to succeed in their cases, but by their nature presumptions are rebuttable by opposing parties.

In certain circumstances, through the operation of judicial notice, a judge is able to "take note" of facts that would otherwise have to be proven.

KEY TERMS

burden of proof

air of reality test

beyond a reasonable doubt

balance of probabilities

prima facie case

directed verdict

non-suit

presumption

reverse onus

judicial notice

notorious fact

rebut

REFERENCES

Baltovich, R v. (2004), 73 OR (3d) 481 (CA).

Canadian Charter of Rights and Freedoms, part I of the *Constitution Act, 1982*, RSC 1985, app. II, no. 44.

Cinous, R v., [2002] SCC 29.

Donoghue (or McAlister) v. Stevenson, [1932] All ER 1, [1932] AC 562 (HL).

Lifchus, R v., [1997] 3 SCR 320.

Moge v. Moge, [1992] 3 SCR 813.

Narcotic Control Act, RSC 1970, c. N-1.

Oakes, R v., [1986] 1 SCR 103.

S. (R.D.), R v. (1997), 10 CR (5th) 1 (SCC).

W. (S.), R v. (1991), 6 CR (4th) 373 (Ont. CA).

Zundel, R v. (1987), 56 CR (3d) 1.

REVIEW QUESTIONS

1. Which party usually bears the burden of proof in a civil case? In a criminal case?

2. What is the air of reality test and what unique position does it play in some criminal defence issues?

3. Explain the difference between a civil standard of proof and a criminal one and why such a difference exists.

4. What is meant by the term *prima facie* case? Give some examples of its significance.

5. What role do presumptions play in both the burden and standard of proof?

6. What does it mean when we say that a presumption is rebuttable?

7. When may a judge take judicial notice of certain facts?

DISCUSSION QUESTIONS

1. Discuss the difficulties that a reverse-onus provision presents in relation to the Charter.

2. Review the reference to a model jury charge offered in *R v. Lifchus*, [1997] 3 SCR 320, at para. 39. Are there any problems with the wording that Justice Cory suggests?

CHAPTER 4

Fundamental Principles

CHAPTER OBJECTIVES

After completing this chapter you should be able to:

- Explain the threshold tests for evidence.
- Distinguish between relevance and materiality and define conditional relevance.
- Understand how evidence is weighed for its probative value and its prejudicial effect.
- Distinguish between direct and circumstantial evidence and explain why relevance is an issue with circumstantial evidence.
- State the general principles of evidence regarding consciousness of guilt and prior judicial determinations.

THE THRESHOLD TEST: RELEVANCE AND MATERIALITY

The determination of whether or not an alleged fact is admissible into evidence, and therefore something that the trier of fact may consider in deciding the case, is based on a series of questions about the fact. The very first of these questions is, Is the fact both relevant and material? Because it is the first question that must be answered, we say that it is the "threshold test" for the admissibility of all evidence. As discussed in chapter 1, the role of the judge is like that of a gatekeeper who decides what evidence gets in through the gate. Evidence that does not meet the test of being relevant and material will not be admitted.

However, just because evidence must be relevant and material to be admitted does not mean that all relevant and material evidence will automatically be admitted. If the trier of law decides that a piece of evidence is relevant and material, she must then ask another series of questions about it, all of which must be answered in the affirmative before the evidence can be considered by the trier of fact. Those questions are the topics of subsequent chapters. But if the evidence is not relevant and material, it will automatically be excluded and no further questions need to be asked about it.

It is important to distinguish between the concepts of relevance and materiality. Many practitioners often fail to differentiate the two concepts when examining the facts, which can lead to confusion in their legal arguments. Proposed evidence can be both irrelevant and immaterial, relevant but immaterial, or irrelevant but material. Thus, potential for confusion abounds in this area.

MATERIALITY EXPLAINED

We begin with the concept of materiality because it is easier to explain and understand than relevance. In any legal dispute, there is something that the parties are arguing about. In a car accident, the parties are probably arguing about who caused the accident, who is at fault. That is the major dispute before the court. There are likely numerous smaller or subordinate disputes as well, such as how fast the defendant was driving before the collision, whether the plaintiff ran a red light, or whether the defendant was intoxicated. In a criminal case, the major issue in dispute between the Crown and the accused is the guilt of the accused. There are also likely to be many smaller disputes in the case. A fact that relates to any matter in dispute between the parties is a **material fact**.

material fact
a fact that relates to any matter in dispute between parties

EXAMPLE ONE

Joe is charged with stealing Frank's car. Joe wishes to introduce evidence that Frank works as a waiter and does not declare all his tips, and therefore is cheating on his income tax. According to Joe's convoluted thinking, Frank bought his car using money that should have gone into the tax system; therefore, the car belongs to all Canadians. Since Joe is a Canadian, he has a right to take the car whenever he wishes.

Assuming that the judge does not agree with Joe's logic, the information about Frank cheating on his taxes will not be admitted because it is immaterial to the proceedings before the court. It does not relate to any matter in issue before the court in Joe's criminal charge. If Frank finds himself in Tax Court at a later date, the information about not declaring his tips would be entirely material—in fact, it could be the main matter in issue between him and the Canada Revenue Agency.

EXAMPLE TWO

Terry is suing Jan as a result of a car accident. There is a dispute about who was at fault. In her cross-examination of Jan, Terry's lawyer demands to know whether or not Jan is retired. Jan's lawyer objects to the question as immaterial. The judge upholds the objection. The information about Jan's retirement cannot assist the trier of fact in determining fault, so the judge must not let it in as evidence.

RELEVANCE EXPLAINED

Relevance is best thought of as a logical support for an argument. That is, for the question, "Is this fact relevant?" we can substitute the question, "Does this fact logically lead to something that is important to prove in the case?" For example, if one wished to prove that a thief was a certain height, would it be logical to establish that he was wearing white running shoes? Not likely. The fact that the accused was wearing running shoes does not have a logical connection to what one is trying to prove—his height. The running shoes would therefore not be a **relevant fact**.

> **relevant fact**
> a fact that logically
> supports a proposition

In determining whether evidence is relevant, the trier of law will sometimes ask whether the existence of the fact makes the proposition it is advanced to support more likely (or less likely). Put another way, imagine what the case would look like without that piece of evidence.

EXAMPLE ONE

The Crown is trying to prove that Eddy is the killer and there is evidence that the killer was seen running down the alley wearing a black toque. The proposition that the Crown is trying to establish is that Eddy is the killer. DNA evidence showing the Eddy's hair was recovered from a black toque in a garbage can in that same alley would make the proposition that Eddy was the killer more likely.

EXAMPLE TWO

In a personal injury case, the plaintiff is trying to prove that the defendant was negligent because he was driving too fast for the road conditions. The plaintiff says that there was frost on the roads and the defendant should have been travelling more slowly, more cautiously. The accident took place in Calgary, Alberta. As part of her case, the plaintiff seeks to introduce into evidence meteorological reports showing that at the time of the accident it was minus –5 °C in Edmonton. Should the judge permit the admission of meteorological evidence that relates to Edmonton into a trial dealing with an accident in Calgary? If the defendant objected to the evidence, would the objection be that the evidence is irrelevant or immaterial?

Let's consider the issue of materiality first because it is usually easier to sort out. Does evidence about the likelihood of frost on roads relate to a matter in issue between the parties? Yes, because the issue is whether the defendant was driving too fast for the road conditions. So, in general terms, the plaintiff is on the right track. The problem is that having information about road conditions in Edmonton before the trier of fact won't assist it in coming to conclusions about the material issues. There is no logical connection between the weather conditions in Edmonton and the road conditions in Calgary. It is illogical to conclude that the road conditions in Edmonton at any particular time were the same as those in Calgary. The plaintiff may want to introduce the evidence about Edmonton because her brother-in-law works for the Edmonton weather channel, so it is cheaper for her to find out this information. Or, even though she knows that the weather was different in Edmonton, she may want to mislead the court into inferring that it was the same. Or she may want to introduce the evidence for any number of other reasons.

In determining the admissibility of this evidence, the trier of law asks, is it logical to conclude that information about the road conditions in Edmonton makes the trier of fact better able to draw conclusions about the road conditions in Calgary? The answer is no, there is no logical connection between the two. More importantly, admission of the evidence is dangerous because the trier of fact may conclude from the fact that the judge let the evidence in that it has some importance or value and may therefore give it weight, even though it deserves no weight. The result could be an unjust decision. In our system of justice, the trial judge must keep out information that will diminish or impair the ability of the trier of fact to render a just and reasonable verdict.

CONDITIONAL RELEVANCE

In a court case, it is often difficult to present evidence in the chronological order in which events occur. One witness is called and tells his or her version of events. Another witness or even several other witnesses must be called to fill in the rest of the story. It is not until all the witnesses have testified that the complete story emerges. Because evidence is often presented in this way, there are times when the relevance of evidence is not immediately apparent.

Recall the murder case involving Eddy and the black toque. The Crown is trying to prove that Eddy murdered the victim. The first witness called says that she saw a man, identified as Eddy, running down the street, near the alley, at about the same time as the murder. This evidence puts Eddy in the general vicinity of the murder, but the witness did not see him wearing a toque or any other type of hat. In fact, she says she is absolutely certain that Eddy was bare-headed.

The next witness called is the police officer who found the black toque in the garbage can in the alley. This black toque seems to have nothing to do with Eddy, because the first witness said he was not wearing a hat when she saw him. The fact that the officer found a black toque does not logically connect, at this point, to the proposition that Eddy is the murderer. It appears to be irrelevant. However, the Crown's third witness, a forensic scientist, will testify that she examined the hat and tested the hair inside it, and found Eddy's DNA in the hair.

When the police officer describes finding the hat, Eddy's lawyer may want to object to the admission of this information into evidence, on the grounds that it is irrelevant. In defending the admission, the Crown would argue that the finding of the hat will be linked to a relevant point but that several witnesses will be needed to do it. The Crown will ask that the evidence be admitted on condition that it is properly and logically tied to a relevant fact by the end of the presentation of the Crown's case. The judge would then admit the evidence on the grounds of its **conditional relevance**. That is, the evidence is admitted on the condition that its relevance will be established as the case goes along and more evidence is presented. If the Crown is unable to establish relevance by the end of its case, the judge will direct the jury to ignore that evidence.

conditional relevance
term describing evidence that may not initially appear relevant but is admitted on condition that its relevance will be established

WEIGHING PROBATIVE VALUE AGAINST PREJUDICE

Besides testing evidence for materiality and relevance, the trier of law also weighs the evidence to ensure that its probative value exceeds its prejudice. **Probative value** is the degree to which a proposed piece of evidence helps prove a proposition. The proposition that a party wishes to prove may be a small part of the case, such as the date the plaintiff signed a contract, or it may be the whole case, such as who murdered the victim. Regardless of whether a proposed piece of evidence is a small or large part of a case, its probative value is how conclusive it is in proving the point in dispute.

Many factors go into the consideration of the probative value of evidence. The credibility of the evidence is important, as is its reliability. These two factors are more appropriately dealt with by the trier of fact than by the trier of law. A factor that bears particularly on the issue of admissibility—and therefore is dealt with by the trier of law—is the strength of the inferences that can be drawn from the proposed evidence. For example, DNA testing of blood on the accused's clothing that shows it matches the victim's blood has very strong inferential value. The evidence establishes the strong likelihood that the accused was close to or in contact with the victim when the victim was bleeding. On the other hand, testing of fibres in the accused's car that shows they match the make of carpet in the victim's home—carpet that was installed in thousands of homes—has less probative value. This evidence does not offer much help at all in proving the Crown's proposition that the accused murdered the victim. The only proper inference to be drawn from such fibre evidence is that the accused or someone else using his car was in one of the thousands of homes that have this carpet.

probative value
the degree to which a potential piece of evidence helps prove a proposition

EXAMPLE

The accused is stopped by the police near the scene of a violent murder. The victim was slashed with a knife and blood was spattered all over the room. The clothes of the accused appear to have dark "blood-like" stains. Testing shows that the stains are in fact blood. However, the blood does not match the victim's or the accused's, but five other people's. Should this evidence be admitted?

If the victim's blood had been on the accused, that evidence would clearly be very probative, because it would place him at or near where the victim suffered an injury. Instead, he has five other people's blood on him, which may be suspicious but is not helpful to the trier of fact, beyond wild speculation. It is that wild speculation that the judge must guard against. The probative value of the evidence is very slight. In weighing the probative value of this evidence, the trier of law must also consider the **prejudice** of the evidence, or the likelihood that a jury hearing this information will give the evidence more weight than it deserves. Clearly, in this instance, the probative value of the evidence is exceeded by the prejudice.

prejudice
the potenial for a trier of fact to give evidence more weight than it deserves

In considerations of the probative value of a proposed piece of evidence, the line between factors that are under the judge's authority (the strength of the inferences that may be drawn from the evidence) and those that are under the jury's authority (the credibility and reliability of the evidence) can become blurred. Where the judge thinks the jury may give the evidence much more weight than it deserves, even if it is otherwise valuable to them, the judge can protect them from this prejudice by excluding the evidence. This commonly occurs with crime scene photos. While such photos are clearly relevant and material to the proceedings, they often cause a very emotional reaction and can lead jurors to distort or abandon the logical processes they are required to carry out. Consider how logical you are when you get into a heated argument. When angry, jealous, frustrated, or hurt, most people say and do things that they would not do in a calm or rational frame of mind. The prejudice inherent in the gory photos is that the jurors may become incapable of objectivity and rational assessment, and reach a decision against the accused regardless of the lack of evidence against him. Thus, a judge needs to consider credibility to a degree, since evidence that is biased or otherwise wholly untrustworthy, if given weight by the trier of fact, can result in a very wrong decision.

Prejudice, then, must be measured and weighed against the probative value of evidence. Historically, prejudice referred only to the potential for the trier of fact to give the evidence more weight than it deserves, and it was usually considered only in criminal matters and only in relation to the accused. More recently, however, the concept of prejudice has been broadened to include other considerations. The concept of fairness to the parties is now being applied to persons other than the accused—the complainant in a sexual assault trial, for example. In weighing the prejudicial value of proposed evidence, judges also consider whether the evidence will absorb an undue amount of court time, whether it was presented by one party with little or no warning to the other, whether it will distract the trier of fact from the issues, and whether it will simply demean the judicial process by insulting or otherwise emotionally abusing witnesses.

The following chart shows the factors that a judge considers in weighing the probative value of the evidence against its prejudice.

Probative Value Versus Prejudice

Probative Value	Prejudice
Strength of the evidence in proving what the party proposes ↓	Potential to be given undeserved weight by the jury ↓
▪ Credibility only where it is so suspect as to be misleading ▪ Reliability only where it is so suspect as to be misleading	Costs of presenting the evidence including ▪ excessive use of court time ▪ fairness to the parties ▪ potential to confuse the issues

It should also be noted that evidence is not automatically excluded just because it is prejudicial. Sometimes, evidence may throw a very negative light on the accused but it has sufficient probative value that it ought to be before the trier of fact. Consider an accused who is charged with breaching a condition of his parole by being at an elementary school. The fact that the restriction was placed on the accused as a result of a conviction for the sexual assault of a child would certainly be prejudicial in the sense that it would show the accused in a bad light, but it would likely be admissible so that the trier of fact could understand the basis for the original order.

RELEVANCE AND CIRCUMSTANTIAL EVIDENCE

Evidence can be categorized as either direct or circumstantial evidence. **Direct evidence** is given when a witness gives testimony about a material fact, and that material fact is something that he actually experienced—saw, heard, touched, etc. As you recall, a material fact is a fact that relates to any matter in dispute between the parties. If the trier of fact believes the witness when he says he saw what he says he did, that's the end of the fact finding on that issue. The credibility of the witness is the deciding point. The trier of fact can believe or disbelieve the witness, but she need not make any logical inference about the direct evidence.

direct evidence
evidence given by a witness about a material fact that the witness experienced

For example, if the Crown is trying to prove that Sam stabbed Joe but Sam is denying his guilt, whether Sam stabbed Joe is a material issue in the case because it is a matter in dispute between the parties. If there is a witness who says she saw Sam stab Joe, her testimony is direct evidence of a material fact. The trier of fact only has to determine whether the witness is credible. If she is, then the trier of fact will decide that Sam stabbed Joe.

Circumstantial evidence is not as straightforward. It is indirect evidence from which the trier of fact can logically infer the existence of a material fact. In other words, there is a chain of facts that can be followed to a logical conclusion about an issue in dispute between the parties even though there is no direct evidence. The trier of fact must make a logical jump or inference to reach the determination of the material fact.

circumstantial evidence
indirect evidence from which the trier of fact can logically infer the existence of a material fact

For example, say the witness in the scenario above, instead of seeing Sam stab Joe, saw a man with one leg stab him. Sam has one leg. There is also evidence that Sam had a long-term grudge against the victim. There is no direct evidence that Sam stabbed Joe. No one can actually identify him as the person who did the stabbing. However, the trier of fact may logically follow the indirect evidence and make a logical inference that Sam stabbed Joe. Circumstantial evidence involves a two-step process. The trier of fact must first decide that the witness is credible and should be believed when she says she saw a one-legged man stab Joe. Second, even if she accepts the witness's testimony, the trier of fact must make an inference that the stabber was Sam and not some other one-legged man.

Relevance is a central issue in circumstantial evidence but not in direct evidence. Direct evidence is always relevant once it has passed the test of materiality.

A fact is always relevant once it passes the test of materiality. Circumstantial evidence must first pass the materiality test but it then must also be tested for its relevance to the matter at hand.

Sometimes TV shows or movies suggest that circumstantial evidence is not as good as direct evidence. That is not necessarily the case. Circumstantial evidence can often be very helpful to a case while direct evidence can be a major problem. For example, it is well established that eyewitness testimony, which is direct evidence, is one of the most unreliable forms of evidence available.

SOME RELEVANCE RULES OF THUMB

Over time, general principles about types of evidence and the issue of relevance have been established. We will look at some of these.

Consciousness of Guilt

In criminal cases, the behaviour of the accused may be admitted as evidence that he was behaving in a "guilty manner." For example, he ran away from the scene of the crime, he lied about his whereabouts on the night in question, or he altered his appearance immediately after the offence was committed. Behavioural evidence is an inference based on circumstantial evidence. The trier of fact is asked to draw the inference that the accused is guilty because of his behaviour in trying to escape the scene or cover up the evidence.

Consciousness of guilt is usually admitted into evidence on the basis that it is relevant. Of course, there may be logical reasons for the accused's behaviour that have nothing to do with guilt. The judge must therefore be extremely vigilant in advising the jury as to the proper use of consciousness of guilt evidence because it could be misused otherwise.

In civil cases, the equivalent to consciousness of guilt is the concept that is often referred to as "subsequent repairs." The defendant has done something following the harm to the plaintiff to rectify the situation that the plaintiff claims resulted in her injury. For example, if the defendant has repaired the broken tiles in the floor that the plaintiff said she had tripped over, this would be evidence of subsequent repairs and would play the same role that consciousness of guilt does in criminal cases. In other words, the evidence is usually admissible, and the trier of fact is asked to infer that the defendant's action to rectify the situation of which the plaintiff is complaining is evidence of liability on the defendant's part.

However, an offer to settle in a civil case is not admissible into evidence. If the defendant has offered the plaintiff an amount of money to settle the case, this is a fact that the trier of fact will not hear. Although one might infer liability on the basis of such an offer, the courts have ruled that offers to settle should be encouraged because of their benefits to the justice system by cutting down on trial time and the attendant costs of litigation.

Prior Judicial Determinations

A single incident can result in both criminal and civil legal proceedings. For example, if a drunk driver hits a pedestrian, the driver will be charged with the criminal offence of impaired driving and it is quite likely that the pedestrian will sue, in civil proceedings, for his injury. If the driver is convicted of impaired driving in the criminal proceeding, the courts have ruled that that conviction is admissible into the civil proceeding, as *prima facie* proof of the act. The defendant in such a civil proceeding thus bears the onus of rebutting or disproving the act. If a person is found criminally responsible for a certain action, it is highly unlikely that a civil court will find otherwise.

However, it is entirely possible for a defendant to be acquitted in the criminal case and still be found liable in the civil case. This can happen because of the different standards of proof required in each type of proceeding, The Crown may not be able to prove beyond a reasonable doubt the guilt of the accused, but a plaintiff in a civil proceeding, relying on the same facts, may be able to establish the defendant's civil liability on the balance of probabilities. In any event, the criminal case is always tried before any civil proceedings in order to avoid undue prejudice to the defendant, whose right to remain silent would be prejudiced in defending the civil action.

CHAPTER SUMMARY

The threshold test for the admission of any evidence requires that the evidence be both relevant and material. It is the very first question one must ask about potentially admissible evidence. While the concepts of relevance and materiality are related, they are not the same. Proposed evidence can be both irrelevant and immaterial, or relevant but immaterial, or irrelevant but material. Thus, potential for confusion abounds in this area. To be material, evidence must relate to any matter that is in dispute between the parties. To be relevant, evidence must have a logical connection to what one is trying to prove.

Evidence may also be conditionally relevant and entered into evidence on the proviso that what appears to be an irrelevant fact will be rendered relevant by the admission of additional evidence.

Once a fact has been found to be relevant and material, the judge may still exercise her discretion to exclude the fact from evidence if its prejudicial effect outweighs its probative value.

Evidence can be either direct or circumstantial. Direct evidence involves a witness's direct, personal knowledge of a material fact. Relevance is not an issue with direct evidence. By comparison, circumstantial evidence is less straightforward. The trier of fact must make an inference, based on the circumstantial evidence, that a material fact exists. Because an inference must be made, relevance is a central issue with circumstantial evidence.

Finally, there are a couple of "rules of thumb" about relevance. First, in both criminal and civil cases, evidence that the accused or defendant attempted to cover up his actions or involvement in the alleged offence or incident is referred to as consciousness of guilt. It is usually viewed as relevant and, therefore, admissible evidence. Second, a prior judicial determination based on the same set of facts is usually admitted into evidence as being relevant. However, it is admitted only as one piece of evidence; it is not necessarily determinative of the decision in the later judicial proceeding.

KEY TERMS

material fact

relevant fact

conditional relevance

probative value

prejudice

direct evidence

circumstantial evidence

REVIEW QUESTIONS

1. Why do we say that it is a threshold test that evidence, to be admissible, must be both relevant and material?

2. What is meant by the concept of materiality?

3. How is it determined whether or not a fact is relevant?

4. What is conditional relevance and why is it necessary to admit some evidence on the basis that it will later be shown to be relevant?

5. When we say that a piece of evidence is more probative than prejudicial, what do we mean?

6. Describe what is meant by the term "direct evidence." Give an example.

7. Describe what is meant by the term "circumstantial evidence." Give an example.

8. Why is relevance a central issue with circumstantial evidence but not with direct evidence?

9. What is consciousness of guilt? Give an example.

DISCUSSION QUESTIONS

The following questions deal with materiality and relevance.

1. The accused has been charged with first degree murder in the killing of an eight-year-old girl who lived next door to him. The Crown wishes to lead evidence from the investigating officer that the attention of the police was drawn to the accused because he looked and acted "weird" when the police first canvassed the neighbourhood to see whether any of the neighbours had seen anything suspicious. The accused refused to participate in the search for the missing child and did not seem particularly upset after her body was discovered. Is the evidence of the police officer admissible? Why?

2. The accused has been charged with the murder of his daughter. The child's dismembered body was found in various places around the city. The first body part found was discovered by a woman walking her dog on the beach. The woman saw a couple acting suspiciously; they left a bag on the rocks and when she went to take a look after they were gone, she found the child's head in the bag. It was obviously a horrible and grisly discovery.

    The accused has admitted to killing his daughter but says it was an accident. He says he dismembered the body after the accidental death because he was an illegal immigrant and was afraid he would be deported. He also admits to going to the beach with his wife and leaving the bag with the head inside. The Crown has refused to accept a plea bargain for either manslaughter or second degree murder and is trying the accused on first degree murder.

    At the trial, the Crown calls the woman who discovered the child's head in a plastic bag on the beach. First, he asks her what her marital status is. Then he asks about the breed of her dog. He then asks her to describe the events of the morning when she saw the suspicious couple and what they looked like. He also asks about the nature of her discovery.

    Are there specific objections the defence can make to any or all of these questions? If so, what are they?

3. The accused and several others were charged with conspiracy to import and traffick in heroin from Hong Kong. The Crown's case is based on surveillance and wiretap evidence. When the accused was arrested, a newspaper article entitled, "The Heroin Trade Moves to Pakistan," written two years prior to the offence, was found in the accused's apartment. Crown counsel argues that the presence of the newspaper article in the accused's apartment raised the inference that the accused had taken preparatory steps to import heroin or had contemplated it, even though the article referred to the heroin trade in Pakistan and not Hong Kong. Defence counsel objects on the basis that the evidence is not relevant. Do you think he is right?

4. The accused is charged with importing a narcotic. The accused had asked his mother if she would store some furniture for his friends who were then travelling in South America. The mother agreed. When she was notified by the airline that the furniture had arrived, she advised them to deliver it to her. Before the furniture was delivered, the RCMP examined it and found marijuana concealed in a cupboard with a false bottom. The RCMP allowed the furniture to be cleared through customs and delivered to the mother's house, and then placed the house under constant surveillance. Four days passed and no one collected the furniture. The RCMP then seized the furniture containing the marijuana. Later in the day, the RCMP conducted a search of the accused's apartment.

    At trial, the examination-in-chief of one of the RCMP officers proceeded in part as follows:

Constable King: So I entered the apartment and found no one at home.

Crown Counsel: Did you find anything relevant to this case?

Constable King: Well, I found a small metric scale, some pipes, some magazine articles talking about sources of marijuana, and a pot that contained a green substance.

Defence Counsel: Your Honour, I object. I fail to see the relevance of all this.

Crown Counsel: Your Honour, the paraphernalia illustrates that the accused is a marijuana user, the scale shows he's a trafficker, and all together this shows a motive to import and from there knowledge of the marijuana in the furniture.

Defence Counsel: The probative value, if any, is weak and the prejudice to my client is enormous. I ask you to exercise your discretion and exclude.

Do you agree with the Crown or the defence regarding the admissibility of this evidence?

PART II

Exclusion of Evidence That May Be Relevant and Material

CHAPTER 5

Hearsay

CHAPTER OBJECTIVES

After completing this chapter you should be able to:

- Define hearsay.
- State the fundamental rule about the admissibility of hearsay.
- Understand when an out-of-court statement may be admitted to show state of mind.
- Distinguish between the two types of implied statement and their admissibility.

INTRODUCTION

Hearsay is a statement, originally made out of court, that is repeated in court for the truth of its contents. The fundamental rule about hearsay is: *Hearsay is not admissible evidence unless it meets a specific exception that permits it to be admitted.*

Hearsay is one of those concepts that are simple and yet elusive. The idea behind restricting the admissibility of hearsay is that a witness should not repeat in court a statement made outside court if the purpose of presenting the statement is to have the trier of fact accept it as true. Hearsay is at best second-hand evidence because the person who made the statement is not making it in court. Typically, someone else is repeating what they heard or what they think they heard.

Think of the game of Broken Telephone, where one person in the circle starts by whispering a sentence in the ear of the person next to her. That person then "repeats" the sentence by whispering in the ear of the person next to him. After going through the twenty people in the circle the statement "Many people are called but few serve" may turn into "Come to McDonald's where billions are served." This may be a fun exercise around the campfire but it is a very dangerous one in a court of law. The reliability of second- or third-hand evidence cannot be tested and examined in court in the same way that first-hand evidence can be tested and examined.

The trier of fact was not there when the events that are the focus of the litigation occurred. In order to come to conclusions of fact, the fact-finder must take the evidence that is presented and weigh it so as to determine what actually occurred.

hearsay
a statement, originally made out of court, that is repeated in court for the truth of its contents

A number of safeguards or tests have been established to ensure that reliable evidence is obtained from witnesses. Chief among these are the following:

1. The person who made the statement is testifying under oath and subject to sanctions or penalties for perjury.

2. The trier of fact can observe the person making the statement and assess her reliability and truthfulness.

3. The opposing part has an opportunity to cross-examine the witness and attack her testimony to test its truthfulness.

In essence, hearsay is generally not admissible because its reliability cannot be tested and examined in the same manner as other evidence. The statement is not made under oath, it cannot be cross-examined, and the trier of fact does not have the opportunity to assess the demeanour of the statement-maker in court. When a witness is merely someone repeating what he or she heard, rather than the actual person who made the statement, all that can be tested is whether or not the witness is giving reliable evidence about hearing the statement. For example, if Joe is giving evidence that Sami told him that Sami's brother had murdered the victim, there is no way for the trier of fact to test whether Sami made the statement that Joe thought he heard, or to understand the basis on which Sami made the statement. To avoid this problem, Sami himself should be called to give evidence. Sami would then be placed under oath and cross-examined.

OUT-OF-COURT STATEMENTS THAT ARE NOT HEARSAY

Generally, an out-of-court statement may not be admissible when it is offered for the truth of its contents. However, it may be admissible for other purposes that have nothing to do with whether the contents of the statement are true. If the statement is not offered for its truth, *it is not hearsay* and may therefore be admitted simply on the threshold basis for the admission of all evidence, its relevancy. One must ask, Is there a relevant purpose for having the statement admitted, aside from for the truth of its contents? If there is such a purpose, the statement may be admissible.

Consider a criminal case in which a police officer, acting on information given to him by an anonymous informant who cannot now be found, searches a suspected drug dealer in a pub and finds her holding a considerable quantity of heroin. The officer had no reason other than the statement of the informant for suspecting that the accused was trafficking in narcotics. At the trial of the accused, the Crown wants the officer to give evidence as to what he was told by the informant in order to show that he had reasonable and probable grounds for conducting a search. The statement of the informant is admissible not for the truth of its contents—that the accused is a heroin trafficker—but rather to show the basis for the arresting officer's actions in searching the accused.

Consider a civil case in which the defendant is being sued by another driver who is claiming the defendant was negligent in backing out of a driveway because he did not look behind him. The defendant states that his passenger got out of the car to direct him because his line of vision was blocked and that the passenger said, "Nothing is coming. It's okay to back up." The statement is admissible not for the truth of whether or not it was actually safe to exit the driveway but for whether or not the defendant had a reasonable basis to believe that it was safe and therefore that he met a reasonable standard of care.

In both of these examples, the statement is used to show what the person who heard the statement was thinking, not whether what he heard was true. When arguing to admit these kinds of statements, counsel are seeking to show the state of mind of the person.

The leading case on the admission of statements to show state of mind is the Privy Council decision in *Subramaniam v. The Director of Public Prosecutions.*[1] The accused was charged with possession of ammunition during a period in Malaysia marked by many terrorist actions. As a defence to the charge, Subramaniam raised the issue of duress. He told the authorities that he had been taken prisoner by terrorists who told him they would kill him unless he assisted them. The trial judge ruled that the statement was hearsay and could not be admitted. As a result, Subramaniam had no way to prove his state of mind—namely, that he felt compelled to help the terrorists—and therefore could not make out the defence of duress. He was convicted and sentenced to death. On appeal, it was held that the statement was admissible. The appeal court ruled that the accused was not seeking to have the statement admitted to prove the fact that the terrorists were going to kill him, but rather to prove what he believed to be the case.

The court held (at 970):

> Evidence of a statement made to a witness by a person who is not himself called as a witness may or may not be hearsay. It is hearsay and inadmissible when the object of the evidence is to establish the truth of what is contained in the statement. It is not hearsay and is admissible when it is proposed to establish by the evidence, not the truth of the statement, but the fact that it was made.

In summary, it does not matter whether someone was carrying drugs, whether it was safe to back out of the driveway, or whether terrorists really would have killed Subramaniam. The statement is not being admitted to prove that it was true. It is being admitted to show what the person who heard the statement thought after hearing it. In other words, the statement is being admitted to show its effect on the person who heard it and his state of mind.

THE ANALYSIS

Let us take a few examples and work through them to see if we can clarify the concept of hearsay.

EXAMPLE ONE

Tim is charged with impaired driving. Sally testifies that she was at a party where Tim was and someone said to her, "I hope Tim isn't planning on driving, he's as drunk as a skunk." Tim was stopped by the police an hour later but the breathalyzer machine malfunctioned and they could not get any blood–alcohol readings for Tim. Can Sally's comment be admitted to prove that Tim was drunk?

In this example, Sally would be testifying about what someone else told her. The evidence would be presented for its truth (that Tim was intoxicated), so it fits the classic hearsay definition and, in the absence of some exception, would be excluded.

EXAMPLE TWO

Douglas Radler collapsed on the street. An ambulance attended. As he was being loaded into the ambulance, Radler was heard to say to the paramedics, "I've got a heart condition but I'm allergic to nitro." On the way to the hospital the paramedics gave him nitroglycerin. He had a massive allergic reaction and died as a result. Radler's family is now suing the ambulance service for wrongful death. At trial, Radler's family wishes to present evidence from a witness at the scene that Radler said those words in order to prove that he was alive and coherent when he was placed in the ambulance. The defendant objects, saying that this evidence is hearsay and inadmissible. Is it?

In this example, the witness would testify about what he heard the deceased say to the ambulance attendants. Because the witness would be repeating in court something heard elsewhere, this evidence is hearsay on its face. Is the potential evidence being offered for its truth? That is, is it being presented to show that the ambulance attendant was warned about Radler's allergy? According to the plaintiff, the evidence is being offered simply to establish that the deceased was alive and coherent when he was loaded into the ambulance. If this is the reason the evidence is being presented, then it should be admitted. The problem is that the plaintiff may claim the information is to be admitted simply to show that the deceased was alive and coherent, but the evidence contains additional information that may be prejudicial to the defence. It would be better if the witness were simply to testify that the deceased was alive and talking in a coherent manner when he was loaded into the ambulance, without getting into the details. The testimony would provide valuable evidence without having a prejudicial impact.

EXAMPLE THREE

Frank and Bob are charged with robbing a bank. Two weeks after the robbery, the police, acting on a tip, intercept a letter sent to Frank in Montreal that has $500 cash in it. The serial numbers of the bills confirm that they are all from the bank robbery. The handwritten note says, "Frank, Here's your share of the loot. Anytime you want to partner up again for some quick money, let me know. Bob." The police conduct a search of Bob's apartment and locate a pad of the same type of paper. The top page has impressions on it, indicating that someone wrote a note on a piece of paper on top of the pad and tore it off. A police expert examines the note and the pad and concludes that the note was written when this paper was on the pad found in Bob's apartment. The Crown wishes to introduce this evidence to establish a connection between Bob and the stolen money found inside the letter to Frank. Bob's counsel objects to the admission of such hearsay evidence. Should it be admissible?

In this example, as in the second example, the issue revolves around why the evidence is being presented. The statement about sharing the loot is clearly prejudicial to the defence's case, but the note does link the stolen money to Bob. The statement could be dealt with by having the police expert testify that the note accompanying the money was written while the note paper was on top of the pad found in Bob's apartment. The content of the note is irrelevant to this analysis. It could have said, "Having a great time in Vancouver, wish you were here." So the evidence would not be hearsay if it were presented for the purpose of establishing the connection between the money and Bob. However, it would be hearsay if it were presented for the purpose of demonstrating the truth of the contents of the note—namely, that Bob and Frank robbed the bank together. If the content of the note is irrelevant, then the evidence should be given without quoting the statement; the expert should simply explain the connection between the note and the pad found in Bob's apartment.

EXAMPLE FOUR

In a family law case, a witness begins to testify that he was standing with his friend when the defendant walked by. The friend commented, "That's the guy I saw smacking his kid around in the parking lot yesterday." The defendant's counsel objects to this as hearsay. Plaintiff's counsel points out that the witness heard it with his own ears, so it is not hearsay at all. Who is right?

This example illustrates a common problem with hearsay. Just because someone heard a statement "with their own ears" does not mean that the statement is not hearsay. Once again, the issue of admissibility turns on the reason for admitting the comment. If the comment is being admitted to show that the friend spoke, then it is not hearsay. However, it is difficult to imagine why the statement should be admitted for that purpose, because the fact that the friend spoke does not itself seem relevant. Rather, it was what the friend said that was important. That is, the witness's evidence is being presented to show the truth that "the guy" did strike his child. Plaintiff's counsel should have called the friend to give direct evidence of what he saw in the parking lot the previous day.

The Test for Hearsay

In assessing whether proposed evidence is hearsay, go right back to the basics and see whether the statement falls under the definition:

1. Is the proposed evidence a statement originally made outside the courtroom?

2. Is it being repeated in court?

3. Is it presented to show what was said is true?

If all three of these questions are answered in the affirmative, then the proposed evidence is hearsay. It should also be noted that hearsay statements do not have to be made orally; they can be made in writing or even implied. In addition, the identity of the person who made the statement is not a factor in determining whether it is hearsay, but it may be a factor in considering whether an exception applies. The statement may in fact have been made by the person testifying. As long as the statement was made previously (out of court) and is being presented for its truth, it is hearsay. In this context, an example of when a statement is presented for purposes other than the truth of its contents is when a prior statement of the witness is introduced to show an inconsistency between what the witness said in testimony and what the witness had said earlier. The purpose of introducing the statement is to attack the witness's credibility or reliability rather than to show whether the statement is true.

IMPLIED STATEMENTS

implied statement
an action, behaviour, or course of conduct that conveys information to observers

An **implied statement** can qualify as hearsay. An implied statement is made when a person performs an action or engages in conduct that conveys information to the observers. There are two types of implied statements and they tend to be treated differently by the courts.

The first type of implied statement involves an action by which a person intends to communicate information non-verbally. For example, nodding the head up and down to answer "yes" and pointing a finger at someone when asked who has the stolen goods are actions intended to convey a message. The person performing such actions intends to convey certain information through his action. When a witness is asked to testify about this kind of non-verbal communication made by another person, the issue of hearsay arises. For example, the witness wants to say, "I accused Tom of stealing the petty cash and he nodded his head up and down, agreeing with me," or, "When Mack heard that I was going to testify against him he stared me straight in the eye and slid his thumb across his throat," or, "The flag person waved her arm in a circle, beckoning us forward." These are all examples of communication by another person without the use of spoken or written language but in a manner that deliberately attempts to communicate a meaning nevertheless. These kinds of implied statements are hearsay and are treated the same as any other hearsay statement. That is, they are not admissible unless they meet one of the exceptions to the hearsay rule (*R v. MacKinnon*).

There is a second kind of conduct that conveys information, even though the actor does not directly intend to do so. Sometimes, a person's action or behaviour implies that she believes certain facts even though the purpose of her action is not to communicate a message. For example, a rich, elderly man has a nightcap every evening before heading off to bed. One night, he falls asleep before he has a chance to even sip his drink. It is later discovered that the drink was spiked with enough rat poison to kill a human being. The day after the drink was poisoned, the niece, who stands to inherit the intended victim's fortune, was observed letting out a cry of shock upon seeing her uncle come down the stairs in the morning. One could argue that the niece's shock implied knowledge of the poison in the uncle's drink because she was totally taken aback by the ordinary morning activity of his coming down to breakfast. Is this type of implied assertion hearsay?

Although there is some judicial inconsistency in and academic debate over the admissibility of this kind of implied statement, generally, Canadian courts tend to treat this type of conduct as admissible. If the action is not *intended* to convey information, then it cannot be a statement. If it cannot be a statement, it follows that it cannot be hearsay either. Therefore, if the action is relevant and not more prejudicial than probative, a description of it will be allowed into evidence.

CHAPTER SUMMARY

Hearsay is a statement, originally made out of court, that is repeated in court for the truth of its contents. Hearsay is not admissible unless it fits within one of the exceptions to the rule, because its reliability is at issue. It is a statement that cannot be tested for reliability because it was not made under oath nor is it possible to cross-examine the maker of the statement in court.

Some statements at first glance may appear to be hearsay but in fact are not. Out-of-court statements that are presented to establish the state of mind of the accused are not hearsay and therefore are admissible if they meet the threshold test for all evidence—namely, that they are relevant and material. The hearsay rule does not apply to them because they are not hearsay.

Implied statements, of which there are two types, may or may not be hearsay. The first type, such as the nod of a head to indicate agreement or assent, is intended to convey information and is therefore treated as a statement. Because it is a statement, it is governed by the hearsay rule and is admissible only if it satisfies one of the exceptions to the rule.

The second type of implied statement also involves actions and behaviour that convey a message. However, this type of action or behaviour is not intended by the actor to communicate information in the same manner as the first type of implied statement. In many instances, the action or behaviour sends a message despite the intention of the actor. This second type of implied statement is usually admissible in Canadian courts. The thinking is that , because the actor did not intend to convey information, it is not a statement in the true sense and therefore is not governed by the hearsay rule. The second type of implied statement is admissible if it is relevant and more probative than prejudicial.

KEY TERMS

hearsay

implied statement

NOTE

1. The Privy Council in the United Kingdom served as the final court of appeal for decisions made in many Commonwealth courts. It was the final arbiter of Canadian law until 1949, when the right to appeal to the Privy Council was eliminated from Canadian law and the Supreme Court of Canada became the final court of appeal for Canada.

REFERENCES

MacKinnon, R v. (2002), 165 CCC (3d) 73 (BCCA).

Subramaniam v. The Director of Public Prosecutions, [1956] 1 WLR 965 (PC).

REVIEW QUESTIONS

1. Define hearsay. What are the three specific facets of this definition?

2. What is the general rule in relation to hearsay?

3. What three safeguards to reliability are missing with hearsay evidence?

4. Give two examples of out-of-court statements that are not hearsay.

5. Explain the difference between the two types of implied statements. Why is the admissibility of one type governed by the hearsay rule and the other not?

DISCUSSION QUESTIONS

1. Two young boys were playing "cowboys and Indians" when one was struck in the eye with an arrow. The statement of claim alleges that the adult defendants were negligent in permitting their son to have a bow and arrows. The plaintiff seeks to introduce evidence that the defendants paid medical bills incurred as a result of the plaintiff's injury. Identify any potential hearsay issue and discuss whether or not the payment of the medical bills is admissible evidence.

2. The plaintiff is suing the defendant for damages for personal injury incurred as a result of the defendant's motor vehicle running her down as she was walking across an intersection. After the incident, a number of spectators gathered and the plaintiff overheard one of them saying, "There's no question that fellow ran the yellow light. I saw him do it." The plaintiff is also prepared to testify that although she was dazed at the time, she distinctly heard a voice, which she could not identify, say, "But I never even saw her until the last moment." The plaintiff also seeks to call a witness who will testify that, shortly before the accident, the defendant's vehicle passed him in an erratic manner and his passenger wife remarked, "He's a driver looking for an accident." Discuss whether any of these statements are admissible into evidence.

3. The accused is charged with credit card fraud. He wants to testify that his friend, who has since died, told him, "This is my card and you may use it if you wish." Is this statement admissible? If so, on what basis?

4. Joe has been accused of public mischief. The allegation is that, as a joke, he shouted, "Bomb! Run for your life!" on a crowded subway platform. A huge panic ensued as people rushed to escape. The arresting officer wants to testify that when he asked the subway passengers to identify who shouted that there was a bomb, several people pointed at Joe. Discuss whether or not the officer will be able to give this evidence.

CHAPTER 6

Traditional Exceptions to the Hearsay Rule

CHAPTER OBJECTIVES

After completing this chapter you should be able to:

- Identify the traditional exceptions to the hearsay rule.

- Explain the circumstances in which the traditional exceptions to the hearsay rule do and do not allow the admission of evidence.

- Explain the reasoning behind the traditional exceptions to the hearsay rule.

INTRODUCTION

As we saw in chapter 5, the common-law general rule that hearsay is not admissible into evidence was developed to address issues of truth and reliability. If a witness did not testify in person and thus could not be evaluated for truthfulness by the trier of fact, could not be cross-examined, and was not subject to sanctions, her statement was viewed as less trustworthy.

However, over time, the courts developed a variety of exceptions to the hearsay rule that became part of the common law. In some exceptional situations, hearsay statements are reliable and it does not make sense to exclude them. The current state of the law is that if a hearsay statement fits into one of the common-law exceptions, it can be admitted into evidence.

This chapter examines these traditional, common-law exceptions.

ADMISSIONS OF A PARTY

admission of a party
anything said by a party by way of word or conduct that the other party wishes to introduce against that party

The general rule regarding the **admission of a party** is that anything said by a party by way of word or conduct may be admitted into evidence and used against him. The rule is applicable to both civil and criminal cases. Although the rule is very broad, there are some limitations on it.

Formal Versus Informal Admissions

The admission process can be either formal or informal. In the formal process, a party to the proceeding admits that certain facts are true, thereby relieving the opposing side from proving those facts at trial. Once a formal admission is made, the party is bound by this admission and usually may not withdraw it. The purpose of formal admissions is to avoid spending valuable trial time proving facts that are not in dispute. For example, in a civil case, the defendant may admit to liability but wish to contest the amount of damages. The defendant is not challenging the factual circumstances of the incident giving rise to the lawsuit, so there is no reason to require the plaintiff to prove them. Formal admission of liability focuses trial time on evidence regarding the amount of damage caused or the degree of injury suffered by the plaintiff. Both parties benefit from this approach because they are not paying lawyers to prepare and argue points that are not in dispute. The rules of civil procedure provide the form, content, and time requirements for formal admissions. In a criminal case, the accused may admit to killing the victim but wish to dispute whether the killing was manslaughter as opposed to murder. By making such an admission, valuable trial time is saved and it is possible for the fact-finder to focus better on the issues in dispute.

In a civil case, the rules of procedure for the superior courts of all the provinces provide for a process of formal admissions. These rules of court require the party seeking specific admissions to give notice to the opposing party, who then has an opportunity to respond. Failure to respond results in a deemed admission of fact. In addition, there may be serious cost consequences for refusal to admit a fact that is subsequently proved to be true at a hearing. Consider a case involving a motor vehicle accident. The notice to the opposing party may include a number of necessary but uncontroversial matters such as dates and times, ownership of vehicles, even who was at fault for the accident. The admission of fault is less common than the admission of other facts, but the real issue between the parties may not be who caused the accident but the extent of the damage caused by it. It is rational to acknowledge the uncontroversial matters and move on to the real issues, thus saving money and court time in the process. A formal admission can come from pleadings, admissions of fact in writing, or simply from the mouth of counsel, thus dispensing with the need for the party to prove the facts admitted to.

Admissions can also be formally used in the criminal process. Consider a case involving a person charged with theft of an automobile. One admission usually sought by the Crown is confirmation of who owns the vehicle and that the owner did not give the accused permission to use the vehicle. After all, the owner is likely to show up and confirm those facts, so why require this person to present such uncontroversial evidence and, along the way, cause her to lose time from work and thus income?

Some defence counsel never make such admissions, simply because the witness may not show up and thus evidence of ownership will be lacking. The tendency today is to make use of certificates authorized by the *Criminal Code* (under s. 655) establishing these facts unless there is contradictory evidence from the accused.

Admissions can also be informal and are often not part of the trial process but arise from relations between the parties. They do not even have to be intended; they simply have to be any statement made by a party that the other party wishes to use against him. An example cited in Paciocco and Stuesser (at 138) that illustrates this point particularly well concerns an individual who bought a car from an elderly couple to commit an armed robbery. The car was identified but the Crown needed to link the accused to the car, which likely was never registered in his name. Long after their dealings with him, the couple could not identify the accused, but they did recall that the person who bought the car from them mentioned that his dog was pregnant and that he worked in chain-link fencing. As it turned out, the accused had a dog that had puppies around that time and he had a job working with chain-link fencing. This information constituted an admission and was used to identify the accused even though when he made the statements he likely had no idea that these words would ever be used against him.

The criteria examined below are used to consider whether a statement of a party will be an admission.

Different Forms of Admission

Admissions may take a number of different forms. They are often formalized and written down but may be just spoken. As we have seen, they do not need to be made with knowledge that they might hurt the speaker in future litigation. But there are unexpected ways that a litigant can be harmed by admissions. The expression "loose lips sink ships" comes to mind because it is often through inadvertent disclosures that a case is mortally wounded.

VICARIOUS ADMISSIONS

A **vicarious admission** is a statement made by an authorized speaker for an individual, business, group, organization, or other recognized entity that may be used against the party in subsequent litigation. When a party authorizes a person to speak on their behalf, the party can be held accountable for what that person says. It is important to note that the content of what the agent, employee, or representative says does not have to be authorized; it is enough that the person is authorized to speak for the party. Carefully worded communiqués that have been approved by a company's legal team seldom provide information that is useful for a plaintiff and damaging to the defendant company. Rather, damaging or incriminating statements usually come from the offhand comments of spokespersons or representatives who have not thought through all the ramifications of their statements.

For example, a few years back one of the major automobile manufacturers was producing a minivan with defects. At certain speeds on the highway, the back door of the van would open when it hit a bump. Not only that, the back seat, which was designed to be removable, would actually pop out of the vehicle. Minivans are often used by families for transporting a lot of passengers, including children, so

vicarious admission
an admission made by an authorized speaker for a party

these were very serious defects. What if, after a mishap, a news crew rushes to the factory to interview the vice-president in charge of safety, but when they get there the only person around is the night watchman? With a looming deadline, the news crew interviews the night watchman, who is happy to share his opinions. He says, among other things, "I keep telling them they have to put safety latches on those vehicles but they say it's too expensive and that they'd rather just settle the lawsuits." Can the night watchman's statement be used as an admission against the car manufacturer? As tempting as it is to say yes, the answer is no, the statement cannot be used, because the night watchman is not authorized to speak about safety matters. If the vice-president had been available and he said the same thing, adding "Those cameras aren't rolling yet, are they?" his statement would be admissible— and damning evidence, indeed.

Finally, it is important to note that vicarious admissions need not be intentionally revealed to the outside world. In fact, admissions are often secret communications within a company. For example, in the Enron litigation, emails that were meant to be kept from regulators, because they exhorted traders to "sanitize" their files, ended up as devastating evidence of impropriety.

In summary, the criteria for determining whether vicarious admissions are admissible are as follows:

1. There must be proof that the speaker was an agent or employee of the party at the time the statement was made.

2. The speaker must have been authorized to speak on the topic in issue.

3. The statement must have been made to a third party.

ADMISSIONS BY ACTION

admission by action
meaning or intention conveyed by an act or gesture

A person can also make an admission without uttering any words. Meaning or intention can be communicated by an act or gesture rather than by spoken or written language. **Admission by action** goes beyond the communication that happens nonverbally when a person answers a question by nodding or shaking her head "yes" or "no," or when a person makes other gestures that communicate meaning. Admissions by action that can be used against a person include the destruction of evidence (as with Enron), lying about material matters (as with Martha Stewart), changing one's name or appearance, asserting a lie, resisting arrest, or failing to appear for a hearing. These admissions can be countered by the party against whom the admission has been made, but the party may be strategically pressed into the defensive position of explaining it away.

For example, in a criminal case, the Crown wishes to introduce evidence of flight as an accused's acknowledgment of a guilty mind. The underlying principle is, Why would an innocent party run from the police? Your response to that question would have a lot to do with your life experience with the police and whether you have an expectation of a fair hearing if you chose to await the arrival of the authorities or turn yourself in. In other words, there may be many reasons why someone would flee the scene of a crime—concern for her personal safety, fear that she will be railroaded into a conviction, or many other factors that have nothing to do with guilt. If there is a rule that permits the admission of an act as evidence of guilt, there ought to be logical consistency regarding the inferences that may be drawn from the act. In reality, the rule says that a person who flees the scene of a crime has abandoned his right to silence, because the trier of fact is entitled to draw the inference that evasive action or effort to cover up implies a guilty motive.

In *R v. Guyatt*, the accused was on trial for murdering his wife. The Court of Appeal approved of the admission of evidence that, some months after his wife's death, the accused had made inquiries at the library about countries that did not have extradition treaties with Canada. He also applied for a passport and told his son that he had cash on hand in case he needed to leave the country. The court stated:

> In my view it was open to the jury to infer from the evidence of the library inquiry and the secreting of a sum of money that Mr. Guyatt planned to leave Canada for a country that would not send him back here to face trial if he was charged with his wife's murder. The jury might then infer that this demonstrated that if it became apparent to Mr. Guyatt that he had not been able to avoid detection he would flee. This could be said to be a consciousness of guilt. In my view the evidence was capable of supporting that inference and was therefore admissible.

In civil matters, a current hot topic is whether subsequent remedial actions of a defendant can be used to prove negligence. Say that, while leaving a grocery store, you slip and fall on the stairs and hurt your back. You complain to the store manager, who looks at your shoes and says that you shouldn't wear heels like that in freezing weather. The next week you pass by the same store and notice a new railing on the stairs and a sign that says, "Caution, stairs may be slippery." Can you use this information to prove that the stairway was hazardous when you fell? There are policy considerations that come into play in answering this question. On the one hand, we want to encourage people and businesses to remedy safety hazards as soon as they become known. On the other hand, people and businesses might be reluctant to take such measures if they knew that these remedial steps could be used against them and contribute to damage awards that they would have to pay.

One solution to this dilemma is to make such measures "off-limits" to litigation. This is the approach that has been taken in the United States, where the federal *Rules of Evidence* state that evidence of subsequent remedial measures is not admissible to prove negligence, culpable conduct, a defect in a product or design, or a need for a warning. Individual litigants may feel hard done by because remedial measures appear relevant and probative to their issue, but the greater good would be served by not admitting this evidence. Moreover, if the evidence were admissible, the remedial measures may never be taken, so potential evidence would never materialize. In that sense, nothing is lost. This same issue arises where a defendant makes a voluntary payment, say, for medical treatment or to compensate the plaintiff for some material loss. Is this an admission of liability? Should it be?

In Canada, we have taken the approach that defendants should not avoid taking remedial measures and thus incur potential greater liability. As outlined in the April 2003 British Columbia Law Institute paper dealing with the issue of remedial measures, historically measures taken after the fact to make an area safer were inadmissible to prove liability. The thinking was that if such measures were admissible, owners of land where hazards existed would not repair them, thus exposing the public to ongoing risk.

The statement by Bramwell B in *Hart v. Lancashire and Yorkshire Ry. Co.* (at 263) is often quoted for this principle:

> People do not furnish evidence against themselves simply by adopting a new plan in order to prevent the recurrence of an accident. I think that a proposition to the contrary would be barbarous. It would be, as I have often had occasion to tell juries, to hold that, because the world gets wise as it gets older, therefore it was foolish before.

However, this rule has been altered over time so that evidence of remedial measures taken may be admissible not as an admission of liability but to support facts that are relevant to the issue of negligence. Essentially, it is circumstantial evidence dealing with the issue of liability.

ADMISSIONS BY SILENCE

Although admissions are most commonly made in words, in some circumstances silence may also be an admission. If a person remains silent in the face of an accusation, the failure to make a denial may be admitted into evidence as an implied admission. However, silence will only be an implied admission if the silence manifestly implies an admission (*R v. Christie, R v. Conlon,* and *R v. Pammer*). Not all statements made in the presence of a party who remains silent amount to an admission, but only those in which denial would be reasonably expected. However, since it is the right of an accused to remain silent, failure to make a denial to a police officer does not constitute an admission because a denial would not be reasonably expected (*R v. Eden*).

Whether or not silence in the face of allegations of wrongdoing is an admission would be determined by way of a voir dire. The judge must determine whether there is sufficient evidence to show that the silence amounted to an adoption of the allegation by the party. This is a difficult proposition to establish and, as a result, silence will only rarely be found to be an admission.

CRITERIA FOR ADMISSIONS

1. Admissions include any statement or act by an opposing party that the other side wishes to use in evidence.

2. The statement need not be knowingly made against interest.

3. The statement can express a belief and not be based on personal knowledge.

4. Admissions include any third-person statement adopted or approved by the other side.

5. Admissions include any statement by an agent or employee authorized to speak on behalf of the other party.

CONSPIRACIES AND ADMISSIONS BY CO-DEFENDANTS

As a general rule, an admission may be used in evidence only against the party who made it. Therefore, an admission against one co-defendant is usually not admissible against anyone but the person who made the statement. For example, if Joe admits that he and Amit robbed the bank, the statement is admissible only against Joe. It cannot be admitted into evidence against Amit. The case against Amit must be made out in some other way.

The exception to this rule occurs when the parties are involved in a common design. For example, in a civil case, when a partnership is suing or being sued, a statement by one partner may be used against all the partners. In a criminal context, **conspiracy** is a common design. When parties are involved in a conspiracy, they are working together to plan a criminal act. Any statements made by any of them in the furtherance of the conspiracy may be used against all the conspirators, not just the one who made the statement. It is important to note that statements that are not part of or in furtherance of the conspiracy are not admissible against anyone but the maker of the statement because the statement does not form part of the conspiracy. Thus, the guilty plea or the confession of one conspirator is not admissible against the other alleged conspirators because the statement is not part of the conspiracy, but is made after the fact.

Proof in a conspiracy trial goes through three stages. In the first stage, the Crown establishes that a conspiracy actually existed. In the second stage, the Crown establishes who members of that conspiracy are. In the third stage, the fact-finder in relation to those proven members of the conspiracy then moves on to consider whether those conspirators are guilty beyond a reasonable doubt. It sometimes happens that the Crown can establish that a conspiracy existed but it lacks sufficient evidence to establish that certain of the accused persons were part of the conspiracy. In that case, those persons are acquitted of the conspiracy charge and free to go unless they are facing other charges. However, if the Crown establishes that a conspiracy did exist and that certain persons were part of that conspiracy, then any evidence that is admissible against one member of the conspiracy is evidence against all members of the conspiracy. So evidence that would usually be inadmissible against one defendant—for example, because it is a tape-recorded telephone conversation between two other defendants—becomes admissible against the first defendant even though it is hearsay in relation to him. The reason for this unique approach is quite simple: because of the intense secrecy surrounding conspiracy offences, the Crown would be handicapped in ever obtaining a conviction without a relaxation in the evidentiary approach. This relaxation of the hearsay rule is referred to as the **co-conspirator exception**.

During trial, hearsay statements by alleged co-conspirators are **conditionally admissible**, meaning that they may be admitted and form the body of evidence that the jury considers when determining whether a conspiracy exists. The conditional evidence cannot be used in determining whether the accused is a member of the conspiracy.

It should be noted that not all statements made by a co-conspirator are admissible, but only those statements made when the conspiracy was active and that can be classified as being "in furtherance" of that conspiracy. It should also be noted that the first stage above involved consideration of "all the evidence," which includes evidence that in the second stage ought not to be considered against individual persons. Hearsay, then, is available to the jury to determine whether a conspiracy existed, but not to determine whether the accused is a member of the conspiracy. However, once the accused is determined to be a member of the conspiracy, hearsay is again admissible to consider whether the accused is guilty beyond a reasonable

conspiracy
a common design or plan by two or more persons to commit a criminal act or omission

co-conspirator exception
rule allowing evidence against one member of a conspiracy as evidence against all other members

conditionally admissible
term describing evidence that is admitted for a specific purpose but that is not at that stage admissible on the larger issue

doubt. It is like a hearsay sandwich—admissible in the first stage and the last but not in the middle.

Some authors argue that the first stage does not involve hearsay at all because the truth of the statements is not the issue, just that they were said, that there were conversations that appear to be in furtherance of a common design or the commission of an offence. This seems to put too narrow an interpretation of the "truth of its contents" aspect of hearsay. For example, say the police wiretap a conversation like this:

Dan: I've got $50,000 to invest in a cocaine smuggling operation but I need some trustworthy people who know how to get through Customs.

Biff: My cousin, Eddie works for Customs and I know he'd turn a blind eye if we paid him $3,000 each time.

Dan: Sounds like a plan.

The argument is that this is not hearsay because it does not matter whether Dan has really got $50,000, or for that matter whether Biff's cousin Eddie works for Customs. They could all be lying about this information but still be conspiring to commit a criminal offence. The difficulty with this approach is that the contents of the statements are in fact the offence. If Dan really has no money or Biff has no cousin in Customs, how can their statements be anything more than exaggeration or bragging? It is not a criminal offence to lie or exaggerate. The contents of the statements are essential to the offence and must be true to the extent that they are not "fantastical"; otherwise, there is no offence. In conspiracy cases, the contents of the statements are relevant and therefore a hearsay exception is necessary in order to consider conversations involving some members of the alleged conspiracy, in order to determine whether a conspiracy exists.

As complex as this all may seem, the Canadian approach is to have the trier of fact, the jury, make the determinations regarding the existence of a conspiracy and membership in the conspiracy, in addition to whether the Crown's case has been proved beyond a reasonable doubt at the end of the day. The mental exercise would be difficult for the legally trained, but it is a very tall order indeed for a jury of lay persons.

In a civil context, the co-conspirator rule is modified to take into account the different standards of proof. In *Insurance Corp. of British Columbia v. Sun*, Grober-man J restated the rule as follows:

- The trier of fact must be satisfied on the *balance of probabilities* that a conspiracy alleged by the plaintiff existed.

- Then, the trier of fact must review all the evidence that is directly admissible against the defendant to see whether it establishes a *reasonable likelihood* that the defendant is a member of the conspiracy.

- If the trier of fact reaches this conclusion, it must then decide whether the plaintiff has established membership on the balance of probabilities. In doing this, the trier of fact can apply the hearsay exception to acts and statements of co-conspirators, making them evidence against the plaintiff.

This analysis must be conducted separately for each defendant and for each conspiracy alleged.

CONSPIRACY AND ADMISSIONS

1. The fact-finder must consider all the evidence to decide whether the Crown has proved beyond a reasonable doubt that the conspiracy existed.

2. If the conspiracy is found to have existed, the fact-finder must consider only the evidence that is directly admissible against each accused to determine whether, on the balance of probabilities, that accused is a member of the conspiracy. (The co-conspirator exception does not come into play yet.)

3. If the accused is determined to be a member of the conspiracy, then the co-conspirator exception applies and any acts and statements of co-conspirators may be used to determine whether the Crown has proved beyond a reasonable doubt that the conspiracy exists and the accused is a member of that conspiracy. (This is the co-conspirator exception.)

DECLARATIONS AGAINST INTEREST

Declarations against interest, or statements made by parties against their own interests, are admissible into evidence if they fit within the criteria for the admissions exception to the hearsay rule that we have just considered. When a person who is not a party to a proceeding makes a statement against his or her own interest, it may be admissible if it falls within the declaration against interest exception. Admissions and statements against interest are similar in that they involve a person making a statement that acknowledges facts that could have negative repercussions, but the declaration against interest exception is essentially used against non-parties.

declaration against interest
a statement made by a party that is against the party's legal interest

There are two categories of "against interest" that have traditionally led to the admissibility of third-party hearsay. One involves statements against pecuniary or proprietary interest. The second relates to statements against penal interest.

Declarations Against Pecuniary or Proprietary Interest

The term **pecuniary or proprietary interest** is another way of saying financial or monetary interest. Where a person makes statements that can cost him money, the statements are considered sufficiently reliable that they should be admitted into evidence. This does not mean that the trier of fact should accept the statements as true without weighing them; it just means that the trier of fact will get to see or hear these statements. The elements of the test for admissibility of statements against pecuniary interest are outlined below, followed by some examples of scenarios that may or may not satisfy the test.

pecuniary or proprietary interest
concerned with financial or ownership matters

DECLARATIONS AGAINST PECUNIARY OR PROPRIETARY INTEREST

1. The person making the statement must be unavailable to testify.

2. The statement must be against the person's interest.

3. The person making the statement must have had personal knowledge of the facts (that is, no "double hearsay").

4. The economic prejudice to the person making the statement must have been immediate.

5. The person making the statement must have known about the prejudice.

SCENARIO ONE

Jennifer is a passenger in Dharma's car when it is cut off by another car and ends up in a ditch. Jennifer is heard to state, "What was that other driver thinking? It's not your fault there are idiots like that on the road." When Jennifer sues Dharma alleging negligent driving, Dharma's counsel seeks to introduce that statement as a statement against pecuniary interest because if Dharma didn't cause the accident, Jennifer can't recover from him for her injuries.

SCENARIO TWO

Allan cashed a cheque from Kay and wrote on the back, "Accepted as full payment for purchase of 1985 Dodge." However, before ownership of the vehicle is transferred, Allan dies and the executor refuses to transfer Allan's 1985 Dodge to Kay's name. When Kay seeks an order requiring the executor to transfer the car to her, she wishes to rely on the notation on the cheque as a statement by the deceased against his pecuniary interest.

SCENARIO THREE

Teresa is a midwife and she delivered a baby for Mr. and Mrs. Rezek. The baby must have been alive on April 1, 2000 in order to inherit a share of Uncle Ian's estate. There is a receipt from Teresa's bookkeeper that states, "Received $200.00 for Teresa's delivery of Rezek baby," which is dated March 31, 2000 and signed by her. By acknowledging the payment, the author of the statement is giving up her right to later claim payment for this service, and thus it is a statement against her financial interest. (See *Higham v. Ridgway*.) It stands to reason that if the midwife is being paid for the delivery, then the child was born at the time and thus the birth requirement for inheritance is proven.

Will the facts in these scenarios satisfy the test for admissibility of statements against pecuniary interest? Let us look at the logic at play here.

1. The person making the statement must be unavailable to testify. The person may be dead, too ill to testify, insane, outside the jurisdiction of the court, or missing. In some instances, evidence against pecuniary or proprietary interest has been permitted when the person making the statement has simply refused to testify.

2. The statement must be against the person's interest. All the scenarios given in the examples appear to fit these criteria. Jennifer, by acknowledging that Dharma was not negligent, may compromise her ability to recover damages from Dharma for personal injuries she suffered. This applies whether or not Jennifer has made a claim; the simple fact that she prejudiced her right to claim is enough. The same reasoning essentially applies to Allan's acknowledgment of payment for the car. By acknowledging full payment, he has given up his right to collect again—it was against his monetary interest that he acknowledged the payment. Finally, Teresa's bookkeeper's acknowledgment of payment for the delivery of the Rezeks' child is against Teresa's interest, but without getting into whether the bookkeeper may have an economic interest in this transaction, we encounter another problem in the following.

3. The person making the statement must be speaking from personal knowledge. There is nothing to indicate that Teresa's bookkeeper was present at the birth, so she would have been relying on what she was told to conclude that the baby was born by March 31, 2000. The bookkeeper's statement would not be admissible under this exception.

4. The economic prejudice to the person making the statement must have been immediate. In such a case, there are too many contingencies that remove the certainty that makes the statement inherently reliable.

5. The person making the statement must have known about the prejudice. Unless the person knows that the statement will cost him money or a chance to recover money otherwise owed to him, then it lacks the force or reliability that would overcome the hearsay rule.

It should be noted that a statement against pecuniary or proprietary interest need not be for public consumption. It could be written in a diary, which the person keeps under lock and key and jealously guards. A private statement against interest that comes to light counts as a statement against pecuniary interest.

Declarations Against Penal Interest

The term **penal interest** implies that the individual could be charged with a criminal offence as a result of the information supplied in the statement. The declaration against penal interest exception to the hearsay rule arises where a person, who is not a party to a proceeding, acknowledges that he or she committed a criminal offence, sometimes even one for which another person is on trial. There are strict rules for the use of such evidence, which may reflect the fact that these declarations are usually made by persons of unsavoury or criminal background. The position

penal interest
a matter that could result in the person's being incarcerated

taken by the Supreme Court of Canada in *Lucier v. R* makes this exception exceedingly narrow and of little practical use.

One early case dealt with by the Supreme Court of Canada provides an excellent example of how this provision will or will not come into play. In *R v. O'Brien*, the accused was charged with possession for the purpose of trafficking (PPT), jointly with a man named Jensen. O'Brien stood trial and was convicted, while his co-accused Jensen fled Canada. Jensen later returned and indicated to his lawyer that he was solely responsible for the drugs and that O'Brien was innocent of the charge. Jensen agreed to testify to that effect in order to provide new evidence for O'Brien's appeal; however, he died before the hearing. The Court of Appeal, though, allowed the statement to be entered and directed an acquittal against O'Brien on the PPT charges. Overturning the Court of Appeal decision, Dickson J for the Supreme Court stated:

> The guarantee of trustworthiness of a statement made out of court flows from the fact that the statement is to the "deceased's immediate prejudice." To be admissible there must be realization by the declarant that the statement may well be used against him. That is the very thing Jensen wished to avoid. He had no intention of furnishing evidence against himself. His obvious desire was not to create damaging evidence, detrimental to his penal interest. Yet, that is the very basis upon which admissibility of extra-judicial declarations of penal interest rests. In my opinion, the statements of Jensen to Mr. Simons failed to meet the requirements for admissibility.

One positive aspect for the accused is that the Crown cannot make use of a declaration against penal interest by a deceased person to implicate the living accused, because it remains inadmissible hearsay.

DECLARATIONS AGAINST PENAL INTEREST

1. The person making the statement must be dead, insane, out of the jurisdiction, or too ill to testify. Refusal to testify is not sufficient.

2. The person making the statement must believe that he or she is vulnerable to criminal prosecution as a result of making the statement.

3. The vulnerability to criminal prosecution cannot be remote (that is, a vague possibility).

4. The court should consider whether there is any other evidence supporting the statement against penal interest and whether there is a connection between the person making the statement and the accused person.

5. The court will look at the totality of the circumstances surrounding the making of the statement to determine its admissibility. Some statements may be somewhat inculpatory (tending to incriminate) and somewhat exculpatory (tending to exonerate) and would not meet the test.

Some examples will illustrate.

EXAMPLE ONE

George tells his lawyer, "You know that pig farmer guy, well, he's going to take the fall for me. I guess I was pretty smart after all to dump those bodies on his farm." Can his statement be admitted as a declaration against penal interest?

EXAMPLE TWO

Tonya admitted to her friend Joey that she robbed the Lower Mainland Savings Credit Union all by herself. Frank is charged with the offence and Tonya promised to come and testify on his behalf, but she became ill with giardiasis (beaver fever) and is in hospital in Oregon. Though lucid, she may not recover in time to testify. Can her statement to Joey be admitted as a declaration against penal interest?

In the first example, George has made his statement that full assurance that it is confidential and will never come to the attention of the authorities. It was not made with a belief that criminal prosecution may result and therefore would not be admissible under this exception. In the second example, Tonya is unable to come to Canada but that does not mean that her evidence cannot be obtained. She could be examined in Oregon under oath with both parties present, or her evidence could be presented through live video conferencing. Unless these options are ruled out, the evidence would not be admissible.

DYING DECLARATIONS

A **dying declaration** is the statement of a dying person. For example, Sameer is bleeding to death from a bullet hole in his chest and gasps out with his last breath, "Robert shot me!" His statement is a dying declaration. The dying declaration exception to the hearsay rule applies only in criminal cases. It has no applicability in civil matters.

dying declaration
a statement made by a person who is certain they are about to die

DYING DECLARATIONS

1. The maker of the statement must be deceased.

2. At the time of making the statement, the person making it must have known that he or she was going to die almost immediately.

3. The statement must be one that would have been admissible if the person who made it had lived.

4. The statement is about who or what caused the maker of the statement to die.

5. The criminal case in which the either the Crown or the defence is seeking to admit the statement is one in which the charge relates to the death of the statement-maker.

IN THE NEWS

Deceased Wife's Statements to Cousin, Doctor Not Admissible Against Husband

In *R v. Czibulka*, the Ontario Court of Appeal considered the admissibility of a deceased woman's statements about her husband. It ruled that Maria Czibulka's complaints of abusive treatment by her husband Louis ought not to have been admitted against him at his murder trial.

Louis and Maria, both alcoholics, had a physically abusive relationship. The scene facing the police when they responded to Louis's 911 call suggesting his wife had overdosed on drugs looked very suspicious. She was lying face down on the living room floor, clad in only a bra and underpants. Her body was covered in bruises and the autopsy confirmed that she had 25 fractured ribs, a fractured skull, a ruptured diaphragm, and internal bleeding. Clumps of her hair had been pulled out and were found in the apartment, and DNA tests confirmed the presence of Louis's skin under her fingernails.

All of that evidence was properly admissible against Louis, but the trial judge went too far in admitting statements she made to her cousin in California and to her doctor. The judge made the mistake of relying on the truthfulness of the contents of the statements to determine their reliability. He also made the classic mistake of concluding that the absence of evidence was evidence of absence.

In overturning the trial court decision, the Ontario Court of Appeal stated (at paras. 35 and 44): "The absence of evidence of motive to fabricate is not the same as evidence of the absence of motive to fabricate. ... In other words, a finding that there is simply no evidence one way or the other that the declarant had a motive to fabricate cannot be converted into a finding in favour of the proponent that the declarant had no motive to fabricate."

Essentially, if the authorities fail to discover a motive to fabricate, that does not mean that the court is entitled to conclude that none existed. The trial judge stated that there was no motive for the deceased to fabricate in her discussions with her doctor. In fact, however, there was substantial motive to fabricate, because she was contemplating litigation against her husband and stated to the doctor that she was visiting him to get the evidence "on the record." In relation to her request for shelter with her cousin in California, the deceased could have exaggerated the abuse she was receiving from her husband in order to "obtain sympathy from her cousin so he might change his mind."

The Court of Appeal ordered a new trial for Louis but without the statements from the deceased.

We can see from the criteria for this exception that the statement must be made when the speaker has lost all hope of living and thus (it is thought) has no reason for worldly gain in lying. The deceased person's comments cannot include hearsay statements and must be directed at the cause of her untimely death. Julius Caesar's dying comment, "Et tu, Brute?" would not work if he had said, "Flavius told me that Brutus was in on the stabbing."

RES GESTAE OR SPONTANEOUS STATEMENTS

res gestae or spontaneous statement
a statement made in an excited state or expressing an existing physical, mental, or emotional state

Res gestae is a Latin term used to refer to what in English have come to be called **spontaneous statements**. These are statements that are made in an excited state or that express an existing physical, mental, or emotional state. There are many variations on such statements and we will look at the most common of these. The idea underlying the exception for such statements is that when an event takes place and a person comments on the event, without having an opportunity to fabricate a story, then the concern about concoction or lying is minimized.

For example, during renovations on your house, a carpenter is in the other room. You hear methodical hammering and then, all of a sudden, you hear what you assume is the hammer dropping and the carpenter shouting, "Ow! my thumb!" If you were to repeat this in court, the statement would be hearsay if you were being called to prove that the carpenter hurt his thumb on the job. If the carpenter tells you three days later, "You know, when I was working on your house, I hit my thumb with the hammer," that statement would also be hearsay and not admissible to prove the fact that he hit his thumb. The hearing of the spontaneous declaration of pain, however, is reliable given the immediacy of the comment and the unlikelihood that a person would drop his hammer and quickly concoct a story about hitting his thumb while working. It is the immediacy and the lack of opportunity to concoct a story that lead to the reliability of spontaneous statements.

Spontaneous statements can include "excited utterances" and statements of present impressions or physical or mental condition.

Excited Utterances

An **excited utterance** is a comment made almost immediately following a startling event. The comment does not have to be immediate, but it must be close enough in time to it that the trier of law can determine that the mind of the speaker was still dominated by the event. The sort of events that qualify as startling are serious accidents, bodily threats, observing a death—anything that would cause the person making the comment to suspend his or her ability to concoct a story. The person's mind must be dominated by the events in question when the words are spoken.

excited utterance
a statement made while the speaker's mind is still dominated by a startling event

One of the problems with this exception is that the meaning of "immediate" in relation to the event being described has been interpreted in different ways. In one case, the statement of a person fleeing from a house screaming, "I've been stabbed," was not considered immediate enough because the act of stabbing was not ongoing (see *R v. Leland*). In another, a stabbing took place, considerable time elapsed, and a statement was made to ambulance attendants, and the statement was still considered sufficiently immediate for the court to allow the exception (see *R v. Andrews* below). While it is true that a judge must consider how startling an event was, one stabbing is probably pretty much as startling as another.

The *R v. Andrews* case is a well-known example of the principles applicable with *res gestae* or spontaneous statements. A couple of robbers, armed with a bread knife and a paring knife and disguised under a sheet, entered Alexander Morrow's apartment and stabbed and robbed him. The sheet came off during the attack and Morrow was able to identify them. After his attackers left, he went upstairs for aid and the police arrived shortly thereafter. Morrow died in hospital a few months later. At trial, the Crown sought to admit his statements to the police identifying his attackers.

The House of Lords identified a number of factors that must be considered in looking at the admissibility of such evidence:

- Can the possibility of concoction or distortion be disregarded?

- Was the event so startling or dramatic as to dominate the thoughts of the victim, giving no real opportunity for reasoned reflection?

- The statement must be so closely associated with the event that it can be fairly stated that the mind of the person making the statement was still dominated by the event.

- Is there anything in the circumstances to imply any special reason for concoction, such as malice or a history of dispute?

- Are there any special circumstances that increase the potential for error, such as excessive alcohol consumption?

Statements of Present Impressions or Physical or Mental Condition

In general, a statement made by a person about their present impressions or physical or mental condition is admissible. However, the statement must relate to an impression or condition that the maker of the statement is experiencing at the time the statement is made. Recalling or remembering the condition will not suffice.

A **present impression** is essentially what it sounds like—a statement such as "I'm cold," "The room is spinning on me," or "The wheel on that truck in front of us looks like it's about to come off." In effect, the person is making a narrative statement in real time, describing events as they unfold. For example, following the volcanic eruption of Mount St. Helens in 1980, a person caught in the fallout zone tape-recorded his experience. He was walking along seeking a clear patch where he would be safe but expecting that he was going to die. As he walked, he commented on the ash burning his eyes and throat, the difficulty he was having in breathing, and everything he could or could not see. His narrative was a simultaneous translation of his experience and precisely what the present impression exception deals with. To meet the exception, a present impression statement does not have to be made in a life-threatening situation, but the comments do have to be almost instantaneous, with no opportunity for concoction.

Statements regarding present physical or mental condition are particular types of present impression statements. In statements regarding present physical condition, the speaker is reporting physical sensations that he or she is experiencing as they happen. Examples of such statements are, "Do you have any Tylenol 3 for this throbbing headache?," "I'm feeling numb on my left side," and "I think my knee just gave out."

Statements regarding a present mental condition include statements of emotion, intention, or planning that a person is experiencing at a particular point in time. Consider someone found dead of a drug overdose who made the statement a while earlier, "I've got nothing to live for." The statement would not be admissible for the truth of its contents—that she had no reason to live—but would be admissible for the inference that she was depressed and perhaps suicidal.

BUSINESS RECORDS

The Common-Law Rule

There are many "mechanical" recordings that are made by individuals in the course of performing their duties of employment. These **business records** can range from the notes made by a nurse about a hospital patient's temperature on his daily chart, to the serial number of a CD player manufactured in Japan, to the sign-in records of the probation office showing whether the accused kept his appointment as re-

present impression
a statement regarding a person's perception of their immediate physical surroundings or actions

business record
a record made in the ordinary course of business by an individual performing the duties of employment who has no motive to fabricate

quired by his probation order, to a multitude of other recordings that are made in any number of different circumstances.

The case of *Ares v. Venner* opened up the admissibility of such business records, in both written and oral form, in recognition that there are many reliable sources of recorded information that can be accessed for litigation purposes, and that calling the person who actually made the recording is not only of little use but a waste of time and the litigants' money. In the absence of the business records rule, the following line of questioning would be necessary:

> Now, Mrs. Masuda, I understand that you work at Toshiba Electronics in Osaka, Japan. You were working on the assembly line on June 23, 2000 recording the serial numbers of CD players being manufactured for the North American market. I am showing you a Toshiba CD player here. Can you tell me what the serial number on this item would be?

Any number of other similarly futile questions could be asked, because the person who recorded the information could only provide specifics by reference to the very records that the party is seeking to admit. Why not then simply admit the records for whatever help they may be to the trier of fact, without having the person employed to record them testify?

As with any other hearsay exception, there should be assurance that the business records will be reliable by reference to the care taken in making and recording the observations.

COMMON-LAW TEST FOR THE ADMISSIBILITY OF BUSINESS RECORDS

To ensure reliability of business records, the judge should consider the following criteria in determining admissibility:

1. the records were made in the ordinary course of the business,

2. they were made by a person whose duty was to keep such records,

3. the person who made the records did so from personal knowledge,

4. the records were made contemporaneously (at the time of the event), and

5. the person making the records had no motive to misrepresent them.

The Statutory Rule

Most provincial evidence statutes[1] as well as the *Canada Evidence Act* contain specific provisions to permit the admission of business records that are in written form, whereas the common-law rule set forth in *Ares v. Venner* applies to both oral and written statements. It is important to note, however, that the statutory provisions do not replace the common-law rule; rather, they work as an adjunct to it.

Unfortunately, the statutory provisions relating to business records are not uniform. Although all the evidence statutes require that written records be made in the usual or ordinary course of business, the statutes differ in their definition of the term "business." For example, the federal, Ontario, and British Columbia statutes do not refer to government in their definition of business. As a result, there is Ontario case law that says that police officers' notes may not be admitted under the statutory provision (*Woods v. Elias*). However, in Manitoba, Prince Edward Island, and Saskatchewan, the decision would likely be quite different, because the evidence acts of these provinces include government activities in the definition of business.

Approximately half of the statutes, besides requiring that records be made in the usual and ordinary course of business, also require that there be an actual duty to make the record. In other words, the person making the written record must be duty-bound to record the "act, transaction, occurrence or event."

Another difference among the statutes is that some require that notice be given to the opposing party prior to a request to the court to admit the documents. Both the *Canada Evidence Act* and the Ontario *Evidence Act* provide that the opposite party must be given seven days' notice, while the British Columbia statute does not specifically require that any notice be given.

Technology and the ways in which electronic records are created and stored have resulted in changes or additions to some of the existing evidence acts to allow for the admission of electronic business records. Given the nature of digital media and how computers operate, some or perhaps all of these electronic documents may not meet current statutory definitions of a "record." To ensure that such records are admissible, the federal government as well as the provincial governments of Ontario, Saskatchewan, Manitoba, and Yukon have enacted uniform electronic evidence provisions. These require authentication of a record to answer the specific questions: What is this document? Where did it come from? Who or what created it? The authentication must be provided by a witness who can give oral evidence to answer these questions

In addition, the party that wishes to have electronic evidence admitted must satisfy the court that the record is the best evidence available. This requirement is necessary because traditional evidence rules have typically required the production of the original document. In computer terms, though, the notion of an "original document" can be problematic. Usually, an electronic record is not the original document. It is most often a printout of information previously stored on a computer, which may only ever exist in document format at the point it is printed out to become evidence in a trial.

PRIOR TESTIMONY

The Canadian legal system often moves quite slowly. In a criminal case, the time between the laying of a charge and the completion of a trial can easily stretch into many years. Civil cases in a superior court may take even longer to work their way to trial. During that time, witnesses in a criminal matter may be called to testify at a preliminary hearing where the accused is represented by counsel and has an opportunity to cross-examine them. In a civil matter, there are likely to be examinations for discovery at which counsel have an opportunity to cross-examine an opposing party under oath.

In addition, the same incident may give rise to both a criminal charge and a civil suit for damages. If Bob gets angry and purposely drives his car into George, causing George serious injury, Bob is likely to be charged with a criminal offence. He may also be sued by George for the damages George suffered—loss of income, medical costs, pain and suffering, and so on. In situations where one incident gives rise to both criminal and civil liability, the criminal trial precedes the civil case.

It sometimes happens that a witness testifies at the preliminary hearing or the examination for discovery but then is unable to present testimony again at trial. The witness may be too ill to testify, or has left the country or disappeared, or has become mentally incapacitated, or has died. If a party wishes to have the absent person's sworn testimony admitted at trial for the truth of its contents, there is a hearsay issue. The prior testimony exception to the hearsay rule was developed to deal with this issue.

The Common-Law Rule

According to *Walkerton (Town) v. Erdman Estate*, oral evidence taken at another proceeding may be admitted at trial for the truth of its contents if:

1. the witness is unavailable for the trial,

2. the material issues and the parties are substantially the same in both proceedings, and

3. the opposite party had the opportunity to cross-examine in the earlier proceeding.

These criteria provide protection against the prejudicial impact of having evidence presented where the other party has no opportunity to test the reliability of the evidence through cross-examination. It is the opportunity to cross-examine that is important, not whether the party actually used the opportunity.

IN THE NEWS

Ellard Jury to Hear Testimony from First Murder Trial

A Crown witness in Kelly Ellard's second trial for the murder of Reena Virk became ill before his cross-examination could be completed, so the evidence he gave at her first trial was admitted at the second.

Justice Selwyn Romilly ruled that the evidence given by Lorne Lloyd-Walters at Ellard's first trial could be heard by the jury. It was the second time in the trial that the jury heard evidence from a witness who was unable to testify. Earlier, the jury heard an audiotape of testimony from a witness in the first trial who later died.

Section 715 of the *Criminal Code* allows testimony from an earlier trial to be used in a subsequent trial, in part to deal with the slow pace of litigation. Without such a provision, the prior testimony of witnesses who die or become incapacitated while a trial decision wends its way through the appeal process would be inadmissible, and without such evidence, a new trial would often be impossible and the administration of justice would fall into disrepute.

Prior Testimony Under the Civil Rules of Court

The procedural rules of most provincial superior courts provide for the admission of testimony in prior proceedings. These rules differ from province to province, but most of them strictly limit the type of evidence that may be admitted. For example, the Ontario *Rules of Civil Procedure* allow only for the admission of prior testimony taken during examinations for discovery:

> 31.11(6) Where a person examined for discovery,
>> (a) has died;
>> (b) is unable to testify because of infirmity or illness;
>> (c) for any other sufficient reason cannot be compelled to attend at the trial; or
>> (d) refuses to take an oath or make an affirmation or to answer any proper question,
>
> any party may, with leave of the trial judge, read into evidence all or part of the evidence given on the examination for discovery as the evidence of the person examined, to the extent that it would be admissible if the person were testifying in court.

This means that, in Ontario, if there had been a prior proceeding such as a criminal trial, any evidence from that proceeding could not be admitted under the rule. Instead, the party wanting to admit the earlier testimony would have to rely on either the common-law rule or s. 5 of the Ontario *Evidence Act*, which provides for the admission of recorded transcripts from prior proceedings.[2]

The British Columbia *Rules of Court* however, provide a much broader rule of admission:

> 40(4) Where a witness is dead, or is unable to attend and testify because of age, infirmity, sickness or imprisonment or is out of the jurisdiction or his or her attendance cannot be secured by subpoena, the court may permit a transcript of any evidence of that witness taken in any proceeding, hearing or inquiry at which the evidence was taken under oath, whether or not involving the same parties to be put in as evidence, but reasonable notice shall be given of the intention to give that evidence.

In civil proceedings in the British Columbia Supreme Court, recourse to the common law or the provincial evidence act would not be necessary because the rule permits the transcript of sworn evidence of "any proceeding, hearing or inquiry" to be admitted into evidence.

Prior Testimony Under the Criminal Code

There are provisions in the *Criminal Code* for the admissibility of prior testimony. As with the common-law rule and provincial procedural rules, the intention appears to be to provide safeguards of necessity and reliability to ensure that the prejudice to the accused is minimized:

> 715(1) Where, at the trial of an accused, a person whose evidence was given at a previous trial on the same charge, or whose evidence was taken in the investi-

gation of the charge against the accused or on the preliminary inquiry into the charge, refuses to be sworn or to give evidence, or if facts are proved on oath from which it can be inferred reasonably that the person

(a) is dead,

(b) has since become and is insane,

(c) is so ill that he is unable to travel or testify, or

(d) is absent from Canada,

and where it is proved that his evidence was taken in the presence of the accused, it may be read as evidence in the proceedings without further proof, unless the accused proves that the accused did not have full opportunity to cross-examine the witness.

In this exception, the necessity criteria are clearly defined as being dead, insane, too ill to testify, or absent from Canada. The judge has the discretion to determine whether the latter three make the accused unable to testify. (The first criterion is something even a judge is powerless to correct.) Note that the evidence must be taken in the presence of the accused and that there must have been *full* opportunity to cross-examine. An accused who absconds before or during his trial is deemed to have been present, so that requirement in the above definition is met, even in the absence of the accused. Thus, a strategy of "taking off" until key witnesses are no longer available will not work.

PRIOR INCONSISTENT STATEMENTS MADE BY SOMEONE OTHER THAN THE ACCUSED

At common law, a prior statement made by a witness who was not a party to the proceeding, may be admitted only to challenge the credibility of a witness, not for the truth of its contents. This is the classic "Are you lying now or were you lying then?" scenario. For example, Sally tells the police that she saw Matt steal money from a classmate's book bag, and then at Matt's theft trial she says she didn't see anyone steal the money. Under the common-law rule, the prior statement—that Sally saw Matt steal the money—may only be admitted to show that Sally is not a very believable witness because she cannot get her story straight. This principle does not involve an exception to the hearsay rule because the prior statement is not being admitted for the truth of its contents.

In *R v. B. (K.G.)*, the Supreme Court of Canada constructed what is essentially a new exception to the hearsay rule by expanding on the use that could be made of a prior inconsistent statement of a non-party. In *R v. B. (K.G.)*, the accused was charged with killing another young person by stabbing him. Three witnesses who were friends of the accused all gave statements to the police implicating the accused. The statements were videotaped, and because the witnesses were under the age of majority, the statements were made in the presence of a parent and in one instance a lawyer acting for the young person. The witnesses subsequently recanted their testimony implicating their friend in the killing, so the Crown had no prospect of convicting the accused without admitting their statements "for their truth."

The Supreme Court ruled that in the following, very limited circumstances, prior inconsistent statements could be admitted for the truth of their contents:

1. The prior statement was "sworn"—that is, made under oath or affirmation—and a warning was given about the consequences of lying in such circumstances.

2. The whole statement was videotaped.

3. The other party was given an opportunity to cross-examine the witness.

The requirement that the statement was sworn at the time it was made is designed to provide the same protection as having a witness give evidence under oath. The requirement that the statement was videotaped is a substitute for having the witness present in the court so that the trier of fact can assess the witness's demeanour. And the requirement that there was an opportunity to cross-examine (the least practical of the criteria because it is logistically unlikely that the accused will have the where-withal to cross-examine or happen to have a lawyer at hand to do so at the time the statement is taken) deals with the most important guarantee of reliability.

IDENTIFICATIONS

In the matter of identifications, the law of evidence takes into account the practicalities of the litigation process and the frailties of human memory. An initial identification often takes place shortly after a crime. The witness may be shown a photo line-up or an in-person line-up, or may even pick out the suspect in a crowd or informal group. Then there will be a passage of time, usually many months or even years, before the witness sees the person again. At this point, the person is typically sitting beside their counsel in a courtroom and is well dressed and well groomed, and to one degree or another looks different from the way they did at the time of the offence. (Male accuseds often have either more or less facial hair; any accused may have a different hairstyle or may have gained or lost weight.) Not surprisingly, witnesses sometimes have difficulty identifying the accused in court.

The usual practice for presenting information regarding the prior identification of the person is as follows. The police officer who took the witness's original testimony testifies about the identification process—say, a photo line-up. The line-up array is presented as an exhibit and the officer testifies about the selection made by the witness from the choices offered. The officer's instructions to the witness are crucial in determining the reliability of the identification. The witness should not have been influenced by the officer or the process and must not have concluded that she had to make a selection, or even that the offender was necessarily in the array. In other words, it is not acceptable for the witness to have picked the *closest* person to the perpetrator rather than the actual offender. Line-up identifications have resulted in many wrongful convictions and, while invaluable for the police, they are not very strong evidence in themselves.

Where the witness can positively identify the accused in court, particularly where the accused has gone through a radical transformation in appearance, the out-of-court identification can be considered by the trier of fact in determining whether identification has been proven beyond a reasonable doubt. This is the case where the witness can testify that she accurately identified the person previously as the offender. Although this evidence is hearsay, its reliability comes from the fact that the identification was made close to the events in question and the witness is available for cross-examination about the accuracy of that identification.

For defence counsel, the essential concern with these identifications is that one can never tell whether the witness is identifying the accused on the basis of her memory of the original incident or of her clearer and more recent memory of picking the accused out of a line-up. The opportunity for observation in a line-up is usually much better than during the actual, often chaotic occurrence of the incident. Since the line-up process takes place outside the view of the court, usually in circumstances where the police have selected someone they believe is the offender, there exists potential for subtle influence of the witness. Subsequently, in the period leading up to the trial and at the trial itself, a witness who does not want to acknowledge a mistaken identification or uncertainty may "dig in" and insist on the truth of her memory.

The rule on the admissibility of prior identifications has evolved out of necessity, given the sometimes very lengthy times between the commission of an offence and the trial. The justice system would be very poorly thought of if a criminal could elude justice after having been positively identified very close to the time of the offence but could not be identified years later, possibly because of his altered appearance.

THE IN-COURT IDENTIFICATION GAME

Defence counsel tend to be cynical about in-court identification of the accused by witnesses. It sometimes seems that a witness looks down at the defence table, passes over the man in the expensive suit, and picks the person beside him as the perpetrator. In an effort to combat this kneejerk identification, some counsel will have the accused sit in the body of the courtroom rather than beside them when identification testimony is being presented. It's hard to say how often this is a successful strategy for the defence. One problem may be that no one else in the courtroom is a likely candidate. The spectators may be elderly or they may not be from the same identifiable racial or cultural group. Defence counsel can overcome this problem by having their client bring a group of friends along with him and giving the witness a real test in identification.

A lawyer had a client who was charged with stealing a car. When he showed up the morning of the trial, the lawyer approached the client and began talking about the case. The person to whom the lawyer was speaking interrupted and said, "I think you want to talk to my cousin." As it turned out, the client had brought his cousin with him and he wanted to see whether the police could pick him out of the body of the courtroom, with his relative there. The family resemblance between the client and his cousin was astounding: they could almost have been twins. The judge, too, was amazed at the family resemblance, but nevertheless he permitted the experiment.

The client, his cousin, and a few other unlikely suspects were in the body of the courtroom when the first officer testified. When the defence counsel got to the issue of identification, the officer unhesitatingly picked out the client. Thinking "Lucky guess," the lawyer continued cross-examination by asking the officer how he could be certain of the identification. The officer replied, "You'll notice, counsellor, that your client has a bit of a curve to his nose and his earlobes are longer than those of his friend. That's how I know he's the one I dealt with." The lawyer was startled, but on closer inspection he found that the officer was right. Not all witnesses are as good at identification as that officer, but he certainly was one whom it would be wise not to challenge in that way again.

PAST RECOLLECTION RECORDED

Sometimes a witness to an incident will, at the time or shortly after, write notes or otherwise record her perceptions of the incident as it occurred. However, given the length of time between the incident and the trial, the witness may not remember the specific details that she wrote down or recorded. The classic example is a situation where the witness writes down the licence plate number of a car speeding away from the crime scene. When called upon to testify months or years later, the witness can no longer remember the exact number and wants to refer to the note that she wrote at the time she witnessed the event in order to refresh her memory.

The note itself is hearsay. It is a written, out-of-court statement, that counsel is trying to admit in court for the truth of its contents. In *R v. Meddoui*, the Supreme Court of Canada upheld criteria summarized by the Alberta Court of Appeal (per Kerans JA, at 352), quoting *Wigmore on Evidence*, as the test for permitting a witness to refer to a written note or other recording:

1. The past recollection must have been recorded in some reliable way.

2. At the time, it must have been sufficiently fresh and vivid to be probably accurate.

3. The witness must be able now to assert that the record accurately represented his knowledge and recollection at the time. The usual phrase requires the witness to affirm that he "knew it to be true at the time."

4. The original record itself must be used, if it is procurable.

In other words, the information the witness wishes to refer to must have been made very close in time to the incident, in some reliable fashion, and the witness must be able to verify that she believed the information to be true when she recorded it.

This test has been explicitly adopted in numerous provincial court decisions and in the Supreme Court's decision in *R v. Fliss*.

ORAL HISTORIES OF ABORIGINAL PEOPLES

The law evolves over time, one hopes in ways that make it fairer and more accessible to the people to whom it applies. Evidence law is perhaps even more responsive to societal change because it is not subject to overtly political considerations but is intended to balance the rights of parties against the interests of society as a whole in seeing that justice is done. In recent times, the Supreme Court has recognized the admissibility of the oral histories of aboriginal people.

Delgamuukw was an aboriginal title claim advanced by the Gitksan and Wet'suwet'en people to a vast area of land in British Columbia. In order to advance this claim, the Gitksan sought to show that they had title to this land prior to 1846 and that they never relinquished this title.

The Supreme Court of Canada laid out the manner of proof of aboriginal right in *R v. Van der Peet* (at paras. 54-59). Stripped to essentials, an aboriginal claimant must prove that a modern practice, tradition, or custom has a reasonable degree of continuity with the practices, traditions, or customs that existed prior to contact.

The practice, custom, or tradition must have been "integral to the distinctive culture" of the aboriginal society, in the sense that it distinguished or characterized their traditional culture and lay at the core of the people's identity. It must be a "defining feature" of the aboriginal society, such that the culture would be "fundamentally altered" without it. And it must be a feature of "central significance" to the people's culture, one that "truly made the society what it was."

The following components summarize the proof needed:

- there must be a modern practice, tradition, or custom (that is, salmon fishing for trade);

- continuity from pre-contact times to the present;

- the practice, tradition, or custom must have been integral to the people's culture; and

- the people must have had a distinctive society.

Proof of aboriginal *title* is more focused on occupation of the land than proof of aboriginal right. It focuses on the time at which the Crown asserted sovereignty over the land, which in British Columbia was 1846. In *Delgamuukw*, the claim of the Gitksan and Wet'suwet'en people was a collective one and supported by collective oral history. The Supreme Court stated that in order to claim aboriginal title, the following must be proved:

1. the land was occupied prior to 1846;

2. continuity exists between present and pre-sovereignty occupation; and

3. at the time sovereignty was asserted by the Crown, occupation of the land was exclusive.

Proof of occupation can be established by showing either actual occupation or that a system of law exists that asserts control over the land.

Oral history was validated by the Supreme Court of Canada in *Delgamuukw* and it was emphasized that no distinction could be made between oral history and documentary history. That is not to say that anything someone says is accepted unquestioningly, but rather that oral history should be assessed for reliability just like documentary evidence and given the weight it deserves:

> Notwithstanding the challenges created by the use of oral histories as proof of historical facts, the laws of evidence must be adapted in order that this type of evidence can be accommodated and placed on an equal footing with the types of historical evidence that courts are familiar with, which largely consists of historical documents. This is a long-standing practice in the interpretation of treaties between the Crown and aboriginal peoples. ... To quote Dickson C.J., given that most aboriginal societies "did not keep written records," the failure to do so would "impose an impossible burden of proof" on aboriginal peoples, and "render nugatory" any rights that they have ... . This process must be undertaken on a case-by-case basis. (para. 87)

Oral histories called *adaawk* and *kungax* by the Gitksan and Wet'suwet'en peoples were admitted at their land claims trial. These histories are recitations of important events for these people, including migrations, origins, traditions, laws, and the territory falling under the jurisdiction of the various houses of the Gitksan and

Wet'suwet'en chiefs. This evidence was offered as proof of historical use and occupation of a specific territory. While the trial judge admitted this evidence, he ultimately gave it no weight, saying that the oral histories were not "literally true," that they included material that was mythological, and that they offered a "romantic view" of the claimants' history.

The Supreme Court of Canada found that the trial judge erred in not giving weight to the oral histories and said that if the oral histories of aboriginal peoples were not treated the same as documentary histories, they would "never be given any independent weight and are only useful as confirmatory evidence in aboriginal rights litigation" and thus would "be consistently and systematically undervalued by the Canadian legal system," making it virtually impossible for First Nations to litigate aboriginal title claims. The court directed a new trial stipulating that this evidence be given weight on the issue of aboriginal title.

CHAPTER SUMMARY

Despite the general rule that hearsay is not admissible into evidence because it cannot be tested in the normal way for reliability, the common law has developed a number of exceptions to the rule. In some exceptional situations, hearsay statements can be viewed as reliable and it does not make sense to exclude them. As a result, if a hearsay statement fits into one of the common-law exceptions, it may be admitted into evidence.

KEY TERMS

admission of a party

vicarious admission

admission by action

conspiracy

co-conspirator exception

conditionally admissible

declaration against interest

pecuniary or proprietary interest

penal interest

dying declaration

res gestae or spontaneous statement

excited utterance

present impression

business record

NOTES

1. Only Alberta (RSA 2000, c. A-18) and Newfoundland and Labrador (RSNL 1990. c. E-16) do not provide a provincial statutory hearsay exception for business records. See the following for the business records provisions: federal—*Canada Evidence Act*, RSC 1980 c. C-5, s. 30; and provincial—RSBC 1996, c. 154, s. 23; CCSM, c. E150, s. 49; RSNB 1973, c. E-11, ss. 49 and 51; RSNS 1989, c. 154, s. 23; RSO 1990, c. E.23, s. 35; RSPEI 1974, c. E-10, s. 32; and SS 2006, c. E-11.2, s. 50.

2. See also *Manitoba Evidence Act*, CCSM c. E150, s. 27; *Alberta Evidence Act*, RSA 2000, c. A-18, s. 27; Nova Scotia *Evidence Act*, RSNS 1989, c. 154, s. 19 ; New Brunswick *Evidence Act*, RSNB 1973, c. E-11, ss. 33 and 35; Saskatchewan *Evidence Act*, SS 2006, c. E-11.2, s. 50.

REFERENCES

Andrews, R v., [1987] 1 AC 281.

Ares v. Venner (1970), 12 CRNS 349 (SCC).

B. (K.G.), R v., [1993] 1 SCR 740.

British Columbia Law Institute, *Report on Post-Accident Remedial Measures,* report no. 28, January 2004. Vancouver, BC: Author.

Christie, R v., [1914] AC 545 (HL).

Conlon, R v. (1990), 1 OR (3d) 188 (CA).

Criminal Code, RSC 1985, c. C-46.

Customs Act, 1985, c. 1 (2d Supp.).

Czibulka, R v. (2004), 189 CCC (3d) 199 (Ont. CA).

Delgamuukw v. British Columbia, [1997] 3 SCR 1010.

Eden, R v., [1970] 2 OR 161 (CA).

Fliss, R v., 2002 SCC 16, [2002] 1 SCR 535.

Guyatt, R v. (1998), 119 CCC (3d) 304 (SCC).

Hart v. Lancashire and Yorkshire Ry. Co. (1869), 21 LT 261 (Eng. Ex. Ct.).

Higham v. Ridgway (1808), 103 ER 717 (KB).

Insurance Corp. of British Columbia v. Sun, 2003 BCSC 1059.

Leland, R v. (1951), 11 CR 152 (Ont. CA).

Lucier v. R, [1982] 1 SCR 28.

Meddoui, R v. (1990), 61 CCC (3d) 345 (Alta. CA), aff'd. [1991] 3 SCR 320.

O'Brien, R v., [1978] 1 SCR 591.

Ontario, *Rules of Civil Procedure*, RRO 1980, reg. 194, rule 51; British Columbia, *Supreme Court Rules*, BC reg. 287/205, rule 31; Nova Scotia, *Rules of Civil Procedure*, rule 21; Newfoundland and Labrador, *Rules of the Supreme Court, 1986*, SNL 1986, c. 42, sch. D, rule 33; Prince Edward Island, *Rules of Civil Procedure*, rule 51; Alberta, *Rules of Court*, Alta. reg. 390/68, rule 230; Manitoba, *Court of Queen's Bench Rules*, Man. reg. 553/88, rule 51; New Brunswick, *Rules of Court*, NB reg. 82-73, rule 51; Saskatchewan, *Queen's Bench Rules*, rules 241 and 242.

Paciocco, D.M., and L. Stuesser, *The Law of Evidence*, 4th ed. (Toronto: Irwin Law, 2005).

Pammer, R v., [1979] MJ no. 149, 1 Man. R (2d) 18 (CA).

Van der Peet, R v., [1996] 2 SCR 507.

Walkerton (Town) v. Erdman Estate (1894), 23 SCR 352.

Woods v. Elias (1978), 21 OR (2d) 840 (Co. Ct.).

REVIEW QUESTIONS

1. What is an admission and when can it be used?
2. In what circumstances does a person make an admission on behalf of a party?
3. Can an employee make an admission on behalf of an employer?
4. Is it possible to make an admission without speaking?
5. What is the difference between an admission and a declaration against interest?
6. Give an example of a dying declaration that would be admissible, and an example of one that would not.
7. List each of the different types of spontaneous statements and state in what circumstances they become admissible.
8. Why is there a business records exception and when will it apply?
9. What is the common-law rule creating an exception for prior testimony? How does it differ from the civil and criminal statutory exceptions?
10. In what circumstances can a prior inconsistent statement be admitted for the truth of its contents?
11. Why is there an exception for prior identification?
12. In what circumstance may a witness rely on a previously recorded statement?
13. Explain the basis for the development of the oral histories of First Nations exception.

DISCUSSION QUESTIONS

1. In a case involving a violation of the *Customs Act* the Crown, in order to establish the country of origin, seeks to introduce the perfume seized from the accused, the bottles of which have attached labels "Made in Paris." The Crown seeks to call Constable Smith, who will testify that the accused told him the perfume came from France and that, when asked how he knew, the accused replied, "Look at the label, dummy!"

   Identify the hearsay statements and discuss whether or not they will be admitted into evidence.

2. The accused is charged with murder. The Crown's main witness, Jones, will testify that the accused's brother advised him some weeks prior to the trial that he should be careful because the accused had "already killed once to save his hide." Jones is also prepared to say that the accused, the night before the trial, phoned him and said, "If you don't want what Smith got, stay off the stand tomorrow." The Crown is prepared to lead evidence that Smith was murdered some two years ago.

   Discuss whether or not each of these statements will be admissible.

3. A witness observes a hit-and-run accident and writes down the licence plate number of the fleeing vehicle. The witness later describes the vehicle to the investigating officer, who makes a note of it. Sometime before the trial the witness lost her note, and now at trial she cannot remember the licence plate number. Discuss whether or not the investigating officer can supply the missing number while giving evidence.

4. The accused, Butch, is charged with the murder of his estranged wife, Jill. The killing occurred in the early morning hours at the deceased's front doorway and was the result of several blows to the head with a small hatchet. Jack, the 14-year-old son of the couple, was roused from his sleep by someone knocking loudly at the front door. He testifies that he heard his mother go downstairs and then heard her screaming: "Butch, what are you doing? No! No! Please don't hurt me, Butch." Will the Crown be successful in having Jack's testimony admitted?

CHAPTER 7

The Principled Exception to the Hearsay Rule

CHAPTER OBJECTIVES

After completing this chapter you should be able to:

- Analyze the traditional exceptions to the hearsay rule in terms of their necessity.

- Analyze the traditional exceptions to the hearsay rule in terms of their reliability.

- Explain the principled exception to the hearsay rule in terms of necessity and reliability.

- Understand the application of the principled exception to the hearsay rule.

WIGMORE'S CRITERIA

Professor Wigmore was one of the foremost experts on Anglo-American evidence law. In the early half of the 20th century, Wigmore wrote a multivolume text on evidence law that is still in use by scholars and practising lawyers today. Besides dealing with the practical applications of evidence in the courtroom, he also did considerable analysis of the historical and academic principles of the common law of evidence. We will come across Professor Wigmore several times in our study of evidence law.

While some people might find the traditional, judge-made exceptions to the hearsay rule to be an unrelated hodgepodge of common-law rules, Wigmore saw a common thread running through all of them, linking them together in a rational manner. Since the rule against the use of hearsay focuses on the difficulties of reliability and trustworthiness, Wigmore asked himself if there was some underlying reason the courts found the exceptions more reliable and trustworthy than hearsay that was not admissible.

The common themes that Wigmore saw as underpinning all the traditional exceptions to the hearsay rule were that the out-of-court statement is

1. *necessary* in the sense that the only way the evidence could be admitted would be through hearsay, and

2. relatively *reliable* in the circumstances in which the statement was made.

The *necessity* of the statement being admitted through hearsay usually arises because the person who made the statement is not available to give testimony in court by the time the case has reached trial. The witness may have died, or left the country and cannot be found, or suffered some deterioration in mental or physical health that makes his or her appearance as a witness next to impossible. In some cases, there may be another evidence rule that prevents the person who made the statement from being summonsed or subpoenaed to give evidence. For example, in a criminal case, a person cannot be compelled by the prosecution to give evidence against his or her spouse.

With regard to *reliability*, the statement must have been made in circumstances where the court has determined that there is some trustworthiness to the statement, even though it was not made under oath and the maker of the statement cannot be cross-examined.

Let us take a second look at the traditional exceptions that we examined in chapter 6. How might they meet the necessary and reliable test?

ADMISSIONS OF A PARTY

This exception to the hearsay rules makes just about everything said by a party to the proceeding admissible against him or her in court.

Necessity

The opposite party must show that the only manner in which the statement can be admitted is by way of hearsay. If the maker of the statement is a party in the case, it is unlikely that he would not be available, but it is the availability of the evidence that is important. For example, in the time between the events that give to the court proceeding and the court proceeding itself, the party may have forgotten earlier statements or changed his story, or, in the case of a criminal charge, the accused may not be testifying at all and so cannot be cross-examined on his out-of-court statements.

Reliability

The type of admissions that an opposing party would want to enter into evidence would be statements that would help his or her case. These admissions would be ones that hurt the case of the party who made them. It seems to be human nature that people tend to lie to help themselves or to make themselves look better. They rarely lie to make themselves look worse. Although false confessions do occur, an accused thief is much more likely to claim that he did not steal the diamond ring than to falsely admit that he did. A defendant who is being sued for damages in tort is much more likely to deny negligence than to falsely admit it. Therefore, when a party makes an admission that would hurt his or her case, generally it is more likely to be reliable than not.

DECLARATIONS AGAINST INTEREST

The two general principles relating to declarations against pecuniary or proprietary interest and declarations against penal interest are:

1. The person making the statement must be unavailable.

2. The statement must be against the statement-maker's interest.

Necessity

One of the criteria for the admission of a non-party statement against interest is that the person who made the statement is unavailable to give evidence at the proceeding. In that circumstance, it is clear that the statement can only be admitted through hearsay.

Reliability

As with admissions of a party, a person is unlikely to make a false statement that harms his or her interest unless it is true.

DYING DECLARATIONS

The test for the admissibility of dying declarations is as follows:

1. The maker of the statement must be deceased.

2. At the time of making the statement, the person making it must have known that he or she was going to die almost immediately.

3. The statement must be one that would have been admissible if the person who made it had lived.

4. The statement is about who or what caused the maker of the statement to die.

5. The criminal case in which either the Crown or the defence is seeking to admit the statement is one in which the charge relates to the death of the statement-maker.

Necessity

The person who made the statement must be dead.

Reliability

The notion of the reliability of a dying declaration probably arose in a time when society was more religious. From the viewpoint of a number of religions, a dying person is likely to tell the truth because she fears the deathbed consequences of going to meet her God. That is fine if we can rely on the statement-maker's belief, but there is no assurance of reliability if the dying person believes that she can lie with impunity. Unlike swearing an oath, which must also be binding on a person's conscience for there to be any assurance of truthfulness, there is no worldly consequence for a dying person who lies.

It might also be argued that a dying person will feel the need to leave this world with a clean slate, regardless of whether she believes that there are consequences in the "great beyond." That is a nice thought but it is little more than a fairy tale—kind of a happy-endings belief. What if a person facing his own mortality is more inclined to get off one last practical joke, delighting in the thought of all the chaos that he will leave behind? We cannot know what goes through the mind of a person on the brink of death, but we have constructed a traditional exception to the hearsay rule that is based on the belief that a dying person's statement is more likely to be true than not. This exception only applies to criminal proceedings.

The statement must be made when the speaker has no hope of living and thus (it is thought) no reason for worldly gain in lying. The deceased person's comments cannot pass on hearsay statements from others and must be directed at the cause of her untimely death. Julius Caesar's dying comment, "Et tu, Brute?" would not work if he had said, "Flavius told me that Brutus was in on the stabbing."

RES GESTAE OR SPONTANEOUS STATEMENTS

In general, the *res gestae* or spontaneous statement exception allows the admission of a statement made in an excited state or a statement expressing an existing physical, mental, or emotional state if the statement is made contemporaneously with, or very close in time to, the event.

Necessity

The party wishing to admit a spontaneous statement into evidence must establish that the statement could only be admitted by way of hearsay. This might be the case if the original maker of the statement is dead or otherwise unavailable to give evidence, or for some other reason, such as he could not remember the statement or had changed his story.

Reliability

The principle underlying this exception is that the statement was made so close in time to the occurrence that the there was no opportunity for the maker of the statement to reflect on it and invent a story. Therefore, he is assumed to have spontaneously stated the truth as he saw it. Of course, the statement may be untrue due to a mistaken perception, but the point is that the maker did not have time to fabricate it.

BUSINESS RECORDS

This exception allows for the admission of business records if:

1. they were made in the ordinary course of the business,

2. they were made by a person whose duty was to keep such records,

3. the person who made the records did so from personal knowledge,

4. the records were made contemporaneously (at the time of the events), and

5. the person making the records had no motive to misrepresent them.

Necessity

It may be necessary to admit a business record through hearsay for several reasons. For example, in the case of hospital records or books of account, if a party was required to call every single nurse or bookkeeper who made entries into the record, trials could last a very long time. In these instances, it is necessary to admit the evidence to ensure that that the justice system can deal with cases in a timely fashion.

Sometimes, it is nearly impossible to determine who actually made the business record. For example, the serial number stamped onto a CD player is a business record. As the player comes down the assembly line, an employee stamps the number onto the item. Three years later, in an attempt to show that the player was stolen, it would be next to impossible to determine which worker stamped the specific player. Instead, a representative of the manufacturer could identify the marking as a business record used by that company and could even specify the date that the player was made by reference to records kept by the manufacturer.

Reliability

The above criteria are designed to ensure reliability. The records were made as part of the usual business of the organization. An organization has an interest in maintaining accurate records. For example, in a hospital, the health and even the lives of the patients depend upon accurate recording. In a profit-making business, accurate records often determine the financial viability of the enterprise. We have additional assurance in the fact that the continued employment of the person who made the record, to some degree, depends on her accuracy in recording. When records are made within a reasonable time of the events, there is some assurance of reliability because intervening factors such as memory loss or third-party influence can be eliminated.

The final factor—that of having "no motive to misrepresent"—is intended to eliminate the prospect that the recording was made by someone who has an interest in the outcome of a dispute and who might doctor or modify the record to support one side.

PRIOR TESTIMONY

Testimony given by a witness in a prior proceeding is generally admissible in another proceeding.

Necessity

The first requirement for the application of this exception, whether it be under the common law, statutes law, or the procedural rules of provincial civil courts, is that the witness be unavailable.

Reliability

As we know, two of the major difficulties with hearsay evidence is that it is not taken under oath or affirmation and cannot be cross-examined. These problems do not exist with prior testimony because it was sworn evidence and there was an opportunity to cross-examine in the earlier proceeding.

PRIOR INCONSISTENT STATEMENTS MADE BY SOMEONE OTHER THAN THE ACCUSED

In the *B. (K.G.)* case, the Supreme Court of Canada ruled that in the following, very limited circumstances, prior inconsistent statements made by witnesses other than the accused may be admitted for the truth of their contents:

1. The prior statement was "sworn"—that is, made under oath or affirmation—and a warning was given about the consequences of lying in such circumstances.

2. The whole statement was videotaped.

3. The other party was given an opportunity to cross-examine the witness.

Necessity

This exception was developed to deal with recanting witnesses—that is, witnesses who tell one story at the time of the investigation which leads to the arrest of the accused, and who then, at trial, tell another story that helps the accused. Much if not all of the Crown's case may depend on the original statements, which cannot be admitted in any other way than through hearsay because the witnesses are now saying something entirely different from what they said initially. If this evidence were to be automatically excluded under the hearsay rule, it would invite witness intimidation by the accused, or by the accused's family and friends.

Reliability

The requirement that the statement was sworn at the time it was made is designed to provide the same protection as having a witness give evidence under oath. The requirement that the statement was videotaped is a substitute for having the witness present in the court so that the trier of fact can assess her demeanour. And the requirement that there was an opportunity to cross-examine deals with the most important guarantee of reliability. As noted by the court in *B. (K.G.)*, the availability at trial of a witness, even a recanting one, goes some distance toward curing the defect of the accused's not having had the opportunity to cross-examine the witness at the time the statement was made.

IDENTIFICATIONS

When a witness has identified the accused from a line-up or a photo array shortly after the incident, the officer conducting the identification process may give testimony that the witness did verbally identify the accused.

Necessity

The rule on the admissibility of prior identifications has evolved out of necessity, given the sometimes very lengthy times between the commission of an offence and the trial. The justice system would be very poorly thought of if a criminal could elude justice after having been positively identified very close to the time of the offence but could not be identified years later, possibly because of his altered appearance.

Reliability

The witness can testify that she accurately identified the person previously as the offender. The reliability comes from the fact that the identification was made close in time to the events in question and the witness is available for cross-examination about the accuracy of that identification.

There are also strict requirements as to how the identification process is to be conducted. The witness cannot be coached or led to the identification in any manner.

PAST RECOLLECTION RECORDED

This exception requires the following:

1. The past recollection must have been recorded in some reliable way.

2. At the time, it must have been sufficiently fresh and vivid to be probably accurate.

3. The witness must be able now to assert that the record accurately represented his knowledge and recollection at the time. The usual phrase requires the witness to affirm that he "knew it to be true at the time."

4. The original record itself must be used, if it is procurable.

Necessity

The witness cannot remember the details of the record he made of the incident. The witness is not able to give the evidence unless he can refer to the record he made of the incident or event.

Reliability

The requirement that the record be made contemporaneously with, or close to, the incident provides some assurance that it was very fresh in the recorder's memory and therefore is more reliable than information recorded sometime after the fact. This is bolstered by the requirement that the record be made in some reliable manner and that the original record be used, if at all possible.

ORAL HISTORIES OF ABORIGINAL PEOPLES

The oral histories of aboriginal peoples have been admitted in land claim cases.

Necessity

Most aboriginal history is based on oral accounts rather than on written accounts. If the courts refused to give oral histories independent legal weight, it would be virtually impossible for First Nations to litigate aboriginal title claims.

Reliability

In *Delgamuukw v. British Columbia*, the Supreme Court of Canada determined that oral histories should be treated in the same manner as written histories in proof of aboriginal land title issues. Oral histories are as reliable or unreliable as written histories. Oral history evidence is to be assessed just like any other fact. It can be tested for reliability in the same way as other evidence—through corroboration, consistency, potential for bias, and so on.

THE DEVELOPMENT OF THE PRINCIPLED EXCEPTION

From their inception, the traditional hearsay exceptions were very rigidly applied by the courts. If the statement did not fit properly into the legal criteria required by the exception, it was not admissible into evidence. This all began to change in the early 1990s when the Supreme Court of Canada heard the case of *R v. Khan*.

In *Khan*, a mother took her three-and-a-half-year-old daughter to see the family doctor. She left the child with the doctor for about half an hour. After leaving the doctor's office, she had a conversation with her daughter. During the chat, it became clear to the mother that Dr. Khan had sexually assaulted the little girl. The child herself clearly did not understand the nature of the assault and had not mentioned it until the mother struck up an innocent conversation. The child was taken to the police, who found physical evidence in the form of semen on the child's clothing. At trial, the judge determined that the child was incapable of giving evidence because of her inability to understand the court process or the nature of the legal requirement to be truthful. Unless the mother was permitted to testify about what the child said to her, there would be no way of convicting Dr. Khan for this offence.

The difficulty was that none of the traditional exceptions to the hearsay rule applied in *Khan*. The Crown attempted to argue that the statement was a spontaneous one, but the statement could not be fit into the *res gestae* exception without doing serious damage to the intention or reason behind the exception. Therefore, the mother's evidence could not be admitted unless the Supreme Court analyzed the basic underpinnings of the exceptions to the hearsay rule and developed a new approach. This is exactly what it did.

In its analysis, the court went back to basics and looked at the reasons for the hearsay rule. Relying on Wigmore's earlier study of the issue, the court concluded that the basic principles supporting the existing exceptions to the rule were, indeed, necessity and reliability. It determined that, in addition to the traditional exceptions, there ought to be an exception that was founded on the principles underlying the development of the hearsay rule. The court called this additional exception the **principled exception**. This new approach stated that where necessity and reliability could be established, hearsay may be admitted, provided that the probative value of the evidence outweighed the prejudice.

principled exception
exception to the hearsay rule based on the principles of necessity and reliability

It must be necessary to rely on hearsay to admit the evidence. If the person who originally made the statement is available to give evidence, he or she must be called to testify in person. In looking at reliability, a court must find replacements for the above-noted credibility and reliability assurances. These replacement guarantees are often referred to as *circumstantial guarantees of reliability*. These can be seen by asking, "What is it about the circumstances of the statement being made that provide a guarantee of reliability?" If there are no circumstantial guarantees of reliability, then the long-standing hearsay dangers cannot be avoided and the evidence should not be admissible.

In the *Khan* case, the child's statements could only be admitted through her mother because the child was too young to testify. On the issue of necessity, the court weighed heavily the concern about the sexual abuse of young children and the fact that these incidents happen in private and often with very small children. Where a child does not satisfy the criteria for giving sworn or unsworn evidence, then his or her evidence, repeated to others, would be lost. In such circumstances, it would not be possible to obtain a conviction against offenders, regardless of the reliability attached to the statements. It was therefore necessary to admit the statements by way of hearsay. The court also stated that in some instances expert testimony about the unacceptably traumatic impact on a child of testifying might suffice to meet the necessity criteria.

With regard to the circumstantial guarantees of reliability, the court found that they could be established by the following:

1. the child's statement was surprising and uncoached,

2. the child used age- and experience-appropriate language to describe an experience she did not fully understand,

3. there was semen on the child's clothing, and

4. her statement, particularly her concern over not getting the candy, had a disarming ring of truth.

The statement was determined by the Supreme Court to be sufficiently reliable to justify its admission.

Since the decision in *Khan*, the principled approach has become the governing exception to the hearsay rule. Evidence that would previously have been excluded automatically by the rigid application of the traditional hearsay exceptions is now admissible if it meets the tests of necessity and reliability.

APPLYING THE EXCEPTIONS

In the years immediately following *Khan*, it was not entirely clear whether this new principled approach replaced all the existing hearsay exceptions or whether these traditional rules still had application in Canadian courts. Was the principled exception to be used only when the evidence did not fit within any of the existing exceptions? If that was to be the rule, there would likely be cases where a statement might fit within one or more of the traditional hearsay exceptions and still not meet the tests of being necessary and reliable.

For example, a spontaneous statement, made in the immediate aftermath of an event, might not be reliable for any number of reasons. Perhaps the maker of the statement was so in shock that any perception he had of the incident was clouded by the physical and emotional trauma he had suffered. Nevertheless, if the traditional *res gestae* exception was applied, the statement would automatically be admissible.

In other words, although the traditional exceptions were developed with the underpinnings of necessity and reliability, there were instances where they might not meet the tests of necessity and reliability. However, if the traditional exceptions were completely eliminated from the law of evidence and only the principled approach applied, the examination of the admissibility of a hearsay statement would be greatly expanded, leading to lengthy trials and unpredictability in the process.

The issue of the traditional exceptions and the principled approach was further canvassed by the Supreme Court of Canada in *R v. Starr*. The difficulty with the *Starr* case is that the court was divided in the end, with four justices in favour of admitting the statements and five against.

In the majority decision, Iacobucci J made it very clear that even the traditional exceptions that apply are to be scrutinized to determine whether the evidence meets the criteria of necessity and reliability. McLachlin CJ (in the dissent) laid out very clear criteria for dealing with hearsay exceptions. She said:

> In my view, the following principles govern the admissibility of hearsay evidence:
>
> 1. Hearsay evidence is admissible if it falls under an exception to the hearsay rule;
>
> 2. The exceptions can be interpreted and reviewed as required to conform to the values of necessity and reliability that justify exceptions to the hearsay rule;
>
> 3. Where the evidence is admissible under an exception to the hearsay rule, the judge may still refuse to admit the evidence if its prejudicial effect outweighs its probative value;
>
> 4. Where evidence is not admissible under an exception to the hearsay rule, the judge may admit it provided that necessity and reliability are established.

In its simplest form, the test that a court will apply in determining whether hearsay will be admissible is as follows:

1. Does the hearsay fall within one of the traditional exceptions?

2. Does it meet the tests of necessity and reliability as set out in the principled approach?

3. If so, it will be admissible as long as it is not more prejudicial than probative.

4. Evidence that does not meet one of the traditional exceptions may be admitted as long as it meets the tests of necessity and reliability established by the principled approach.

CHAPTER SUMMARY

The traditional common-law exceptions to the hearsay rule can be looked at in terms of their necessity and reliability. Professor Wigmore's analysis of these criteria in the traditional exceptions provided the basis for the principled exception as established by the Supreme Court of Canada in the case of *R v. Khan*. The application of the principled exception was clarified in the *Starr* decision.

The principled exception does not replace the traditional exceptions but rather is used to ensure that the traditional exception being applied in a particular case is in fact necessary and reliable. Only if the facts of the case do not permit the application of the traditional exceptions does the court look to the principled exception to determine the admissibility of a hearsay statement.

KEY TERM

principled exception

REFERENCES

B. (K.G.), R v., [1993] 1 SCR 740.

Delgamuukw v. British Columbia, [1997] 3 SCR 1010.

Khan, R v., [1990] 2 SCR 531.

Starr, R v., [2000] 2 SCR 144.

REVIEW QUESTIONS

1. What are the two cornerstones of the principled exception to the hearsay rule?

2. Explain how necessity and reliability are applicable to each of the traditional exceptions to the hearsay rule.

3. How is the principled exception to be applied?

DISCUSSION QUESTIONS

1. Go back to the Discussion Questions at the end of chapter 6. Discuss how the principles of necessity and reliability apply to each of the hearsay statements in questions 1 to 4.

2. Parminder was rushed to the hospital by her sister with a suspected case of severe tetanus poisoning. She could not speak but her sister told the nurse that Parminder was allergic to penicillin. Parminder was given penicillin and is now in a coma from which she may never recover. Tragically, in an unrelated incident, her sister was later killed in a car accident.

    The parents of the girls are now suing the hospital for the damage suffered by Parminder. They want to call another patient who was in the emergency waiting room the day Parminder was admitted to hospital. He will testify that he heard Parminder's sister tell the nurse that Parminder was allergic to penicillin.

    Discuss whether or not you think this evidence will be admitted.

3. Max was charged with impaired driving after he was stopped as a result of a 911 call. The person who called 911 was another driver who had been following Max on the highway and was extremely concerned about his driving. The caller said that Max was driving erratically, was weaving over the lines on the highway, and had already almost hit three other cars. The Crown wants to admit the tape of the 911 call as evidence of just how badly Max was driving.

    If you were the judge, would you allow this evidence? On what basis would you admit the evidence or exclude it?

CHAPTER 8

Character Evidence

CHAPTER OBJECTIVES

After completing this chapter you should be able to:

- Understand the value and danger of character evidence.

- Recognize when character evidence is admissible and when it is not.

- Understand that similar fact evidence can be very useful but also very dangerous.

- Recognize the difference between character evidence and evidence of propensity.

- Understand the role of third-party evidence.

- Identify the "rape shield" provisions in the *Criminal Code* and the Supreme Court of Canada's ruling on the admission of a complainant's sexual history in cases involving sexual offences.

OVERVIEW OF CHARACTER EVIDENCE

When considering the reliability of the information put before it by a witness, would the trier of fact be assisted if it had reliable information about the witness's character? It would, because there is some truth to the proposition that bad people do bad things and good people do good things. This is the main reason why early English juries were chosen from people who were familiar with the parties to the dispute.

In our present legal system, the courts view character evidence with suspicion, not because it has no value, but because it may be given far greater value than it deserves. The courts have recognized a strong human inclination to speculate and to jump to conclusions based on available information, and with this in mind have imposed strict limits on the admissibility of character evidence. Where the available information casts the accused in a bad light because of his unrelated behaviour, a great risk exists that the trier of fact will leap to the conclusion that the accused is guilty even though the reliable evidence is not sufficient to support such a conclusion.

Character evidence is presented to try to establish that a person who holds certain characteristics either did or did not act a certain way on a specific occasion—in other words, that the person "acted in character." The proposition is not without merit, because people are creatures of habit and tend to repeat the same type of actions—they tend to act in character. However, people act "out of character" as well. People do things that we never would have thought they were capable of. Therefore, one has to be very careful when asked to extrapolate consistent behaviour from past behaviour. Such extrapolations can lend to incorrect conclusions, as shown in the example below:

> Elly is charged with stealing a car.
> Elly has a criminal record for shoplifting.
> Elly must have stolen the car.

Similarly, extrapolations from presumed behaviour can lend to incorrect conclusions, as shown in the example below.

> The man is charged with molesting young boys.
> The man is a priest.
> Priests are celibate.
> The man could not have molested young boys.

WHAT IS CHARACTER EVIDENCE?

Character evidence is evidence of the type of person someone is—honest, dishonest, calm, ill-tempered, generous, selfish, and so forth—as demonstrated by the person's past conduct. It is really all about drawing inferences from past conduct—did Sam kill on this occasion because he has killed in the past?

THE DANGERS OF CHARACTER EVIDENCE

probative value
the value or strength of a fact in proving what the party seeks to establish

potential prejudice
the potential for a piece of proposed evidence to be misused (usually, given too much weight) by the trier of fact

Although character evidence may have **probative value**, the courts are reluctant to admit this type of evidence because of its **potential prejudice**. As stated above, people tend to give greater value to character evidence than it deserves and draw incorrect conclusions on its basis. They also show a tendency to want to convict an accused of the crime in question for his past crimes. This topic is described more fully in the sections below.

AGAINST WHOM MAY CHARACTER EVIDENCE BE PRESENTED?

Although it is usually the accused against whom character evidence is presented, character evidence may be presented against a complainant as well.

The distinction that has just been raised between leading evidence of bad character against a person accused of a crime or against the complainant is an important one. How the common-law rules that govern the admissibility of character evidence are applied is largely dependent on the context within which the evidence is being offered. The important considerations that a judge takes into account in deciding to admit or refuse evidence are whether the evidence is being tendered in a civil or criminal trial, who the evidence would be used against, and whether the evidence is of good or bad character, because these considerations will determine the degree of injustice that will flow from the misuse of evidence. For example, in a criminal trial, the liberty of an accused is at stake and the courts have always treated this as a more important consideration than the loss of money that is usually at stake in a civil trial. Finally, character evidence can be led against third-party witnesses. This topic is discussed below under the heading "Testimony and Credibility of Third Parties."

CHARACTER EVIDENCE OF A PERSON CHARGED WITH A CRIMINAL OFFENCE

Generally, in a criminal trial, prosecutors are not permitted to introduce information about an accused's bad character in order to assist the trier of fact in concluding that the accused was also bad on this particular occasion. An accused who has broken into houses in the past to rob them may be more likely than a person on the street to be the person who robbed a little old lady at the automated teller. However, there are a lot of people who fit into the category of persons who rob houses and quite a lot who have even robbed little old ladies, so establishing that the accused robs houses does not help much in proving he robbed the woman at the automated teller. It does show that he belongs to that group of people capable of stealing, but this group is so large that it would be dangerous to give significant weight to this fact. The danger is that the trier of fact, when presented with this evidence, will give it much more weight than it deserves. In the opinion of the courts, on a scale of 1 to 100, where 1 is the tiniest bit of proof, barely registerable, and 100 is absolute certainty, this sort of information deserves about a 3.

In assessing the value of such information, the court needs to ask: in what way is the house robber more likely to have robbed the old lady than the person who cheats on his income taxes, buys a colour television for $50 out of the back of somebody's car, or neglects to report a bank error that is $150 in his favour? All these people are arguably stealing and are, at the least, guilty of moral lapses that show they are capable of taking from someone else for their own advantage. The Minister of Forests in British Columbia accused a senator from Montana of stealing because he introduced a bill to pay out softwood lumber levies to American producers in spite of numerous North American Free Trade Agreement (NAFTA) rulings that said the levies contravened NAFTA. Does this mean the senator from Montana is more likely to have robbed the little old lady than any other person on the street? No.

The house robber may in fact be less likely to have robbed the little old lady because she may remind him of his own grandmother whom he dearly loves, or he may choose to rob only empty houses because he is terrified of confrontation with people, no matter how old or frail. So, while there may be some value to the information that the accused has a record for robbing houses, the value it provides is far outweighed by the danger it poses in a criminal case, where it may be assigned more weight than it deserves by the trier of fact. Thus, the judge performs a gate-keeping function by screening out this information because it is dangerous.

BAD CHARACTER AND AN ACCUSED

A recent Ontario case, *R v. Soikie,* dealt with the issue of the admissibility of bad character evidence against an accused. Mr. Soikie was charged with murder. He claimed to have killed the deceased in self-defence and as a result of provocation. He did not suggest in his testimony that he was a man of good character but his counsel attacked the character of the deceased by leading evidence of prior violent acts perpetrated by the deceased. In response, the Crown was permitted to lead evidence of the peaceful disposition of the deceased. The issue was whether the Crown would be permitted to attack the accused's character by showing him to have a violent disposition. The trial judge declined to permit such an attack, stating that admitting the Crown's evidence would result in both moral and reasoning prejudice and tend to distract the trier of fact because the evidence was inflammatory. The judge ruled that evidence of the accused's character did not advance the issue whether the deceased was the aggressor, and its probative value did not exceed the prejudice that would result from its admission.

Source: *R v. Soikie,* 2004 CanLII 1849 (ONSC).

Criminal Record and the Accused

Because an accused has a right to be presumed innocent, a criminal record may not be admitted into evidence by the Crown, *except* where the accused chooses to testify. In this case, it is felt that the record goes to the issue of general credibility of the accused. In other words, the criminal record is not to be used to show that the accused is more likely to have committed the offence for which he is charged, but to show that his sworn testimony is less worthy of belief in light of his past dishonest behaviour. As the gatekeeper, the judge still has the discretion to disallow the criminal record, though in practice almost all judges allow the record to be admitted. One judge, who was seen by the police as pro-defence, would only allow that portion of the criminal record to be admitted that went to the veracity of the witness. Accordingly, convictions for perjury were admissible in his court room, as were convictions for fraud or false pretenses because they had an element of dishonesty.

Whether the accused's criminal record is admitted is particularly important where the Crown's case is circumstantial and the record is one that casts the accused in a particularly bad moral light, as with someone charged with sexual offences who has one or more convictions for similar offences.

An accused who does testify is taken to have put his credibility in issue, and by taking the stand to tell his story, the accused places himself in a position where his criminal record may be introduced into evidence. This can strongly discourage an accused from testifying. For example, in a sexual assault case, once the jurors learn that the accused was convicted of rape eight years ago, it will be difficult for them to dispassionately listen to the evidence in relation to the sexual assault charge, ignore the criminal record, and impartially weigh the evidence of guilt presented by the Crown. The jury's inability to overlook a similar conviction undoubtedly contributed to the conviction of Norman Fox in Vancouver on June 21, 1976. He was convicted of sexual assault largely based on his previous conviction for rape. He spent six years in jail for a crime that someone else committed. This was one of the earliest well-publicized wrongful conviction cases. Interestingly, the commissioner who reviewed the case, to determine whether compensation should be paid to Mr. Fox for his wrongful conviction, pressured him into agreeing to share the compensation award with the woman he was legitimately convicted of raping many years before. His prior offence still tarnished him to the degree that the commissioner, rather than simply compensating him for the wrong done to him by the system, made it clear that he felt it was distasteful giving money to a rapist.

Other Dangers of Character Evidence

There are other dangers in presenting bad character evidence to the jury. The jurors may use it to justify a conviction for the wrong reasons. There is a significant danger that the accused will be convicted as additional punishment for past wrongdoings, or that he will be punished because he is not likeable, or that the jury will convict him simply to bring closure to the matter. The jury, out of laziness, may be unwilling to conduct a thorough and exhaustive analysis of the evidence, particularly when the accused is viewed as an undesirable element in society. Their thinking may be, "It's not like we're convicting Snow White here, look at his record."

I'VE DONE PLENTY OF BAD THINGS, BUT …

The following example demonstrates how it is possible to turn evidence of prior convictions into a positive. The complainant knew the accused—indeed, they had been lovers—but the accused claimed that the complainant made the allegation against him because he was a spurned lover. The accused chose to testify at his trial and the Crown, in cross-examination, had him acknowledge a string of criminal offences, from break and enter to assault. These offences went back over a period of about 10 years. This is usually a bad sign for an accused, who hopes to create a doubt in the jury's mind that he committed the particular offence he is charged with. After the Crown prosecutor concluded his questioning about the accused's lengthy record and confirmed that the accused actually committed all these offences, he made a classic mistake. He asked, "So why should the jury believe that you didn't commit the offence you are charged with?" The accused, in a very convincing speech, said words to the effect, "I pleaded guilty to every one of those offences, because I did them, but I won't plead guilty to this one because I didn't do it." The Crown recognized the damage that was done to his case by catching the reaction of the jury, but it was too late. His efforts to challenge the sincerity of the accused's assertion of innocence were unsuccessful. In the end, the jury could not reach a verdict, and a new trial was directed.

Good Character Evidence

People charged with criminal offences will often claim to their lawyers that they can get two dozen character witnesses to testify on their behalf. In reality, presenting good character evidence does not happen very often. This is partly because the criminal courts are filled with people accused of crimes who don't stand to gain much from a character contest with the Crown. But the main reason is that, at the heart of it, good character evidence is not very meaningful because even people of good character do bad things. Who among us has not been guilty of some transgression in the past? It may be impossible to find a person who has led a life filled with only positive acts and has not committed a wrongful act at some point in her life. Entire novels have been built on morally upright persons succumbing to temptation.

In spite of the fact that such evidence has limited merit in the eyes of the court, some accused persons do present evidence to try to show that they are not the kind of people to commit the type of offence they have been charged with. Generally, evidence of good character is restricted to the accused's reputation in the community rather than specific past good deeds.

Most often, when an accused chooses to lead evidence of his good character, he calls friends and neighbours to testify about his reputation in the community. Such testimony can be helpful, although a cardinal rule is to be sure that the people chosen to testify know the substance of the charge facing the accused. It undermines the accused's case if the Crown in cross-examination asks, "Did you know that four women have testified that the accused exposed himself to them while performing a solitary sexual act?" and the witness reacts with surprise and revulsion. The jurors are likely to discount entirely the friend's or neighbour's good character evidence, or worse, think badly of the accused for not being forthright with his chosen witness. They conclude, "If he can't be honest with his friends, then he surely must be lying to us."

An accused person can also testify about his own good character, but such testimony is likely to be greeted with cynicism. Jurors are likely to think, "What else would you expect him to say?" Another approach is to present expert evidence on the topic of good character, but a good character expert sounds a little silly to most jurors, who feel they don't need an expert to tell them what constitutes good character. Instead, what experts usually testify about is very specific behaviour and the accused's predisposition toward it. For example, a person charged with sexually assaulting a child who can demonstrate through an expert that he does not have the psychological profile of a pedophile would stand a better chance with a jury than another person who cannot advance this sort of evidence. Similarly, a man charged with performing an indecent act with another man in a public washroom who presents evidence to show that homosexual activity is repugnant to him improves his standing with a jury.

However, once the accused calls good character evidence, he is taken to have put his character in issue and the Crown is entitled to attack his character by cross-examining the accused's witnesses, by calling its own witnesses who can challenge this version of the accused's character, and by calling its own experts. In other words, once the accused has opened the door by calling evidence of good character, the Crown is free to lead evidence of bad character. The accused will almost certainly have his criminal record put to him and may have to answer to other evidence showing that the accused committed similar crimes in the past. An accused can even put his character in issue inadvertently, as happened in *R v. McFadden*. In this case, the accused, who was married, was charged with the indecent assault and murder of another woman. In defending the charge, he stated, "I have the most beautiful wife in the world." He was taken to have implied that he would never become sexually involved with another woman. This would permit the Crown to explore any infidelities or even marital problems that the accused might have.

In another matter, *R v. Tierney*, the accused stated that he was not the sort to commit sexual assault of a woman. A psychiatrist for the Crown then testified that the accused possessed an abnormal disposition to react violently if rejected by a woman, providing devastating evidence against the accused. Of particular danger to an accused is the fact that since reputation evidence is by its nature hearsay, then rebuttal to reputation evidence can also be hearsay. Witnesses for the accused can therefore be asked what rumours they have heard about the accused. These rumours can be plentiful and vicious, and can damage the character of the accused. As these examples show, the decision to call good character evidence is one that should be considered cautiously.

SIMILAR FACT EVIDENCE

Although a general prohibition exists against the use of bad character evidence, there are some instances where the evidence is so valuable, so convincing, that to deny it to the fact finder simply because it shows the accused in a bad light would be unjustifiable. The classic example is the case of *Makin v. AG for New South Wales*. The Makins presented as a lovely couple with four daughters of their own ranging in age from 11 to 17. They advertised in the *Sydney Morning Herald* that they would adopt or take in children for a fee. This was an appealing prospect to many young unwed mothers who could not adequately provide for their babies but wanted to ensure that they got a better deal in life than what they could offer. The Makins took in many such babies; however, few survived the guardianship of this pair. On October 11, 1892 a workman was digging in the backyard of a house in Macdonaldtown, a suburb of Sydney, trying to clear a blockage in a drain. His gruesome discovery was that the blockage was caused by two bundles of baby clothing containing the decaying remains of two infants. The police dug up the backyard and located another five putrefying corpses of infants. Tenancy records soon revealed that John and Sarah Makin were the former tenants of the cottage. The police also determined that the Makins had a former address in Redfern, where more bodies of babies were discovered. The Makins were eventually tracked to another home in nearby Chippendale and yet more baby bodies were found in the backyard of that property. In all, the grisly total grew to 12.

In the sensational trial of the Makins, evidence was presented through Amber Murray and numerous other mothers who had entrusted their children to the Makins for a weekly fee of 10 shillings. In the end, the Makins's own daughter Clarice testified against them, linking clothing found on the buried corpses to her parents and confirming that Amber Murray's infant child Horace did not survive to make the move to Macdonaldtown from Redfern. This evidence was significant because it helped establish the monetary motive for the killings—John Makin had continued to collect the 10 shillings from Amber Murray well beyond Horace's death. Though the Makins testified on their own behalf, their credibility was destroyed when the prosecution caught them up in lies and inconsistencies. Both were convicted and given the only sentence available, death. John was hanged, but Sarah had her sentence commuted to life imprisonment. She was released after 19 years, in 1911.

Given the primitive state of forensic evidence at the time, a conviction against the Makins was by no means a certainty. After all, infant deaths were quite common and it was not unheard of for children who died in childbirth or shortly after to be buried in backyards. The contribution that *Makin* made to the law of evidence is that the case gave birth to the principle at the root of **similar fact evidence**. The court developed the principle in the following passage:

> It is undoubtedly not competent for the prosecution to adduce evidence tending to shew that the accused has been guilty of criminal acts other than those covered by this indictment, for the purpose of leading to the conclusion that the accused is a person likely from his criminal conduct or character to have committed the offence for which he is being tried. On the other hand, the mere fact that the evidence adduced tends to shew the commission of other crimes does not render it inadmissible if it be relevant to an issue before the jury, and it may be so relevant if it bears upon the question whether the acts alleged to constitute the crime charged in the indictment were designed or accidental, or [if the evidence is used] to rebut a defence which would otherwise be open to the accused.

Evidence that some infant corpses were found in the backyard of a home that the Makins occupied was not admitted to prove that they committed the act for which they were standing trial. Rather, the evidence was used to rebut an argument that the deaths were accidental. In other words, coincidence could be ruled out because there were a dozen similar deaths. The strength of the evidence lay in the sheer unlikelihood that the Makins innocently happened to rent out houses with backyards filled with baby corpses.

Development of the Similar Fact Evidence Rule

Similar fact evidence is evidence that shows that the accused committed similar offences in the past. It is very tempting for a prosecutor to see great value in similar fact evidence because it will help the jury come to the conclusion that the prosecutor feels is just. However, the fact remains that a person charged with a crime is not on trial for past transgressions. It is essential to avoid drawing the prohibited inference that the accused is guilty of the offence simply because he has committed similar acts in the past. On the other hand, if it can be clearly shown that the accused has demonstrated in his behaviour a pattern or design, then it is logical to admit similar fact evidence to imply that it is likely that the same person who committed similar acts in the past committed the outstanding offence. Although there may be some appeal in this proposition, the law is quite settled that while similar fact evidence may indeed be admissible for certain purposes, it is not permissible for the Crown to lead the evidence for the prohibited inference that due to a predisposition the accused is more likely to have committed this particular offence.

similar fact evidence
evidence that shows that an accused committed similar offences in the past, which may be admitted provided that it is relevant to establishing an important matter other than the accused's predisposition to commit that type of offence

The leading case on similar fact evidence in Canada, and the one that developed the test for the admissibility of similar fact evidence, is *R v. Handy*. In this case, heard by the Supreme Court of Canada, the accused was charged with sexual assault causing bodily harm. He claimed that the complainant consented to the manner of sexual interaction but she stated that she had initially consented and withdrew her consent when the sexual interaction became violent. She stated that Handy would not take no for an answer. At trial, the Crown sought to introduce evidence from the accused's former wife stating that he had sexually assaulted her seven times and enjoyed inflicting pain on her when they had sex. The accused alleged that the complainant and his wife had colluded in their stories. In rejecting the Crown's request to introduce the evidence, the Supreme Court set out the test for admissibility:

> Similar fact evidence is … presumptively inadmissible. The onus is on the prosecution to satisfy the trial judge on the balance of probabilities that in the context of the particular case the probative value of the evidence in relation to a particular issue outweighs its potential prejudice and thereby justifies its reception.

Using this test, a trial judge starts from the proposition that similar fact evidence should not be admitted. In assessing whether an exception should be made for evidence that the Crown seeks to admit, the judge requires the Crown to first show that the evidence is relevant to some other issue beyond the disposition or character of the accused. The Crown must then establish that the inevitable prejudice that accompanies such evidence is outweighed by the value of the evidence—its contribution to proving the Crown's case. Any evidence that merely shows prior convictions can only be seen as general propensity evidence, and cannot have greater probative value than the prejudice it introduces. The Crown's task is even more difficult when the accused has numerous convictions, because the greater the number of convictions, the more likely the jury will see them as conclusive of guilt in the outstanding offence and abandon the arduous task of weeding through the maze of evidence admitted against the accused.

Finally, the judge must assess the similarity of the evidence of prior bad acts to the case before the court by applying a number of criteria. The distinctiveness of the events is one such criterion. For example, the fact that two sexual assaults were committed does not meet the criterion of distinctiveness, but two sexual assaults where the assailant is wearing a gorilla suit and eating bananas during the assault is strikingly distinctive. Another consideration is the number of similar incidents. The probative value increases with the increase in the number of incidents. The number of details that match will enhance the probative value of the evidence, provided, however, that there is a link to the accused. Another important criterion is proximity in time.

Generally, the greater the period of time between the present offence and past similar offences, the more caution must be exercised in determining the admissibility of the similar fact evidence. In a recent case, *R v. Atlin*, an appeal from a conviction for sexual assault from the Yukon, the appeal court considered what impact the passage of time should have in the weight given to the similarity of facts. There was evidence that the accused had committed similar acts between 1972 and 1975 and the matter in issue took place around 1987. The court stated:

One matter that seems to me troubling in the instant case is the temporal aspect. By that I mean that the incident involving M.J. occurred at a time when the appellant was quite a young person and the incidents involving S.J. occurred when he was an adult. It is entirely possible that as an individual matures there can be a change in their attitude, way of life and such. While it is not always going to be a conclusive fact where there are other very cogent badges or indicia of similarity, it seems to me that in general the greater the temporal space between the alleged similar acts and the acts that are alleged in the counts before the Court in the indictment, the more care or caution that will have to be exercised by the [judge] in analyzing the question of how that circumstance will impact on admissibility. It is fair to say that this will often be a very salient factor in the analysis concerning admissibility.

For a good example of the reasoning process that judges follow in considering whether to admit similar fact evidence, see the case of *R v. Tyhurst*, excerpted at www.emp.ca/evidence.

Using the above criteria for similar fact evidence in sexual assault trials, courts have rejected evidence that shows prior violent activity that was not sexual. In addition, courts have prohibited evidence of other sexual assaults where consent, not the identity of the assailant, is the only issue before the court because the accused admits engaging in sexual activity but denies it was forced.

THE TEST FOR ADMISSIBILITY OF SIMILAR FACT EVIDENCE

1. The judge starts from the proposition that evidence of bad character should not be admitted.

2. The Crown must establish that bad character evidence is relevant to some other issue beyond the disposition or character of the accused.

3. The Crown must show on a balance of probabilities that the probative value of the evidence outweighs the prejudicial effect.

How Similar Is Similar?

If a court is prepared to look at an accused's past acts to detect a pattern or design, then the admissibility of such evidence must in part be determined by the degree of similarity between the past acts and the circumstances of the present case. Simply put, similar fact evidence put forth by the Crown must be evaluated to determine how similar the acts are to one another. In such instances, the court will look for unique characteristics of the acts—a fingerprint, so to speak. There have been cases, however, where the court has made dubious conclusions in this regard. One such case is *R v. Arp*, where the judge allowed evidence to be admitted regarding two incidents, over three years apart, where young intoxicated women were taken to remote locations near Prince George, British Columbia and killed, and their naked bodies left at the site. Their clothing was scattered about, some of which had been cut by a sharp tool. Unfortunately, there is not much that is unique in these incidents. The kidnapping and murder of young women, their sexual assault, and the abandonment of their naked bodies are by no means "fingerprints." The only somewhat uncommon incident is the cutting of the clothing, which is not a rare occurrence in crimes of this kind. In Arp's situation and others like it, the accused is faced with the additional hurdle of overcoming the prejudice generated by being linked in the mind of the trier of fact to another horrific crime. The prejudice is compounded if there are many similar crimes that the accused is linked to.

There is really no hard and fast rule when it comes to the question of how similar the similar facts must be before they can be introduced as evidence against an accused. Obviously, the greater the similarity between the similar facts and the facts of the present case, the more likely it is that the similar facts will be admitted. But is partial similarity sufficient? If an accused has demonstrated a bad temper in the past by yelling and screaming at the slightest provocation but not resorting to violence, then can that evidence be introduced if the present allegations are that the accused lost his temper and killed in a blind rage? Most of us would probably have great difficulty accepting a link between those similar facts and an accused charged with murder. Although both situations clearly relate to a bad temper, the accused never demonstrated any physically violent acts in the past. If anything, his past actions demonstrate that the accused possesses the ability to refrain from violence even when in an angry and agitated state.

Thus, the lawyer should focus on the degree of similarity when arguing in court for or against the admissibility of similar fact evidence. Often, it is possible to make a persuasive argument either for or against the admissibility of the same set of similar facts. Many courts have adopted the phrase "striking similarity" when determining whether a set of similar facts are sufficiently similar to the case at hand. It is conceded that the "striking similarity" test falls short of establishing a definitive and objective standard of comparison. However, the same can be said for the concept of reasonable doubt.

Assessing the Degree of Prejudice in Similar Fact Evidence

In *Handy*, the Supreme Court of Canada described two types of prejudice that can result from the admission of similar fact evidence and instructed the courts to weigh such prejudice against probative value. The first is **moral prejudice**. Moral prejudice results when the evidence of bad character shows the accused in a bad light, as a morally bad person, and leads the fact finder to infer guilt. If the fact finder reasons that the accused must be guilty because she is the kind of person who commits immoral acts, there is a prejudice to the accused.

The second type of prejudice is **reasoning prejudice**. This form of prejudice results when evidence that is presented to establish identity or rebut innocent association interferes with the trier of fact's reasoning process. The evidence is a kind of red herring that distracts the trier of fact from the task of objectively evaluating the legitimate evidence. The trier of fact can become confused or distracted and decide the issue on the basis of evidence that is not legitimately before him. Judges may be tempted to admit the evidence because the more similar the evidence is, the stronger the probative value. But this also means that there is a greater chance that the trier of fact can mistakenly mix together the two matters, weighing information from the similar fact matter as if it were evidence in the present matter. In such

moral prejudice
prejudice that results from the admission of evidence of bad character showing the accused to be a morally bad person and leading the trier of fact to conclude that he is guilty

reasoning prejudice
applies to evidence that, if admitted, may confuse the trier of fact or distract the trier of fact from the issue it must decide

instances, the trier of fact has blended the two offences and not limited the similar fact offence to consideration of issues of identity or innocent association that it was admitted to establish.

Although the Crown must establish that the similar fact evidence is admissible for some other purpose than to show bad character, the evidence is not inadmissible simply because it does show bad character, particularly when the evidence has high probative value. In a recent murder case, the Crown's theory was that a number of young teens beat to death one of their friends at the direction of one boy's mother because she thought that the victim had told the authorities she was running a stolen goods fencing operation from her house. To support this theory, the Crown sought to present evidence that she was fencing stolen goods from her home. Because she was not charged with fencing—the trial was for murder—defence counsel objected to the admission of this evidence that would show her in a bad light. However, the judge admitted the evidence, stating that an accused is not entitled to keep relevant evidence away from the trier of fact simply because it makes her look bad and that the probative value of the evidence exceeded the prejudice it would create.

Thus we see another important aspect of similar fact evidence. While such evidence is presumed inadmissible because of its potential for prejudice, if it has high probative value it will be admissible, in spite of the prejudice that it has. It would not serve the cause of justice if a truly bad person were permitted to wear a blanket of protection that kept out highly relevant evidence, simply because it made him look bad. As with most aspects of evidence law, a balancing of the accused's rights and the need for society to protect itself is at play.

Prior Acquittals and Similar Fact Evidence

What of the situation where an accused committed a prior similar act but was acquitted? Should evidence of the prior act be admissible to prove that the accused is the person who committed the alleged offence? The position in Canada is that an acquittal places the similar fact evidence off-limits in future prosecutions. Even a stay of proceedings, where the Crown chooses not to proceed with the charges (usually because a conviction is unlikely), has been determined to have the same result as an acquittal in relation to similar fact evidence. Some theorists argue that the probative value of the evidence is independent of whether a conviction or acquittal arose. In other words, the similar nature of the evidence can support an inference that the same person committed both offences and assist the trier of fact in its determination regardless of whether the accused was acquitted. The argument is that the trial judge in the present matter should be entitled to look behind the acquittal when a completely unrelated issue resulted in the acquittal, such as a breach of the accused's right to counsel, because there is no diminishment of the probative value of the facts from the prior trial.

Others have had considerable difficulty with this reasoning. They contend that to categorize acquittals differently or to create a hierarchy of acquittals is a slippery slope and would be a serious setback to the presumption of innocence. If an accused is truly entitled to be presumed innocent, then an acquittal makes the first allegation a nullity, as if it never existed. Fortunately for accused persons, similar fact evidence from a prior acquittal or stay of proceedings remains off-limits at this time.

CHARACTER EVIDENCE AND EVIDENCE OF PROPENSITY

Character evidence and evidence of propensity are two different things. The concepts may appear to be similar but they are fundamentally different. As stated earlier in this chapter, character evidence is evidence of the type of person someone is as demonstrated by the person's past conduct. **Propensity evidence** is proof of a person's psychiatric tendencies, as provided by an expert. Because propensity evidence is given by an expert, it is taken as psychiatric fact. For example, character evidence may show, on the basis of a person's past violent acts, that the person has a disposition for violence, while propensity evidence may show, on the basis of a psychiatric assessment, that the person has violent tendencies. Sometimes this distinction may be blurred, but it is important to keep in mind that while anyone can testify as to character, only a properly qualified expert can offer evidence of a person's propensity to act in a certain manner.

propensity evidence
evidence of an accused's past history or tendency to act in a certain way

Propensity evidence creates extreme prejudice for the accused and for this reason will not be admitted to merely demonstrate the propensity of an accused to act a certain way. This may sound illogical, but it makes perfect sense if we look at the rationale behind the rule against admitting evidence of bad character. It is dangerous to conclude that someone committed an act because he acted the same way in the past. Similarly, in the case of propensity evidence, it is equally (and perhaps even more) dangerous to conclude that an individual acted in a certain manner simply because of a psychological predisposition.

The common-law position is that propensity evidence may only be admitted if it is analogous to a physiological fact. Therefore, it would not be permissible to lead evidence that the accused had abnormal violent tendencies to support an inference that he killed the victim. However, it may be permissible to lead such evidence to demonstrate that the accused had the capacity to kill in a certain manner. For example, if a crime showed clear signs of psychopathological origin, it may be permissible for the Crown to demonstrate that the accused shares these specific psychopathological tendencies with the perpetrator. Thus, a perpetrator who tortures his victim with electric shocks as a precursor to sexually assaulting her would likely demonstrate a very specific psychological profile. In any event, evidence of propensity would only be admitted if the probative value of the evidence is so high that it displaces the extreme prejudice that the accused would suffer from the admission of the evidence.

CHARACTER EVIDENCE AND CO-ACCUSED PERSONS

In an interesting twist, in cases where the Crown is not entitled to present bad character evidence, a co-accused may be entitled to present evidence that the other person charged is of bad character, provided that the judge does not conclude that the prejudicial effect is greater than the probative value. By doing so, the co-accused attempts to show that the other person charged is more likely to have committed the crime, essentially saying, "The other guy did it—after all, look at his record."

The impact of taking this course of action, however, is that the co-accused person puts his own character in issue and is open for attack by the other person or the Crown. Often, these character battles work to the advantage of the Crown, with both accused pointing fingers at each other and damaging the character of the other. Sometimes, though, it can turn out badly for the Crown if the jurors find both accused to be lacking in credibility and conclude, "These guys are both bad news but we can't tell which one of them did it." An acquittal of both accused where the jury is certain that one of them committed the offence is necessary in such cases but certain to leave a bad taste for the public.

CHARACTER EVIDENCE AND PRIOR CONVICTIONS IN CIVIL MATTERS

Character evidence is rarely led in civil cases and is usually not admissible. Most of the common-law rules that relate to character evidence and virtually all of the statutory modifications to the common law have arisen in the context of criminal cases. However, evidence of a party's character is admissible if the character of the party is at issue. For example, in a defamation case where the plaintiff is claiming that the defendant has made negative remarks that damaged the plaintiff's reputation, it is a full defence to an allegation of defamation that the statements made by the defendant about the plaintiff are true. It is only defamation if the statements about the plaintiff are false. It would therefore be appropriate for the defendant to lead evidence that such statements are true. Apart from those situations where the character of a party is at issue, evidence that a party is of bad character is generally inadmissible in civil cases. Similarly, rarely will a party be entitled to present evidence of her good character.

There is, however, a special rule that has been developed to deal with circumstances where a person has acted in such a way that he attracts both criminal and civil liability. If the person is convicted of a criminal offence, say, sexually assaulting the complainant, the complainant can then sue the perpetrator in civil court, using the conviction as *prima facie* proof that the defendant committed the assault. What this means is that, absent proof to the contrary, the trier of fact must conclude that the sexual assault has been proven in the civil matter. In this instance, the "prior" bad act alleged is in fact the same act but proven to a criminal standard, so in the subsequent civil case, the trier of fact may start from the proposition that the defendant has already been convicted of the alleged assault beyond a reasonable doubt.

TESTIMONY AND CREDIBILITY OF THIRD PARTIES

Witnesses who are not parties in a trial are presented as truth-tellers and will be accepted as such unless the opponent challenges the witness's credibility or general character. As seen in chapter 3, the person calling the witness is not entitled to bolster that witness's credibility with evidence of the witness's good character or honesty. It is common to provide a brief introduction of the witness to the trier of fact so that the evidence of the witness may be put in context, but it is not permissible to attempt to enhance the witness's credibility through this avenue. The dialogue below illustrates a permissible introduction of a witness:

Counsel: Calling Frances Moorley to the stand. … Now Ms. Moorley, I understand that you are an accountant and have been for the past ten years.

F.M.: Yes, I work at General Motors in the Finance Department.

Counsel: And you are a mother of two teenaged children and have resided in Littletown for the past eight years.

F.M.: That's correct, we moved here from Bigtown just over eight and a half years ago.

Counsel: Now, you observed a matter on June 21 that brings you to court today, could you tell us about that.

This exchange gives the trier of fact a sense of the witness without going overboard and attempting to enhance the witness's credibility. If counsel were to take it a step further and go into the witness's church attendance, volunteer work, and medal for bravery, that would constitute an attempt to present the witness as being more believable than a typical witness and would not be acceptable.

CLOTHES MAKE THE WITNESS

In a recent jury trial, the accused was charged with insurance fraud by claiming to have a passenger in his car when he was involved in an accident. It was a very rainy October night and the other vehicle came through an intersection, striking the accused's car as he was turning left. The drivers pulled their vehicles to the side of the road and exchanged information in the rain at the back of the other driver's vehicle. At trial, the accused stated that his passenger remained in the vehicle because it was raining. It was not until a year later and medical benefits had been provided to the person alleged to be the passenger that a new insurance adjuster noted that the other driver stated that there was only a driver (and no passenger) in the vehicle he collided with. Thus, the adjuster concluded that it was an attempt to obtain "no fault" benefits by fraud. The issue at trial was whether the other driver could have been mistaken in concluding that there was no passenger in the accused's vehicle. The problem was that the other driver was an off-duty police officer; therefore, the police and Crown believed him. Although it was clear that the other driver could be mistaken, particularly given that it was raining and dark outside, no amount of arguing by the defence would dissuade the Crown from proceeding with the charges. On the first day of the trial, the Crown called its first witness, the police officer, who showed up for court in uniform, even though he was off duty at the time. So why was he wearing his uniform? If he had been a painter, would he have turned up in paint coveralls, or if he had been a doctor, would he have turned up in scrubs? Obviously not. This was a thinly disguised attempt to bolster his credibility. The defence objected, but the judge, particularly because the officer was there and ready to testify, permitted him to give his testimony in uniform. As it turned out, the officer had to be recalled later in the trial, and this time the judge directed that he not wear his uniform. Interestingly enough, his evidence was much less impressive the second time around. The accused was ultimately acquitted.

Witnesses who are not parties to a criminal trial are not entitled to the same protection against bad character evidence that an accused is. The particular protection against bad character evidence afforded an accused stems from the fact that his liberty is at stake. Witnesses who are not parties to a criminal trial do not have their liberty at stake, and their credibility can be attacked as long as the questions asked of them are relevant to the testimony they give. An exception is made where the witness is caught lying. In such instances, the general credibility of the witness can be attacked. For example, in the novel *A Time to Kill*, by John Grisham, defence counsel calls a psychiatrist to testify that the accused was insane when he killed the two men who raped his daughter. The prosecution attacks the character of the psychiatrist, asking whether he has any criminal convictions. The defence lawyer makes the mistake of not objecting to this question about his past criminal history, which is irrelevant to his testimony. The psychiatrist states that he has no criminal convictions, but it comes out that he has a 30-year-old conviction for statutory rape. Because the psychiatrist has lied, evidence of his past criminal history is admitted because it becomes relevant to the issue of his general credibility.

The testimony of third parties has been used in murder trials to show that the victim had a disposition toward violence, thus supporting the accused's plea of self-defence. This sort of evidence has been admitted even where the accused was unaware of the deceased's violent tendencies because it supports the proposition that the accused had little choice but to defend himself when faced with a violent attack. However, when an accused calls a third-party witness to testify about the deceased person's predisposition for violence, he risks putting his own character in issue, and as a consequence the Crown will now be in a position to attack the character of the accused in much the same manner as it could attack any other witness.

Third-Party Character Evidence in Sexual Assault Cases

There is a specific subset of third-party character evidence that has been the subject of legislative and judicial intervention. This relates to complainants in trials for sexual offences. The **rape shield provisions** in ss. 276 and 277 of the *Criminal Code* state that the prior sexual conduct of the complainant is presumptively inadmissible. Section 276(1) states:

rape shield provisions
provisions in the *Criminal Code* that forbid the admission of evidence of a complainant's sexual history to support an inference that she is more likely to have given consent or is less worthy of belief

> [E]vidence that the complainant has engaged in sexual activity, whether with the accused or with any other person, is not admissible to support an inference that, by reason of the sexual nature of that activity, the complainant
> (a) is more likely to have consented to the sexual activity that forms the subject-matter of the charge; or
> (b) is less worthy of belief.

Although the argument that sexually experienced persons will have sex with anyone or cannot be believed is absurd, it has proven to be very persuasive to juries. Time and again, juries, even juries predominantly composed of women, have acquitted persons accused of sexual offences after the credibility of the victim was undermined by the testimony of third parties. This was done through questioning: how often she had sex, whether she had sex with more than one partner, whether she had sex more than once an evening—even questions about fantasized sex were sometimes allowed.

This era of victim abuse was finally put to an end with the Supreme Court decision in *R v. Seaboyer; R v. Gayme*. Although the decision does not say that a complainant can never be questioned about prior sexual history, it does regulate such questioning by putting the onus on the accused to convince a judge that such questions are relevant to a legitimate issue for the defence. It explicitly prohibits questioning that is directed toward the twin myths that sexually experienced complainants are either less worthy of belief or more likely to have consented because of their sexual history. By way of example, Seaboyer sought to question the complainant about prior sexual activity that might explain bruising that she claimed resulted from the alleged sexual assault, and Gayme, an 18-year-old student, sought to question the 15-year-old complainant about her sexual history in relation to other students at the same school where the alleged assault took place. He claimed that she was the sexual aggressor. In both cases, the accused were denied the right to question the complainants on their prior sexual history.

CHAPTER SUMMARY

Character evidence is evidence of the type of person someone is, as demonstrated by the person's past conduct. Although character evidence has probative value, it also carries the potential to create prejudice in the eyes of the trier of fact and is only admitted by the court under strict circumstances. Similar fact evidence can have great probative value, but it has a very high potential to create moral prejudice and reasoning prejudice and will only be admitted if it passes the test set out by the Supreme Court of Canada. Evidence of propensity is distinct from character evidence in that it is evidence of a person's psychiatric tendencies as attested to by an expert. Third-party character evidence has been limited in sexual assault cases by the rape shield provisions in the *Criminal Code* and by the Supreme Court of Canada.

KEY TERMS

probative value	reasoning prejudice
potential prejudice	propensity evidence
similar fact evidence	rape shield provisions
moral prejudice	

REFERENCES

Arp, R v., [1998] 3 SCR 339.

Atlin, R v., 2003 YKCA 5.

Criminal Code, RSC 1985, c. C-46, as amended.

Handy, R v., [2002] 2 SCR 908.

Official Report of the Debates of the Legislative Assembly (Hansard). March 26, 1985 (Afternoon sitting), pp. 5463-66.

Makin v. AG for New South Wales, [1894] AC 57 (PC).

McFadden, R v. (1981), 65 CCC (2d) 9 (BCCA).

Seaboyer, R v.; R v. Gayme, [1991] 2 SCR 577.

Tierney, R v. (1982), 70 CCC (2d) 481 (Ont. CA).

REVIEW QUESTIONS

1. What are the dangers of admitting character evidence?

2. What is the value of character evidence?

3. What is similar fact evidence and what criteria apply to its admissibility?

4. What are the rape shield provisions and how would an accused get evidence of a complainant's sexual history admitted?

DISCUSSION QUESTIONS

In the following scenarios, (a) determine whether the evidence is admissible and if not, why not, and (b) if the evidence is admissible, determine for what purpose it's being admitted.

1. Glen Bainbridge is charged with murder in the death of his wife. The prosecution wishes to lead evidence that Glen had beaten his wife on two previous occasions.

2. Allen Abdi is charged with sexually assaulting a young boy who visited him at his home. The prosecution wants to lead evidence that the accused molested five other boys, two of whom obtained multi-million-dollar settlements to buy their silence. The alleged past activities include hugging, kissing, and fondling the other boys. These incidents go back in time between 12 and 15 years and only one of the boys will testify in person. The other evidence will be provided by third parties.

3. Peter Savard is charged with the murder of a 17-year-old cheerleader, whose killer carved the number "66" into her flesh. The prosecution wants to lead evidence that Peter has just been paroled after serving 20

years for killing a 17-year-old cheerleader and carving the number "66" into her body.

4. Scott Nardella is charged with sexual assault. The defence wishes to lead evidence that Scott had a past sexual relationship with the complainant and evidence about the complainant's other past sexual relationships.

5. Ronald Pritchard is charged with common assault. The defence wishes to lead evidence that Ronald had been beaten by the complainant in the past and evidence about the complainant's past violent acts.

6. Trevor McDonald has been charged with smuggling diamonds into Canada. His defence is that he "forgot" to declare the goods and lacked criminal intent. His lawyer wishes to lead evidence that Trevor is a deeply religious and honest person.

7. Nadia Ali was a passenger in a motor vehicle that was driven by her boyfriend, Steven Ancheta. Steven drove under a transport truck and Nadia was decapitated. Nadia's parents sued Steven and the truck driver, Joe Dietrich. During his discovery, Joe stated that he is not presently working because he lost his licence after being convicted of drunk driving while taking his mother to bingo.

8. Reginald Stein, a police officer, has been charged with second-degree murder in the death of Ellen Selkirk. The defence is based on "justifiable force." Reginald wishes to lead evidence that he was awarded a citation for Top Cop after saving three children from a burning car. He also wishes to lead evidence that Ellen is known to have a terrible temper. The Crown wishes to lead evidence that Reginald was once suspended for hitting a motorist and charged (but acquitted) of assault.

CHAPTER 9

Opinion Evidence

CHAPTER OBJECTIVES

After completing this chapter you should be able to:

- Understand when the opinion evidence of a lay witness can be admitted and when it cannot.

- Understand the process of qualifying an expert witness.

- Understand when the opinion of an expert witness can be admitted and when it cannot.

- Understand the limitations on expert evidence.

GENERAL RESTRICTIONS ON OPINION EVIDENCE

The primary purpose of evidence law is to ensure that reliable information is put before the trier of fact. With this purpose in mind, the courts developed the rule that witnesses are not to express opinions, but merely state facts that are within their knowledge, observation, and experience. If you have seen reruns of the 1950s TV series *Dragnet*, you will recall Joe Friday's urging of excited witnesses, "Just the facts, ma'am." In the courtroom, the witness and the finder of fact have clearly differentiated rules: the witness supplies the facts, and the trier of fact evaluates them and determines what to make of them. This differentiation of roles is particularly important, given that in most instances the witness has only a piece of the puzzle, whereas the trier of fact is given information from many sources and can see how the pieces fit together. The trier of fact is thus better positioned to draw conclusions from the evidence put before it. But as with most rules that arise in evidence law, this one has significant exceptions. Where the trier of fact is in need of help from a witness that can only come in the form of an opinion, the witness may, in certain situations, be permitted to express an opinion. Mostly, this will happen when the witness is determined by the judge to be an expert in a particular area, but lay people are also permitted to express their opinions in certain circumstances.

THE RULE AGAINST OPINION EVIDENCE

The rule against opinion evidence can be stated in simple terms:

> Opinion evidence is not admissible unless it is either the opinion of a layperson that is helpful for a clear understanding of his or her testimony or the opinion of an expert.

If the rule against opinion evidence were as straightforward as it appears to be in the above passage, there would be no need to continue reading this chapter. However, the details and the application of the rule can be confusing. The first question that arises is, What do we mean when we talk about an opinion?

WHAT IS AN OPINION?

opinion evidence
evidence given by a witness that is based on conclusions or inferences drawn from facts or observations; generally, the witness is not permitted to state the conclusions or inferences themselves, only the observations

The best way to understand what is meant by "opinion evidence" is to first look at what it is not. It is not evidence of fact. Rather, **opinion evidence** is evidence that is based on conclusions or inferences that are drawn from facts or observations. If a witness states that she observed a dead body being placed into the trunk of a vehicle, she is stating her opinion as to the state of the body. She may have drawn this conclusion from the fact that the person was not moving or that his clothes were bloodstained, but it is unlikely that the witness was able to observe as a fact that the person being put into the trunk was deceased. The witness will be permitted to state her personal observations, but not her inferences or conclusions based on those observations. The conclusions of the witness are only her opinion, not matters of fact. It is up to the trier of fact to look at all of the evidence and then to draw the appropriate conclusions. However, this does not mean that a witness would never be able to testify that a person was deceased, even if it involved the drawing of an inference from personally observed fact. This situation is discussed below under the heading "Layperson's Opinion."

An excellent illustration of prohibited opinion evidence is the true story of a witness testifying at an assault trial. During direct examination, the witness testified that the accused bit the victim's ear off in the fray. When cross-examining the witness, defence counsel challenged the witness, "Now, you didn't actually see the accused bite the complainant's ear off, did you?" "No," replied the witness. "Then how can you say for sure that it was the accused who bit the complainant's ear off?" "Because I saw the accused spit out the ear," was the reply. The observed fact was the spitting out of the ear. The opinion was that the accused had bitten off the victim's ear. The point is that the witness can only testify about what he saw, the spitting out of the ear, and not the inference he drew, that the accused bit off the ear.

layperson's opinion
opinion given by an ordinary witness on a matter of ordinary experience; permitted where the opinion does not unnecessarily encroach on the trier of fact's role

LAYPERSON'S OPINION

What if, in the first example, the witness had instead observed a decapitated body being placed in the trunk of car? Is there any real danger in permitting the witness to offer a **layperson's opinion** as to whether the victim was alive or deceased at the time? Is the trier of fact in any better position than the witness to conclude that the victim was indeed dead when placed in the trunk? Clearly, the witness is in as good a position as the trier of fact—if not better—to conclude that the victim was deceased where the signs of death are obvious and overwhelming.

There are certain instances where allowing opinion evidence to be admitted can help the trier of fact and where there is little potential for harm. For example, lay witnesses are permitted to offer an opinion that a layperson could ordinarily be expected to arrive at. Lay witnesses are thus permitted to offer an opinion on such matters as a person's age, height, race, or other physical characteristics. It is understood that the trier of fact will regard these opinions as approximations or best estimates rather than exact statements or gospel truths.

Similarly, where the subject matter of the opinion is within the knowledge and expertise of the average person, an opinion will usually be permitted. Thus, lay witnesses are permitted to answer such questions as "What speed was the car travelling at?," "What time of day was it?," "What colour was her dress?," and "How far away was the shooter?" A lay witness can even express an opinion on whether an accused was intoxicated on a particular occasion (see *Graat v. The Queen*). The trier of fact knows, or is reminded by the judge that the witness is only giving her best estimate and that different witnesses have different abilities to judge or approximate and different experiences on which they base their opinions. However, if the information provided by the witness requires specialized knowledge that is beyond the average person's, the witness must be qualified as having the expertise to make those conclusions.

The courts apply the following general criteria to determine whether the opinion evidence of a lay witness can be accepted:

1. The opinion is one that a layperson could ordinarily be expected to arrive at.

2. The lay witness has sufficient experience to draw these conclusions.

3. The lay witness is better situated than the trier of fact to form the conclusions.

In addition, a lay witness may be permitted to present his evidence in opinion form where it is difficult for the witness to express the information without stating an opinion. For example, "He was drunk" is clearly an opinion but it is more easily expressed than "His eyes were bloodshot, he was weaving back and forth, he stank of alcohol, and he had urinated in his pants." The latter presentation of facts (although those facts still contain some opinions) is far more helpful to the trier of fact, but many witnesses, particularly those who are testifying for the first time, would have difficulty expressing the precise basis upon which they came to the conclusion that the person was drunk. The statement "He was drunk" has some value but should be given less weight than the other, more factual description of what was observed. Where a witness includes opinions in her testimony, this is sometimes referred to as a **compendious mode of expressing facts**, and permitting the witness some latitude in testifying is a way of making the legal process approachable to the average person.

compendious mode of expressing facts
testimony in which the witness mixes opinion into his narrative in order to express himself; permitted by the court where it is difficult for the witness to express the information without stating an opinion

EXPERT OPINION

expert opinion
testimony given by a
properly qualified person
with specific expertise in
an area that is in issue
before the court; permitted
in order to assist the trier
of fact in coming to
conclusions of fact in
that area

Expert opinion is just what it sounds like. It is where a person with specific expertise in an area that is in issue before the court testifies in order to assist the trier of fact in coming to conclusions of fact in that area. The trier of fact will almost never be expert in blood spatter analysis, accident reconstruction, stress loads in bridge construction, DNA analysis, breathalyzer readings, or any number of scientific or knowledge-based fields. Because litigation often involves understanding and interpreting complex and narrow fields of study, experts can be extremely helpful to the trier of fact. The rule permitting expert evidence can be summarized as follows:

> A properly qualified expert will be permitted to provide his or her opinion if specialized knowledge will permit the trier of fact to better understand the facts or evidence before it.

Experts are helpful in sorting out some of the issues facing the trier of fact in litigation and in criminal trials. Often they are essential. However, some safeguards exist to ensure that the trier of fact is not unduly influenced by the opinions of expert witnesses and that the persons testifying are indeed experts in their fields. In *R v. Mohan*, the Supreme Court of Canada developed four criteria to help determine whether a witness may be qualified as an expert and thus give opinion evidence:

1. *Relevance:* There are two aspects of this determination. The first is simple, logical relevance. Does the information that counsel seeks to introduce via the expert logically promote the proposition advanced? Second, even if the information is relevant, do the benefits of this sort of evidence outweigh the risks?

2. *Necessity:* Is the expert needed to assist the trier of fact in coming to conclusions on the issues before the court?

3. *Qualifications:* Is this particular expert qualified in the field he would provide evidence in? It is noteworthy that some experts are presented and qualified to give evidence in one area but in the course of their testimony stray into areas that are beyond their area of expertise.

4. *The absence of any exclusionary rule:* There cannot be a rule prohibiting the evidence. In other words, counsel cannot use the expert to get information before the trier of fact that is otherwise inadmissible, such as hearsay evidence or evidence obtained in violation of a person's Charter rights.

Relevance

In assessing whether the relevance requirement has been met, a judge starts with the basic assessment of relevance, asking, Does the information help make the point it is being presented to prove? If it does not, then it is not admitted as evidence and that's that. If it does, then the judge goes on to weigh the information to determine whether it ought to be admitted. This process is similar to a cost–benefit analysis. The judge asks, What cost or potential for distortion or damage does the information represent and what benefit exists for the trier of fact in hearing the proposed evidence? In short, Does the probative value exceed the prejudice? The same assessment takes place in both criminal and civil matters, although in criminal matters, because the cost for a criminal defendant may be imprisonment, the information is only excluded when the prejudice far outweighs the probative value.

In considering the probative value of the evidence, the court uses three criteria:

1. *The connection between the expert opinion and facts proven in evidence.* The closer the connection, the more weight the opinion deserves.

2. *The strength of the expert evidence.* How important is the evidence in proving the proposition it is presented to support?

3. *The importance of the evidence.* Is the issue being proved central to the proceedings? The more significant or important the issue is, the more likely the court will find there to be a benefit in allowing the evidence.

In relation to the last point, counsel that hopes to have expert evidence admitted needs to avoid the "so what" factor. The trier of law says, "If I admit the evidence or not, so what? How will that have any impact on the outcome of the proceedings?" Remember that the trier of law, in considering prejudice, must also weigh the risk that admitting too much evidence will overwhelm the trier of fact, or that the proposed evidence will confuse the trier of fact.

Necessity

A judge cannot simply look at the expert evidence and determine that it would be helpful to the trier of fact. Setting the bar that low invites the admission of all kinds of evidence that the trier of fact might like, because it would make its job easier, but also invites reliance or dependence on evidence that provides easy answers but not necessarily the right ones. Necessity means what it implies: unless the trier of fact cannot reasonably come to the right conclusion without the expert evidence, the evidence should not be permitted. There must be the potential for a wrong determination or an inability to understand or "access" the information before expert evidence can be admitted. From this perspective, a wrong determination in a criminal case implies the potential for a wrongful conviction, and thus the courts have been broad in their interpretation of necessity when considering the evidence of criminal defence experts. This approach ensures that the accused has the opportunity for "full answer and defence."

Qualifications

In order for expert evidence to be admitted, the expert must be qualified in the field he provides evidence in. Thus, counsel that seeks to have an expert testify about the effect of glue sniffing on the accused's state of mind when he assaulted his teacher would likely be successful in convincing the judge that expert evidence regarding the toxicology of glue is both necessary and relevant. If the witness is a toxicologist with advanced degrees, publications on the subject, and 20 years of experience, the judge will very likely qualify the expert to testify. If counsel attempts to have one of the client's glue-sniffing friends give evidence about the impact of glue on the brain, the judge is likely to refuse the testimony, notwithstanding that the witness will have a basis for testifying far more intimate than the conventionally schooled expert.

The Absence of Any Exclusionary Rule

The issue here is that a party should not be able to present evidence through an expert that it could not present directly. So, where an accused speaks to a psychiatrist, who is later called to testify, the psychiatrist should not be able to relate an excuse or a justification given by the accused for his actions ("He attacked me with a shovel, so I stabbed him"), thus permitting that information to get before the trier of fact without the accused's facing cross-examination. Or, where a Crown expert makes reference to a confession from the accused that was beaten out of him and thus is not admissible, the expert's comment should not be admitted. In both cases, the expert evidence would not be admissible to the extent that it violates an exclusionary rule.

Limits on the Number of Expert Witnesses

One of the problems with expert testimony is that, on any topic, a plaintiff or the Crown can find a dozen experts to support its contention while the defendant or the accused can find an equal number whose evidence leads to the opposite conclusion. As a point of fact, many jurisdictions limit the number of experts who can testify on a point so that the exercise does not become simply a numbers game, leading the trier of fact to conclude that the side that presents the most experts must be right.

Exceptions can be granted to permit more experts to be called than are provided for in the *Canada Evidence Act* and provincial statutes. The *Canada Evidence Act* limits the number of experts that can be called by any party without leave of the court to five. Leave may be granted even after a party has called expert witnesses.

Hired Gun Syndrome

A related issue is the "hired gun" syndrome. It is remarkable (and not entirely coincidental) how often the same expert will testify in many different trials but only for the defence, or only for the Crown. Certain toxicologists are well-known defence witnesses and have never testified for the Crown. Similarly, there are doctors who consistently will provide evidence for defendants while others are known as "plaintiffs' doctors." Experts are usually paid by the party who has retained their services. This is not to suggest that expert evidence can be bought, but that some experts may be predisposed to viewing matters in a way that is helpful to the plaintiff or to the defendant. In instances where the court determines that an expert is biased or has adopted an adversarial stance toward the other party, that evidence can be excluded or given diminished weight.

Provincial and Territorial Rules Regarding Expert Evidence

Many provincial/territorial evidence acts have special provisions that are designed to streamline the presentation of expert evidence and accommodate experts. Most experts are busy practising in their fields and may find it difficult to fit a trial into their schedules. For example, a doctor may have a waiting room filled with patients or may be scheduled for surgery on the same day that she is expected to testify in court. Under s. 52 of the Ontario *Evidence Act*, a party may, with leave of the trial judge, use the report of an expert at trial instead of calling the expert as a witness. In Manitoba, a medical report is admissible without leave of the court by virtue of s. 50(1) of the *Manitoba Evidence Act*. Prince Edward Island and Saskatchewan also have provisions in their legislation permitting the use of medical reports. In s. 10 of British Columbia's *Evidence Act*, any expert report is admissible as evidence. Both the Yukon and the Northwest Territories have adopted provisions similar to those of British Columbia. All of these statutes generally permit a party to compel the attendance of a medical practitioner or other expert if it is necessary to hear from him or her or to test his or her evidence by cross-examination, but many provide cost sanctions for calling the expert unnecessarily. Any party that wishes to rely on any of these statutes should review the applicable provisions carefully because there are special procedural and notice requirements. At the time of writing, Alberta, Nova Scotia, New Brunswick, and Newfoundland did not have any provisions in their evidence acts permitting the use of medical or expert reports.

The Process of Qualifying an Expert

Before a witness will be permitted to provide expert evidence, the judge will need to determine whether the evidence that is being adduced is admissible, and whether the witness is properly qualified to provide the evidence. If there is no jury and there is no dispute regarding the admissibility of expert evidence in the circumstances, the process of qualifying the expert is usually brief. Counsel usually leads the witness through her resumé and may ask a few questions pertaining to the witness's qualifications. Opposing counsel will be provided with the opportunity to ask questions, and the judge may question the witness as well. Counsel then requests that the judge qualify the witness as an expert.

If there is a jury, or if the necessity for expert evidence or the witness's qualifications are in dispute, the process of qualifying the witness as an expert may be more rigorous. The party attempting to put forth the evidence will have to demonstrate that the evidence meets the four criteria set out in *R v. Mohan*.

Limitations on Expert Evidence

Even when an expert's testimony is admitted by the court, it is still subject to several limits that determine the weight it is given by a judge or a jury.

1. FOUNDATION OF THE EXPERT'S OPINION

In order for an expert's opinion to have any value, it must be based on proven facts. An opinion based on facts not proven is of very little value and will be given very little, if any, weight by the trier of fact. Where the trier of fact is a jury, the judge will instruct the jury to give the opinion little or no weight. If an expert states that the deceased died from stab wounds without first examining the deceased or her medical records, that opinion is of very little help to the trier of fact since it is little more than speculation or conjecture. It is therefore crucial that both sides understand the factual underpinnings of any expert's opinion. The evidence of many experts can be attacked by skillful cross-examination that uncovers the absence of a factual basis for the expert's opinion. Similarly, it is equally important for a party calling an expert to properly build a foundation upon which the expert can base her opinion or risk having the evidence be given very little weight.

The foundation of an expert's testimony is usually established by posing a hypothetical question for the expert to answer. That way, it is relatively easy for the trier of fact to determine how much of the information contained in the hypothetical question is based on evidence presented to the court. The trier of fact will weigh the evidentiary foundation of the opinion before ultimately deciding the degree, if any, to which the opinion is accepted. The hypothetical question is usually formulated by asking the expert to assume certain facts upon which to base her opinion. Later, if the facts are not proven at all or the trier of fact rejects the assumed facts, the opinion is treated with far less deference.

The hypothetical question will often be worked out ahead of time with the expert's help and will carefully track the evidence that has come out in court. So, for example, where an expert is called in an impaired driving trial, the purpose is usually to challenge the accuracy of the breathalyzer readings. The hypothetical question would establish a pattern of drinking and ask the expert what the blood-alcohol level would be in light of those facts. In this example, the hypothetical question might be phrased as follows:

> Hypothetically, if a person weighing 220 pounds were to begin drinking at 8:30 p.m. and consume eight ounces of alcohol at an even rate between 8:30 p.m. and 11:00 p.m. and the person was detained by the police as the driver of a vehicle at 11:25 p.m., what would this person's blood-alcohol level be at the time of driving?

2. HEARSAY

Sometimes, the foundation of an expert's evidence is based on hearsay evidence. Experts may testify in innumerable areas of specialized or scientific endeavour. In preparing a report to be used in litigation, an expert will often obtain information from sources that are not presented in evidence by either side in the litigation. The expert has thus relied on information that is not before the trier of fact. This can be problematic for the trier of fact, who is usually faced with two different expert opinions on the same topic and must evaluate which opinion deserves more weight. If the opinions are based solely on the evidence that is before the trier of fact, then the trier of fact simply weighs the evidence presented by the two experts and determines which opinion is more persuasive.

Where an expert has conducted an interview with a person who does not testify in court or where, for example, a psychologist has spoken with an accused who does not testify, then the expert's opinion must be influenced to a degree by this inadmissible hearsay evidence. To safeguard the trier of fact from being unduly and indirectly influenced by inadmissible hearsay evidence, the courts have developed a rule that the expert's evidence is to be discounted according to the degree to which the inadmissible hearsay evidence has influenced the expert's opinion. In order for the expert's opinion to be given any weight, there must be some admissible evidence that goes to the foundation of the expert's opinion. The more that the expert relies on hearsay evidence, the less weight the evidence can be given. Where the expert opinion is based mainly on inadmissible hearsay evidence, the trial judge may in fact instruct the trier of fact to give it no weight at all (as occurred in *R v. Lavallee*).

3. ULTIMATE ISSUE OPINIONS

Generally, no expert witness, or any other witness, should express an **ultimate issue opinion**—that is, an opinion on the ultimate issue that is before the trier of fact. Here are some examples:

> "He was obviously insane at the time of the offence."

> "They must have known that dumping those chemicals would kill the fish."

> "The plaintiff caused the accident and now he's trying to rip off the system."

> "The building collapsed because the contractor used shoddy materials."

ultimate issue opinion an opinion on the ultimate issue that is before the trier of fact; generally, witnesses are not permitted to give an ultimate issue opinion because the trier of fact could be swayed by it

The reason the courts do not permit this type of evidence is that the trier of fact is charged with the responsibility of drawing conclusions based on the facts. If the trier of fact is exposed to opinions on the ultimate issue between the parties, it may be swayed by those opinions and not decide the issues on the basis of the admissible evidence. This can occur when the expert witness is persuasive, when the trier of fact is lazy, or when the matter is so confusing to the trier of fact that a clearly stated opinion on these issues is welcomed. In other words, by having witnesses express their own opinions on the ultimate issues, they are usurping the role of the trier of fact.

However, experts may express opinions on the ultimate issue where such evidence will be of assistance to the trier of fact. It is not, however, appropriate for the witness to say, "He's as guilty as hell." That is clearly for the trier of fact to determine. But the expert witness may say, "In my opinion, Mr. Abbey was insane at the time that he killed his wife." This is an opinion that will assist the trier of fact in determining the accused's criminal responsibility for the offence with which he is charged.

As the expert's evidence begins to drift into areas normally reserved for the trier of fact, less weight will likely be placed on the evidence. The witness may be permitted to continue his testimony, but the judge will try to prevent him from stating any opinions on the issues or questions reserved for the trier of fact, and any that slip through are likely to be given very little, if any, weight.

On occasion, especially in jury trials, the expert evidence may be excluded entirely. The Supreme Court of British Columbia recently ruled on the limitations that should be imposed on expert witnesses commenting on the ultimate issue before the trier of fact. In *Brough v. Richmond*, a case involving a motor vehicle accident, McKinnon J noted that the medical expert who wrote a report in the litigation concluded that the patient was "malingering," clearly a conclusion that the trier of fact must make. The report of the expert was more what one would expect from an advocate for the insurer than from an independent expert. In relation to the expert's comments about the patient's reticence and vague and noncommittal responses, McKinnon J stated (at para. 18):

> In these circumstances an expert is expected to state that the person interviewed declined to provide certain information, leaving the reason(s) for this lack of co-operation to the trier of fact. Whether or not someone was "highly evasive and vague" or whether their reticence was "obvious" is a question of fact best avoided by expert witnesses. In my view, these comments are somewhat deprecatory, and of an editorial nature, inappropriate for an expert. As well, they comment directly on the plaintiff's credibility.

Accordingly, the judge excluded the report in its entirety.

Another example of an expert treading too heavily into the area reserved for the trier of fact is found in *Murray v. Galuska*. The plaintiff sued the defendants for negligence and malicious prosecution because he was criminally charged in relation to an accident that occurred in a pulp and paper operation where he was director of manufacturing. The opinion came from Richard Peck, a highly respected and experienced criminal lawyer who is often sought out by the BC attorney general to provide independent opinions and to prosecute cases where the Crown has a conflict of interest. The problem lay in the instructions given to Mr. Peck, which asked his opinion on the ultimate issue in the case:

> 1. Provide an opinion as to whether counsel of ordinary competence, in British Columbia in 1997, would have approved charges against Ian Murray in the circumstances of this case; and
> 2. Provide an opinion as the whether a Crown Counsel of ordinary competence, in British Columbia in 1998, would have continued the prosecution of Mr. Murray to verdict, given the evidence heard at trial.

These are, of course, the findings that a trier of fact must make in determining whether the plaintiff has made out his case. How can it assist the court to have an opinion on the above questions? Such an opinion can only be designed to sway the court and, if permitted, could improperly influence the judge's decision. The judge concluded that such an opinion would effectively usurp her role and it was not admitted.

4. RULE AGAINST OATH HELPING

oath helping
testimony by a witness in which he approves of, or comments favourably on the credibility of, another witness; generally prohibited because, in the view of the courts, a witness should have her testimony evaluated on its own without the need for another witness bolstering that testimony

In the view of the courts, a witness should have her testimony evaluated on its own without the need for another witness bolstering that testimony. When one witness enhances the evidence of another by approving of him or commenting favourably on his credibility, the witness has engaged in the prohibited practice of **oath helping**. The following is an example of oath helping: "My good friend, Dr. Freud, who testified earlier, is the most prominent and respected psychoanalyst in the field." Statements such as these hinder the trier of fact and raise a number of concerns. Would the trier of fact then be weighing the expert witness's credibility or would the trier of fact be swayed by the oath helper's opinion that the expert witness is the salt of the earth? Would the trial be distracted if a battle of the supporting witnesses ensues? Would the trier of fact defer to the opinion of the expert who is the most highly spoken of by the other witnesses, thus determining the dispute on the basis of the expert's popularity rather than the facts relating to the dispute that were before the trier of fact?

There is an exception to the rule against oath helping. In certain situations, it is permissible to lead evidence from expert witnesses that is general in nature where the evidence provides information to the trier of fact that will assist it in evaluating the general credibility of certain types of witnesses. For example, where there are allegations of sexual abuse against family members, and a child complainant testifies to the abuse before the trial begins, it is quite common for the child complainant to retract her allegations between the time of her testimony and the trial. She may do so for a number of reasons: family members may pressure her to withdraw the allegation for fear that the family bread winner will be jailed; she may have been removed from her home and misses her siblings and parents; the family may have been thrown into chaos with the revelations of abuse and she may decide that things were better off for everyone before the disclosure; or family members may deny that the abuse occurred and she may become confused and uncertain about what, if anything, did happen. The trier of fact will ultimately have to evaluate the validity of the initial allegation and will have to decide what to do with the fact of the retraction. This is where expert evidence comes in. An expert can testify that such retractions are quite common in situations of familial sexual abuse, although the expert must not specifically comment on whether any particular witness is telling the truth in her testimony. Thus, the trier of fact will be able to put the retraction in context—it may be a valid retraction or it may be a manifestation of the factors mentioned above. At least the trier of fact will not feel compelled to treat the retraction as conclusive on the issue of whether or not the abuse took place. It becomes one factor to consider among all the other admissible evidence.

5. NOVEL SCIENCE

New and emerging scientific endeavours may become relevant in a dispute. Because the judge is charged with the task of determining what information will be admitted on the basis of whether it will help or hinder the trier of fact, she will have to determine whether to accept expert evidence in new and somewhat untested sciences. In her role as gatekeeper, she must give special scrutiny to the proposed evidence so that the trier of fact is not subjected to unreliable evidence cloaked in the mystique of science. Expert evidence is routinely admitted in proven scientific areas. Fingerprint experts testify about whether a print lifted from a crime scene matches the accused's and inform the jury regarding the uniqueness of a person's fingerprints. Even with this well-established science, there is some dispute about how many matching characteristics are required before the expert can confirm a match. Where fingerprint experts testify on both sides of an issue, it will all come down to the trier of fact determining which expert to give more weight to.

DNA EVIDENCE

DNA evidence was first admitted into evidence in England in the late 1980s and has since exploded in use and popularity all over the world. It has been responsible for the location and conviction of numerous violent offenders and, of equal importance, it has been responsible for the exoneration of many wrongfully convicted persons.

Although DNA evidence has found a significant place in police work and is routinely accepted in expert evidence in courts of law, there continues to be some controversy about how definitive the results are. Some proponents put the probability of wrongful identification in the range of one in several billion, while critics point out that within certain more isolated communities where marriages between close relatives are common, the certainty plummets to one in 100,000. To put this in perspective, if the real certainty of a mismatch is one in 100,000, this means that in a place the size of Canada there are potentially more than 300 other people who would also be matches. This and other factors will influence the ability of scientists to give definitive statements about the certainty of a match, including the population that the accused comes from and the quality of the sample being tested. Clearly, DNA evidence has been shown to be helpful to triers of fact, but the courts are mindful of its limitations in deciding whether to admit DNA evidence that is presented in the course of expert testimony.

The Supreme Court of Canada recently dealt with the issue of the admissibility of novel science in *R v. J.-L.J.* This was a case where the accused sought to lead expert evidence to address his contention that the sexual offences he was charged with were performed by a particular type of sexual deviant and that he did not demonstrate those deviant sexual characteristics. The psychologist he wished to have testify was a pioneer in Canada of a device known as the penile plethysmograph. This device measures changes in the flow of blood to or circumference of the penis in response to the subject's being presented with visual stimuli—for example, pictures of a child in a sexual context. If the subject reacts to such stimuli, then the theory is that his true sexual interests are revealed notwithstanding his protestations to the contrary.

The Supreme Court referred to the US case of *Daubert v. Merrell Dow Pharmaceuticals, Inc.* in commenting favourably about the factors that would be helpful in evaluating the soundness of novel science. The US Supreme Court identified four factors (at 593-94):

(1) whether the theory or technique can be and has been tested:

Scientific methodology today is based on generating hypotheses and testing them to see if they can be falsified; indeed, this methodology is what distinguishes science from other fields of human inquiry.

(2) whether the theory or technique has been subjected to peer review and publication:

[S]ubmission to the scrutiny of the scientific community is a component of "good science," in part because it increases the likelihood that substantive flaws in methodology will be detected.

(3)   the known or potential rate of error or the existence of standards; and,

(4)   whether the theory or technique used has been generally accepted:

> A "reliability assessment does not require, although it does permit, explicit identification of a relevant scientific community and an express determination of a particular degree of acceptance within that community." ...
>
> Widespread acceptance can be an important factor in ruling particular evidence admissible, and "a known technique which has been able to attract only minimal support within the community," ... may properly be viewed with skepticism.

In commenting on this last factor, the Supreme Court of Canada concluded (at para. 34):

> Thus, in the United States, as here, "general acceptance" is only one of several factors to be considered. A penile plethysmograph may not yet be generally accepted as a forensic tool, but it may become so. A case-by-case evaluation of novel science is necessary in light of the changing nature of our scientific knowledge: it was once accepted by the highest authorities of the western world that the earth was flat.

In assessing whether *J.-L.J.* had met the special scrutiny test outlined by Sopinka J in *Mohan*, the Supreme Court analyzed the matter as follows (at para. 35):

> The penile plethysmograph, as noted by Fish JA, is *generally recognized by the scientific community* and is used by psychiatric facilities such as the Institut Philippe Pinel de Montréal to monitor the result of treatment for sexual pathologies. The plethysmograph enables the medical staff to assess the progress of therapy of known and admitted sexual deviants. This is inapplicable to the respondent. He denies he is part of such a group. He is not undergoing therapy. *Dr. Beltrami is a pioneer in Canada in trying to use this therapeutic tool as a forensic tool where the problems are firstly to determine whether the offence could only be committed by a perpetrator who possesses distinctive and identifiable psychological traits, secondly to determine whether a "standard profile" of those traits has been developed, and thirdly to match the accused against the profile.* Dr. Beltrami's evidence is therefore subject to "special scrutiny." While the techniques he employed are not novel, he is using them for a novel purpose. *A level of reliability that is quite useful in therapy because it yields some information about a course of treatment is not necessarily sufficiently reliable to be used in a court of law to identify or exclude the accused as a potential perpetrator of an offence.* In fact, penile plethysmography has received a mixed reception in Quebec courts. ... Efforts to use penile plethysmography in the United States as proof of disposition have largely been rejected ... . [Emphasis added.]

Another factor that was very important in this particular case was that, by Dr. Beltrami's admission, the penile plethysmograph only detected a sexual deviant 47.5 percent of the time. In other words, in a population of sexual deviants, the plethysmograph worked in detecting the deviant less than half of the time. This level of reliability did not impress the Supreme Court. This case provides an excellent example of how courts will go about the process of assessing novel science using the special scrutiny test.

CRITERIA FOR THE ADMISSION OF NOVEL SCIENCE

In order to be admissible, the novel science must meet the following criteria:

1. **It must be essential.** The trier of fact cannot come to a satisfactory conclusion without this aid.

2. **It must withstand special scrutiny.** The reliability of the science must be established because the scientific community has not generally accepted it yet.

3. **It must satisfy even stricter necessity and reliability requirements** where it approaches the ultimate issue in the matter.

THE CASE FOR POLYGRAPH EVIDENCE

Polygraphs of one sort or another have been in use since 1924. Police forces across the world use polygraphs as an investigative tool to assist them in narrowing their list of suspects. In most violent offences, the perpetrator is someone close to the victim. Thus, if six close friends and family take the polygraph test and five pass according to the technician, the police will focus their efforts on the remaining person. The courts, however, have treated polygraph evidence with suspicion. They have not been prepared to take the leap of faith that the police forces have and have not accepted polygraph evidence in courts of law.

The courts have perceived a great danger in the admission of evidence from a device that is commonly referred to as a "lie detector." If the trier of fact hears that an accused failed the lie detector, then the trier of fact may conclude that the accused is lying and convict the individual on this basis. The danger is that the trier of fact will take this information as absolute and abandon its task of weighing all the evidence for and against the accused. What the polygraph does is measure a number of physiological responses in the subject. The responses are correlated to the questions being asked and graphed to determine whether there is a relation between false responses and the graph. Ideally, a certain pattern on the graph that is the same pattern that resulted from responses when the subject is known to have lied would appear when other questions are being asked. This then points to further lies. Typically, the polygraph plots at least three physiological responses: blood pressure, pulse, and respiration.

Polygraphs may also test muscular movement and the electrical conductivity of the skin, which is reduced if the subject perspires. Critics of the polygraph point out that emotional stress generated by the test itself can cause heightened blood pressure, pulse rate, and respiration and changes in the electrical conductivity of the skin. They also point out that a pathological liar would not react to the questions in the manner that a "normal" person would, thus eliminating the validity of the test for this group.

Polygraph evidence has not found general approval or acceptance by the scientific community and an argument for the admissibility of this evidence must be determined having regard to the principles of novel science. It may very well be that polygraph testing will evolve and become much more reliable at some future date.

Even if it does, it is unclear whether the courts would ever be prepared to admit polygraph evidence to help the trier of fact make findings of fact or credibility.

CHAPTER SUMMARY

The courts are reluctant to permit witnesses to express opinions or come to conclusions based on evidence that is presented in court because this function is reserved for the trier of fact. A lay witness is qualified to testify as to what he actually saw or heard, but is usually in a worse position than the trier of fact to draw conclusions on the facts. Experts are provided with more leeway, but before expert evidence is admitted, the four criteria of relevance, necessity, qualifications, and the absence of any exclusionary rules must be met. The rationale for permitting expert evidence is that this evidence allows the trier of fact to make better sense of technical matters or ones requiring specialized knowledge. However, in light of the inherent dangers of placing too much reliance on the evidence of experts, the courts have placed limitations not only on the admissibility of this evidence, but also on the weight that the evidence is given by the trier of fact.

KEY TERMS

opinion evidence

layperson's opinion

compendious mode of expressing facts

expert opinion

ultimate issue opinion

oath helping

REFERENCES

Brough v. Richmond, 2003 BCSC 512.

Canadian Charter of Rights and Freedoms, part I of the *Constitution Act, 1982*, RSC 1985, app. II, no. 44.

Daubert v. Merrell Dow Pharmaceuticals, Inc., 509 US 59 (1993).

Evidence Act, RSBC 1996, c. 124.

Evidence Act, RSO 1990, c. E.23.

Graat *v. The Queen*, [1982] 2 SCR 819.

J.-L.J., R v., [2000] 2 SCR 600.

Lavallee, R v. (1990), 76 CR (3d) 329 (SCC).

Manitoba Evidence Act, CCSM, c. E150.

Mohan, R v., [1994] 2 SCR 9.

Murray v. Galuska, 2002 BCSC 1532.

Reid v. Watkins, [1964] 2 OR 249 (HCJ).

REVIEW QUESTIONS

1. Give some examples of novel science and explain how its admissibility would be tested.

2. Explain the two rules or principles that argue against the admissibility of opinion evidence.

3. What is the *Mohan* test for the admissibility of expert evidence?

EXERCISES

Review the following scenarios. For each, determine whether the testimony is admissible. Why or why not? If the testimony is not admissible, is there any way for the statement to be rephrased so that it would be admissible?

1. Ricardo Thanderys testified, "I knew that the guy did it because he was the only one in the bunch who was shaking."

2. George Jankowski testified, "The car was obviously speeding, maybe 120 kilometers an hour, before it struck the deceased."

3. Baligha Ahmed testified, "I knew the guy was dead because the piano fell on him."

4. Dr. Hans Everthen, a cardiologist, testified, "The victim died of natural causes as a result of a heart attack, not from the blow to his head."

5. Dr. Mary Distu, a toxicologist, testified, "The victim was drunk and probably attacked the accused first."

6. Rob Dapur, an expert in alienology, testified, "The accused could not have been present when the deceased died because the accused had clear and obvious signs on her body that she had been abducted by aliens at that time."

7. Susan Holgado, a handwriting expert, testified, "The deceased did not write the words 'Kent did it' in her own blood shortly before succumbing to her injuries. The words were written by someone else."

8. Albert Mackay, a highly respected psychiatrist, testified, "The accused could not be guilty of murder because he was clearly and obviously insane at the time."

CHAPTER 10

Privilege

CHAPTER OBJECTIVES

After completing this chapter you should be able to:

- Define privilege.

- Understand that all forms of privilege are subject to a public safety exception.

- Understand the differences between solicitor–client privilege and litigation privilege.

- Understand the distinction between privilege by class and privilege by case and identify relationships that may attract privilege on a case-by-case basis.

- Understand Wigmore's four criteria for assessing privilege.

PRIVILEGE AND THE BALANCING OF VALUES

We have already seen that not all evidence that is relevant and material is admitted in court. If it were, evidence law would be very simple. The courts choose to operate in this manner, not to unnecessarily complicate the litigation process, but for the very good reason that if the process operated with no exceptions, there would be some very unfortunate unintended consequences. The legal system must be fair, and wherever fairness comes into play, there is usually a balancing of interests. In some instances, certain communications—for example, letters or conversations—will be kept from the trier of fact. This information is often reliable and probative—it may even contain confessions of guilt or information that would resolve a civil dispute with a high degree of certainty. The reason for excluding this information is based on the balancing of interests—not only those of the parties but those of society as well. There are some situations where another value is seen as more important than the principle of maximizing reliable information placed before the trier of fact. In these cases, the value of preserving the confidentiality of certain communications is seen as more important than the value of placing reliable and probative information before a judge or a jury.

PRIVILEGE DEFINED

privilege
status accorded communicated information that makes the information unavailable to the trier of fact

The concept of **privilege** is that certain information is off limits to the litigation process. No matter how relevant and material, the information cannot be available to the trier of fact. Indeed, some privileged information is so valuable that it would determine the outcome of the litigation and allow the trier of fact to easily make a determination in that the right disposition of the litigation had been arrived at.

For this reason, judges are hesitant to endorse claims of privilege except in situations where there are clear historical grounds for the claim and where the competing interests are substantial. Privilege can attach to verbal or written communications, and once a judge has determined that the communication is privileged, it cannot be introduced into evidence no matter how valuable or determinative. In this respect, the judge acts as gatekeeper by shielding the trier of fact from information that it should not hear or see.

privilege by class
privilege based on the relationship between the communicator of information and the recipient

privilege by case
privilege extended to communication on a case-by-case basis

Privilege is generally placed into two categories: privilege by class and privilege by case. **Privilege by class** is based solely on the type of relationship between the communicator and recipient of the communication. It arises upon the establishment of any class of relationship that has been accorded this privilege. In other words, to invoke the privilege, a party need only show the court that the communication was made within a prescribed class of relationships. After privilege by class is established, all communications within that class are protected, subject only to situations where public safety is endangered. On the other hand, **privilege by case** is determined on a case-by-case basis. It is not primarily dependent on the type of relationship between the person making the communication and the person to whom the communication was made. However, this is not to say that the nature of the relationship is not important. It clearly is, but whether privilege extends to any communication is determined by the court on a case-by-case basis.

It is important to understand that although privilege is an exception to the rule that relevant and material evidence is generally admissible, there are many situations where courts refuse to exclude evidence that appears to attract a claim of privilege. This is done either by applying the privilege exceptions narrowly and thus saying that privilege does not apply to the unique circumstances before the court, or by carving out exceptions to the exception itself.

PUBLIC SAFETY EXCEPTION

public safety exception
an exception to privilege when the otherwise protected communication poses a threat to public safety

All forms of privilege are subject to the **public safety exception**. Basically, this means that privilege is overridden when there is a threat to public safety. Although the issue usually arises within the context of the doctor–patient relationship, it can exist elsewhere. For example, if a client confides to his lawyer that he plans to murder his wife, the public safety exception is invoked and the intended victim must be warned. The Canadian case that set the standard is *Smith v. Jones*. In this case, the Supreme Court of Canada laid out clear criteria for the exception to privilege. The duty to warn intended victims exists where

1. the risk is to a clearly identifiable person or group;

2. the risk of harm includes severe bodily injury, death, or serious psychological harm; and

3. the risk is imminent.

All three elements must be present. Because the standard is high, this exception to privilege is applied infrequently and only to the extent necessary to warn the intended victim or victims of the danger. Furthermore, the exception cannot be used to disclose past acts, only intentions to commit future acts.

PRIVILEGE BY CLASS

Because privileged communications are generally not admissible as evidence, and it is the aim of the courts to put as much relevant and material information before the trier of fact as possible, courts and judges take a very narrow or restrictive approach when privilege is claimed by class. If the relationship does not clearly and obviously fall within a prescribed class, the claim will fail. (Keep in mind, however, that if privilege cannot be established by class, it may still be made out in an individual case, as discussed below under the heading "Privilege by Case.") The following are some classes of privilege that have developed over time.

1. Solicitor–Client Privilege

Solicitor–client privilege is one of the oldest and most entrenched forms of privilege. It protects communications between a lawyer and her client. The reason this form of privilege is so universally respected is that it is accepted that a client could not obtain proper legal advice if he were afraid of telling his lawyer the whole truth about the matter. Once the client does reveal the whole truth, the lawyer is in a position to give proper advice. Not only does this serve the best interests of the client, it often translates into great savings of court time and efficiency in the process if an early resolution of the matter is achieved. One notable feature of solicitor–client privilege is that the privilege belongs to the client and survives his death. Thus, the lawyer is not released from her obligations to keep her client's secrets even after the client dies. This rule exists because the client's interest in privacy can extend beyond his death, as when an action against an individual is pursued through an executor. It is not up to former counsel to determine what would have been or should be waived in terms of their communications.

Solicitor–client privilege is one major exception to the rule that relevant and material evidence is always admissible. But, as with many areas of evidence law, there are exceptions to the exception. There are a number of situations where communications between a lawyer and someone else are not privileged, or where the law has carved out an exception to the rule that communications between a lawyer and her client are excluded as evidence. In those instances, the communications can be disclosed to the court.

Not everything that anyone says to a lawyer will attract privilege. Even where it is established that the communication was made or received by a client, this fact is

solicitor–client privilege
privilege that protects communications between lawyer and client made for the purpose of obtaining legal advice

not sufficient to establish privilege over disclosure of the communication. To attract privilege, the communication must be confidential and be in relation to the seeking, forming, or giving of legal advice. So, it is only where a client is communicating with a lawyer in order to get legal advice that the conversation or written communication is protected.

In addition, a client who wishes to claim privilege is responsible for protecting the information. If the client has a loud conversation with his lawyer in a restaurant or at a party, and details of the matter are overheard, the client has let the information out into the public and privilege cannot be restored. The analogy of closing the barn door after the horse has fled applies here. In the view of the courts, the privilege holder has essentially waived his right to rely on privilege by either intentionally or inadvertently letting the information out into the public. Thus, the concept of privilege is applied to the source of the information—lawyer contact with client—but not the information itself, if it is not properly guarded. Even so, the use of privilege has generally been very narrowly interpreted so as to minimize the loss of relevant and material information to the finder of fact. Although careless handling of documents may affect whether privilege will continue to apply to them, documents that have made their way into other hands by theft or trickery will likely maintain their privileged character in Canada.

Privilege does not attach simply because someone is a lawyer. A lawyer working as the president of a company does not have privilege attach to communications made or received in her capacity as president. (Of course, communications she has as president of the company with the company's lawyers to obtain advice on a legal matter are protected.)

A recent decision of the Supreme Court of Canada confirms that in-house counsel who provide opinions for administrative tribunals will have those communications protected by solicitor–client privilege. In *Pritchard v. Ontario (Human Rights Commission)*, Ms. Pritchard was appealing a decision of the Human Rights Commission not to deal with her complaint that her former employer, Sears Canada, had discriminated against her. Ms. Pritchard wanted to have disclosure of a legal opinion provided to the commission by in-house counsel on the issue whether her claim ought to be dismissed as a bad-faith application because she had signed a release against Sears Canada dealing with these same complaints. The court treated the situation the same as with corporate in-house counsel or in-house counsel for a government department dealing with litigation against it. In the appeal, the court found that the Human Rights Commission is a party to the proceedings before the court and thus in no different position from any other litigant. It therefore ruled that the "communication between the Human Rights Commission and its in-house counsel is protected by solicitor–client privilege."

Often in legal matters, a strict application of legal principles by a judge would result in an absurdity. Fortunately, common sense usually prevails. Such is the case where communications between a solicitor and client are criminal in themselves. These conversations are not protected. An example would be the case where a lawyer is involved in a criminal conspiracy, as has happened on occasion where lawyers have been involved in drug-conspiracy or money-laundering schemes. Lawyers are also not ethically permitted to advise clients on how to commit crimes so that clients can get away with criminal acts. For example, advice to a client on how to circumvent money laundering laws would not be protected by privilege.

> ## SOLICITOR–CLIENT PRIVILEGE
>
> Communications between a solicitor and client that
>
> 1. are of a confidential nature,
>
> 2. relate to the seeking, forming, or giving of legal advice, and
>
> 3. are not criminal in themselves and do not facilitate criminal activity
>
> are privileged, *except*
>
> > a. where they are necessary to establish the innocence of an accused person
>
> *or*
> > b. where public safety is at risk.

There is a distinction to be made, however, between past and future crimes. A client can expect his solicitor to keep his communications confidential even where he admits to horrendous past crimes. Unless and until the client indicates he will go out and harm another person or group of persons *in the future*, his acknowledgments of past offences cannot be repeated in court. As well, telling a lawyer about future non-violent crimes will not trigger the public safety exception and the communication will continue to attract protection from disclosure. Where, however, the lawyer has received information that public safety is at risk, the duty to warn intended victims set out in *Smith v. Jones* applies. The lawyer must then take whatever steps she can to protect the person or group exposed to the threat. Usually this means calling the police. However, the lawyer may only reveal as much confidential information as is necessary to protect the threatened party.

EXCEPTION TO SOLICITOR–CLIENT PRIVILEGE WHERE THE INNOCENCE OF AN ACCUSED IS AT STAKE

An accused may seek to have third-party communications between a solicitor and her client admitted in order to help establish his innocence. This exception to solicitor–client privilege is referred to as **innocence at stake** and is consistent with the accused's right to make full answer and defence, as afforded by s. 7 of the *Canadian Charter of Rights and Freedoms*. The exception also reflects the view of the court that an accused cannot be seen to properly defend himself where a lawyer, an officer of the court, withholds information that could clear him.

However, the innocence at stake exception to solicitor–client privilege is applied narrowly by the courts because of the deference given to protecting these communications. It is clear from *R v. McClure* that before the courts will even consider the exception, an initial threshold must be met whereby "the accused must establish that the information he is seeking in the solicitor-client file is not available from any other source and he is otherwise unable to raise a reasonable doubt as to his guilt in any other way" (at para. 48).

What this means is that the courts will not consider an innocence at stake exception if the accused is able to raise a reasonable doubt without violating solicitor–client privilege. In other words, the innocence at stake exception is not open if other evidence is available to the accused that would raise a reasonable doubt. This

innocence at stake exception
an exception to solicitor–client privilege when the otherwise protected communication is necessary to establish the client's innocence

is in keeping with the purpose of the exception, which is to prevent wrongful convictions, not to permit the accused to mount a more complete defence.

Some commentators have argued that the initial threshold set out in *McClure* is too stringent. In order to pass the threshold, the accused must demonstrate an inability to otherwise raise a reasonable doubt. This is essentially an acknowledgment that the accused has a weak defence. How can an accused later put forth a credible defence if the *McClure* test is not met?

If the accused is able to meet this initial threshold, there follows a two-part test, as set out in *McClure*. The accused must first pass a less stringent hurdle—establish that communications exist that could raise a reasonable doubt. If this test is met, the judge must then look at the solicitor–client communications in order to decide whether they are likely to raise a reasonable doubt. All of the above must be shown by the accused on a balance of probabilities.

If the accused is successful, the judge orders that only those communications that are necessary to establish the accused's innocence be admitted into evidence. Note: If those communications in fact establish that another person committed the crime that the accused is charged with, the communications will not be made available to the Crown in a subsequent trial against that other person. They continue to be protected in relation to that person by solicitor–client privilege and that person is not taken to have waived that privilege.

One thing to remember is that throughout this whole process, the accused is "shooting in the dark"—he will likely have some reason to suspect that this information will assist him, but he will not know for sure. If he did have positive proof, then the privilege would likely have already been waived by the other party. Let's say Winston is asked to hold a briefcase for a friend. It turns out that the briefcase was stolen in a particularly violent robbery and the police find the briefcase when conducting a lawful drug search of Winston's apartment. Winston ends up being charged for the robbery but before he can convince his friend to testify that he was the one who committed the robbery, the friend dies. This friend has a criminal lawyer that he has been dealing with. Winston surmises that the friend would have told his criminal lawyer about his involvement in the robbery, so Winston wants the lawyer to tell the court about the friend's involvement. We know that the friend cannot waive the solicitor–client privilege—he is dead—so Winston would have to rely on the innocence at stake provisions and convince the judge that the lawyer has evidence that would assist his case and that he would otherwise likely be convicted. Note, though, that Winston is focusing his energy on trying to convince a judge that he will likely be convicted without this evidence when there is no guarantee that the evidence will be admitted.

2. Litigation Privilege

litigation privilege
privilege that protects communications between a client's lawyer or law firm and third parties

Similar to solicitor–client privilege, **litigation privilege** is a concept that has developed to facilitate a smooth-functioning legal system. This class of privilege applies to communications between a client's lawyer and third parties, provided that the litigation was commenced or anticipated at the time of the communications and that the dominant purpose of the communications was to obtain information for the litigation. This group is usually composed of persons who provide expert opinions on some aspect of the litigation, which the lawyer then uses to formulate legal

INNOCENCE AT STAKE TEST

1. Threshold

   a. The accused must establish that there is no other source for the exonerating information.

   b. The accused must establish that he would otherwise be unable to raise a reasonable doubt.

2. Two-Part Test

   a. The accused must establish that communications exist that *could* raise a reasonable doubt regarding his guilt.

   b. If the accused establishes that such communications exist, then the judge will examine them to determine whether they are *likely* to raise a reasonable doubt.

advice to the client. The reports containing the expert opinions may be released to the other side, in which case privilege no longer attaches, but if they are kept secret, they are protected from disclosure. The reason for this rule is that, with the increasingly complex litigation today, no lawyer is in a position to properly advise all clients at all times without the assistance of third parties. If clients were afraid to obtain this information for fear that opposing counsel would use the information against them, that would undermine the ability of the parties to pursue legal remedies and, almost as importantly, it would limit the lawyer's or law firm's ability to achieve a settlement without the need for a trial.

Although litigation privilege does remove some relevant information from review by the finder of fact, it is information that might not exist at all without the rule and it is greatly beneficial to all parties to have such a provision in place. There are a few distinctions between litigation privilege and solicitor–client privilege that are worth noting. Litigation privilege can only be claimed if the information was requested because of or in contemplation of litigation. This is not the case with solicitor–client communications. These must be in relation to obtaining legal advice, but litigation need not be involved. As well, third-party communications gathered for the purpose of litigation are more broadly protected than third-party solicitor–client communications where the third party is an agent of the lawyer, such as a translator or psychiatrist. A good example of how the question of admissibility arises is an accident involving a railroad authority. The authority always investigates the accident and produces an occurrence report. If the authority is sued, the report may assist its counsel in litigation. If it is simply a safety report, then it is discoverable, but if its dominant purpose was in contemplation of litigation, then it is not discoverable. However, because these reports are routinely produced for every accident, the courts have been wary of excluding them when litigation privilege is asserted. The reasoning is that these authorities cannot be expected to be sued for every accident, regardless of severity or fault, and therefore the reports do not meet the requirement of having been requested in contemplation of litigation.

Another interesting difference between litigation privilege and solicitor–client privilege is that solicitor–client privilege lasts forever. Litigation privilege dies with the litigation because, after the litigation has ended, there is no longer an interest to

LITIGATION PRIVILEGE

1. Applies to communications between a lawyer or law firm and third parties.

2. Litigation must have been commenced or anticipated at time of communication.

3. Dominant purpose of the communication is to assist in the litigation.

protect. With litigation privilege, the communications need not be confidential. Finally, litigation privilege may be more easily overridden than solicitor–client privilege on the basis of fairness or process arguments. The rationale of litigation privilege is to facilitate the litigation process rather than to protect the solicitor–client relationship. The Ontario Court of Appeal in *General Accident Assurance Company v. Chrusz* stated that "litigation privilege is being defined by the rules as they are amended from time to time." The rules provide for disclosure of privileged documents to ensure a fair trial.

A comparison of solicitor–client privilege and litigation privilege is provided in the table below.

Comparison of Solicitor–Client Privilege and Litigation Privilege

Solicitor–Client Privilege	Litigation Privilege
Protects confidential communications between a lawyer and her client.	Communications need not be made in confidence, just in the process of litigation.
Applies to communications made in order to obtain legal advice.	Applies only to communications made in the context of litigation and is not applicable to pre- or post-litigation communications.
Does not expire with the end of the relationship or the death of the client or lawyer.	Only exists during the subsistence of the litigation.
Great deference is given to solicitor–client communications, so solicitor–client privilege is not easily overridden.	More easily overridden on the basis of fairness or process arguments.
Third-party communications are protected where the third party is an agent of the lawyer such as a translator, or a psychiatrist examining the client for the lawyer.	Third-party communications are much more broadly protected where information is being gathered for the purpose of assisting the lawyer with anticipated or ongoing litigation.

3. Settlement Negotiations

Settlement negotiations enjoy a form of privilege that serves an important purpose in litigation. This class of privilege protects both sides from having sensitive information about settlement discussions revealed to the court. Settlement privilege by its nature implies that the information has been revealed to the other side, usually in the form of settlement discussions, a letter, or an offer to settle. This information is not provided to the judge, specifically so that each side can explore settlement without fearing that it is raising or lowering its bottom line in court with each concession that it makes. Thus, these mediations are **without prejudice**—none of the discussions, offers, or compromises may be used in subsequent court proceedings. In Ontario, rule 49 of the *Rules of Civil Procedure* specifically protects formal offers to settle from disclosure to the trial judge for the purpose of establishing liability. However, the rule allows disclosure after judgment when dealing with the issue of costs.

> **without prejudice**
> protection claimed for information provided by a party that prevents the information from being used in court

One important distinction that is quite important, but sometimes overlooked, is that although settlement discussions are protected, admissions of liability are not unless it is made clear that all settlement discussions are privileged. For example, the statement "I'm sorry, don't worry, I'll pay to have your car repaired" may very well be admissible as an admission of liability. It is therefore advisable for parties to make it clear that any settlement discussions are to be privileged. This is usually accomplished by prefacing any offers with the words "without prejudice." Similarly, most mediators will have their clients sign a confidentiality agreement prior to the mediation session. In such instances, an ounce of prevention is indeed worth a pound of cure.

4. Government Privilege or Public Interest Immunity

The immunity enjoyed by governments used to be unassailable; it was a blanket class immunity that flowed simply from an assertion by the responsible minister that the documents were privileged "in the public interest." This is no longer the case. Today, the interests of the justice system are balanced with the public interest. On the one hand, the administration of justice depends on the availability of reliable information, whatever the source, even if that source is government documents. On the other hand, protecting sensitive governmental information may be in the public interest. Let's say that the federal government decides to bid out a catering contract for one of the international airports. A losing bidder sues the government, claiming racial profiling and discrimination as the basis for not getting the contract. The plaintiff's counsel seeks Cabinet documents dealing with airport security. The government declines, claiming public interest in keeping airport security measures secret. Depending on the specific documents being sought, public interest may well trump the plaintiff's right to know.

In fact, the one area where absolute privilege continues to apply is with Cabinet documents. Any communications to Cabinet fall under a blanket "class" privilege and cannot be disclosed. There is a strong policy argument in favour of this. If bureaucrats and others who advise the Cabinet had to constantly look over their shoulders and hedge their language, then the government would not be getting clear and honest advice in order to make decisions, and if these advisers avoided blunt language for fear of lawsuits or other repercussions, the government would be left without the tools it needed to make appropriate decisions. This rationale is similar to that for solicitor–client privilege.

5. National Security Matters

In the wake of the September 11, 2001 terrorist attacks on the United States, additional security measures have been put in place in Canada that appear to permit various government agencies and departments to operate under a veil of secrecy by claiming that there are national security interests to protect. Where an issue of disclosure of potentially sensitive information arises, the parties are obliged to inform the attorney general. The judge is required to seal the information or otherwise give direction that will prevent disclosure. A hearing is then held to determine the validity of the national security claim. The novel aspect of this procedure is that the hearing is in camera, without notice to any parties, and without the right by any party to make representations unless the judge so determines. No one is permitted to disclose the existence of the application. Even if the judge determines that the government has not made out its case for protection of the information, the attorney general can override that decision by the simple filing of a certificate. The certificate is good for 15 years. The danger with this kind of power is that the government, for political reasons, can restrict information that might injure it. Although the Federal Court of Appeal has the power to override the certificate, the criteria to override are extremely difficult to meet. The national security claim will stand as long as the government can show some relevance of the certified information to the area that the government claims protection for.

6. Informants

Another class of privilege that protects the public interest is privilege that protects against disclosure of an informant's identity. Informants are a "necessary evil" within the justice system. Police investigations often turn on information that is provided by criminals who obtain some kind of benefit for cooperating with the police. If this source of information dried up for the police, many serious crimes would remain unsolved. In exchange, the informants, often petty drug dealers, thieves, and other miscreants, are able to ply their trade under an umbrella of immunity. They may be caught committing less serious offences, but they have confidence that if they have some information to exchange or if they have been valuable to the police in the past, their case will not proceed to trial. Occasionally, money is exchanged for information, but the greatest inducement to helping the police is that the police will forgive the charges for their low-level criminal activity.

The reason for providing protection from disclosure of the informant's identity is twofold. First, without this protection, the informant would be useless to the police in future investigations. He would be marked in the criminal community and would no longer have access to helpful information for the police. The reason why informants are so valuable and necessary is that they have access to places and information that the police do not. Second, if the informant's identity were disclosed, he might be murdered for having assisted the police. Disclosure of an informant's identity at a preliminary inquiry increases the likelihood that the informant will not live to see the trial. Without this protection, few people would be willing to work with the police, even where they receive some consideration in the form of forgiven charges in exchange for their help.

7. Spousal Privilege

Generally, husbands and wives, as well as married same-sex spouses, cannot be compelled to disclose to the court any communication's between them made during their marriage. This class of protection is known as **spousal privilege**. The principle of spousal non-compellability is an old one and likely born of the concept of the unity of husband and wife. According to this concept, the wife is not a separate person in the eyes of the law, and spousal non-compellability is simply an extension of the right not to be compelled to testify against yourself. Additional policy considerations evolved over time, including the support or respect that society has for the family unit and the importance of safeguarding the relationship and preserving the marriage. However, in 1853 the British Parliament passed the *Evidence Amendment Act*, which made married spouses competent and compellable in civil proceedings. Before this, spouses were not able to testify either for or against their wife or husband. But it was not long before marital communications attracted privilege in criminal proceedings. Today, spousal privilege is codified in the *Canada Evidence Act* as well as in various provincial acts. Section 4(3) of the *Canada Evidence Act* states:

> No husband is compellable to disclose any communication made to him by his wife during their marriage, and no wife is compellable to disclose any communication made to her by her husband during their marriage.

The precise wording of s. 4(3) is very important. Note that in order to claim privilege, the parties must be legally married. It has been determined that privilege does not apply to irreconcilably separated married persons. It also does not apply to common-law spouses. So, in essence, persons married for two weeks have greater protection from being compelled to testify than common-law couples who have been together for 40 years. Interestingly, this section previously gave no protection to same-sex couples, because they could not legally marry. Therefore, same-sex couples were discriminated against on the basis of their sexual orientation.

Another important component of s. 4(3) of the *Canada Evidence Act* is that spousal privilege only attaches to communications. Thus, a spouse can be compelled to testify about anything dealing with her mate, except interactions that qualify as communications. Therefore, a husband or wife may be compelled to testify about things that he or she has observed. For example, a wife whose husband hands her bloody clothes with the instructions, "See if you can get that nasty stain out of my favourite shirt; that Alfred bled like a stuck pig," could not be compelled to repeat his words, but could be compelled to disclose her observations about the bloody laundry.

An interesting distinction between spousal privilege and other forms of privilege is that although the spouse who receives the communication cannot be compelled to disclose it, if she volunteers the information the court welcomes it. This rule appears to be a compromise that attempts to maximize the amount of information available to the court. In effect, the court is saying, "We won't make you talk about it, but if you want to, we're happy to hear it."

spousal privilege
privilege based on the spousal relationship that prevents one spouse from testifying against the other

> ## SPOUSAL PRIVILEGE IN BRIEF
>
> 1. The persons in the relationship must be married.
>
> 2. Privilege only applies to communications during the marriage and does not survive the ending of the marriage.
>
> 3. Privilege only applies to communications, not observations.
>
> 4. The spouse who receives the communication cannot be compelled to disclose it, although she may volunteer it.

Note that the communications must have originated during the marriage and only survive as long as the marriage does. So, if the marriage is dissolved through divorce or the death of the spouse making the statement to the court, privilege no longer applies. The idea here is that there is no longer a relationship to safeguard, so there is no longer a need to restrict the available information in order to protect the marriage. This rule is another nuance designed to maximize the amount of information available to the trier of fact.

Spouses who are careless and talk about their secrets in public are not protected, although communications that are intercepted by wiretap pursuant to a wiretap authorization are protected.

8. Judges' Privilege

judges' privilege
privilege that protects judges and administrative tribunal members against disclosing information behind their decisions

Judges and members of administrative tribunals cannot be compelled to testify or disclose any information regarding their deliberations or reasoning in coming to a decision. This class of protection is known as **judges' privilege**. This makes perfect sense given the independence of the judiciary. Judges must be free to make what are often difficult decisions without fear that their conduct in coming to a decision will be placed under a microscope.

Similarly, deliberations by jurors are also protected by law. It is only when there is a concern regarding juror misconduct or the veracity of those deliberations that jurors are required to disclose what went on during their deliberations. The extent of any such disclosure is confined to dealing with those concerns only.

PRIVILEGE BY CASE

There are other classes of relationships that appear to be of sufficient importance to attract privilege. However, the courts have been reluctant to extend privilege to other classes. In *A. (L.L.) v. B. (A.)*, the Supreme Court of Canada expressed its view that "class privilege presents many impediments to the proper administration of justice and … has not been favoured in Canada" (at para. 65).

There exist many relationships where a layperson, or even a person in a relationship, may form the erroneous opinion that any communications within the relationship are privileged. Communications that arise within these relationships may indeed give rise to a claim of privilege, but whether privilege attaches or not is determined on a case-by-case basis, not simply as a result of the existence of the relationship. It is crucial to keep the distinction between privilege by class and privilege by case clear. In the former, privilege arises automatically. However, there are a great many relationships where privilege is determined on a case-by-case basis. Some of these may be relationships where it is commonly assumed by the parties, or even by the general public, that communications are protected by class, although the reality is that courts will apply privilege only on a case-by-case basis in these circumstances.

An American jurist, John Henry Wigmore, developed four criteria for assessing claims of privilege in areas where the claim has not been traditionally accepted by the courts on the basis of privilege by class. These criteria have been adopted by the courts in Canada and are commonly referred to as the **Wigmore test**. The criteria are as follows:

> (1) The communications must originate in a confidence that they will not be disclosed.
>
> (2) This element of confidentiality must be essential to the full and satisfactory maintenance of the relationship between the parties.
>
> (3) The relation must be one which in the opinion of the community ought to be sedulously [persistently and diligently] fostered.
>
> (4) The injury that would inure to the relation by the disclosure of the communications must be greater than the benefit thereby gained for the correct disposal of litigation.

Wigmore test
four criteria for assessing case-by-case claims of privilege

Wigmore's Four Criteria

(1) THE COMMUNICATIONS MUST ORIGINATE IN A CONFIDENCE THAT THEY WILL NOT BE DISCLOSED

In assessing whether privilege should attach to communications between individuals in a circumstance where there is no legislated or historically recognized privilege, the first criterion identified by Wigmore was whether the communication originated in confidence. In other words, if the parties at the time did not think that the communications were confidential, then there is no confidential relationship to protect and a litigant cannot claim privilege as an afterthought. What kind of communications originate in confidence? In fact, there are a great number of relationships that are confidential in nature. Take, for example, the relationship between an accountant and his client. Not only will the client often have information that is disclosed to the accountant that he does not want the taxation department to know about, but he likely also does not want this information shared with his neighbours or co-workers. Therefore, communications with an accountant almost certainly originate in confidence. Similarly, communications with a banker, doctor, or escort service are confidential in nature. Even communications with a hairdresser, personal trainer, or car mechanic are confidential. In these and other such relationships, individuals want to know that their privacy is respected. All these communications will likely originate in confidence that the professional will not disclose the private information.

(2) THIS ELEMENT OF CONFIDENTIALITY MUST BE ESSENTIAL TO THE FULL AND SATISFACTORY MAINTENANCE OF THE RELATIONSHIP BETWEEN THE PARTIES

The second of Wigmore's criteria deals with the importance of confidentiality to the maintenance of the relationship. The court considers whether it is necessary to protect the communication in order to preserve the relationship. Take the classic situation of the confessional. Great deference is given to communications between a person who is unburdening her conscience and the religious figure that she confides in. Similarly, the Greenpeace activist who drives a high performance car that has some of the anti-pollution devices circumvented would require discretion. Disclosure of this information might be very embarrassing to the activist and would undoubtedly damage the relationship with the mechanic. However, if the court were to grant privilege, relevant and material evidence would be lost to the trier of fact, so this claim of privilege would fail.

(3) THE RELATION MUST BE ONE THAT IN THE OPINION OF THE COMMUNITY OUGHT TO BE SEDULOUSLY FOSTERED

This aspect of Wigmore's criteria deals with the value that the community places on the relationship. For example, a bookie and his client would satisfy the first two criteria because their communications would originate in confidence and confidentiality is essential to the relationship. However, the community does not value this relationship above the correct disposal of litigation. The same is true of the relationship between a hit man and his mob boss or a drug addict and his dealer. There are many relationships where confidential communications are essential to a relationship but do not attract any protection from disclosure. Relationships that may attract protection include therapeutic relationships, such as the relationship between a psychotherapist and a patient that has been abused. The court must weigh the benefit to the victim of being able to trust that her innermost thoughts will be protected from exposure, particularly to the abuser. Clearly, the court must weigh the value that the community puts on this relationship and the importance of having information available for the correct disposition of the dispute.

(4) THE INJURY THAT WOULD INURE TO THE RELATION BY THE DISCLOSURE OF THE COMMUNICATIONS MUST BE GREATER THAN THE BENEFIT THEREBY GAINED FOR THE CORRECT DISPOSAL OF LITIGATION

This is the overall balancing criterion. With this, the court must assess whether the damage to the relationship that would result from the release of the information is greater than the benefit that would be gained by having this information available to correctly dispose of the litigation. For example, in *R v. R.J.S.* a father was charged with sexual assault of his stepchild. He agreed to participate in therapy sessions to help the child, and in those sessions accusations of sexual assault were levelled at him. He did not respond to the allegations, through a denial or otherwise. The Crown sought to introduce the allegations and lack of a denial as evidence against the accused, and the accused sought to have the communications designated as privileged. In looking at the therapeutic nature of the communications, the court determined that Wigmore's first three criteria were met. However, the court found that the importance to the correct disposal of the litigation outweighed the potential for injury to the relationship between the father and the therapist.

In the example above, it seems obvious that allowing evidence that will aid in convicting a child abuser outweighs any damage to the relationship between the father and the therapist. However, it is important to consider carefully what is gained and what is lost. It can be extremely important for an abused person to have an opportunity to confront the abuser in a safe and professionally supervised setting. This may be key to the abused person's recovery. If the communications in the therapy sessions are disclosed, the accused person knows that his continued involvement in this forum could be used against him in court and he would not continue to involve himself in this process. Thus, by making such a ruling, the court captures information on one occasion but scares away all future positive involvement of accused persons in the recovery of their victims. This could translate into a net loss when weighed by the court.

RELATIONSHIPS NOT PROTECTED BY CLASS

Most patients mistakenly assume that what they have told their doctor is private and protected from disclosure. Similarly, both priest and penitent often share the view that confessions cannot be disclosed. However, courts have traditionally been reluctant to expand the classes to which privilege attaches because this evidence is usually highly probative and very reliable. Often, it is the best evidence available to the trier of fact. Communications from such relationships may be privileged, but only on a case-by-case basis and if they meet the Wigmore test. Because many relationships enjoy widespread popularity, the courts have struggled with preserving the integrity of some of these relationships while also attempting to ensure that relevant and probative evidence is not excluded without sufficient justification.

1. Relationship Between Doctor and Patient

Doctors, psychiatrists, and psychologists all have strict codes that forbid them from revealing confidential information provided to them by their patients. As far back as the time of Hippocrates and the Hippocratic Oath, doctors were exhorted to keep secret those confidences entrusted to them:

> Whatsoever things I see or hear concerning the life of men, in my attendance on the sick … I will keep silence thereon, counting such things as sacred secrets.

Yet this duty to respect the secrets of the patient is not absolute. It has become increasingly clear that society is prepared to intercede in the relationship between doctor and patient where there is a risk to an identifiable person or group. However, the dilemma facing the physician remains. By breaching client confidentiality where a risk to an identifiable person is revealed, the physician exposes herself to sanctions for professional misconduct if her governing body second-guesses her decision. In addition—and this is one of the more compelling arguments put forth by medical persons—the more often doctor–patient confidentiality is breached, the less likely it will be that sick people will seek help.

The position of the courts with regard to doctor–patient privilege is set out in *Smith v. Jones*, which was discussed earlier in this chapter under the heading "Public Safety Exception." After *Smith*, there can be no doubt that in law the duty to protect outweighs patient confidentiality.

As a result of *Smith*, a psychiatrist must take effective steps to warn an intended victim or the authorities but should only reveal as much information as is necessary to protect the potential victim. In the psychiatrist's assessment, probably the most difficult task is to determine the degree of risk. Psychiatrists have applied a standard of "more likely than not." For example, if a patient who is involved in a billing dispute with the telephone company confides to a psychiatrist that he would like to "blow away some of the telephone repairmen," the psychiatrist will assess whether it is more likely than not that the patient will kill or seriously harm the repairmen. The Canadian Psychiatric Association has expressed concern that it is not possible to treat serious psychiatric disorders if the patient is not free to discuss his problems with his therapist. However, the duty to warn remains, which could have devastating financial repercussions through civil suits against the psychiatrist if her assessment of the patient turns out to be wrong.

Physicians also find themselves in circumstances where their duty of confidentiality to their patients is in conflict with their duty to the public at large. Such is the case where a person with a sexually transmitted disease is not prepared to treat it or avoid unprotected sexual contact. The same criteria that apply to psychiatrists would apply to other physicians in those circumstances.

2. Relationship Between Religious Leader and Adherent

Many Canadians feel very strongly about what Catholics would call the "sanctity of the confessional" or protection from disclosure of communications between an individual and her religious leader or adviser. Yet the law does not treat such communications as privileged in the way that solicitor–client communications are privileged. The law in Canada remains as it was decided in the case of *R v. Gruenke*. Although the case was not unanimously decided, Lamer CJ, writing for the majority, stated (at p. 386):

> [A] prima facie privilege for religious communications would constitute an exception to the general principle that all relevant evidence is admissible. Unless it can be said that the policy reasons to support a class privilege for religious communications are as compelling as the policy reasons which underlay the class privilege for solicitor-client communications, there is no basis for departing from the fundamental "first principle" that all relevant evidence is admissible until proven otherwise.

The argument of the majority that distinguishes solicitor–client communications as more deserving of the application of privilege than religious communications is that this relationship is essential to the functioning of the legal system. It is, of course, a matter of perspective. Judges, first being lawyers, naturally are inclined to see communications between lawyers and clients as having greater importance than any other communications. But a priest, rabbi, or imam were charged with determining which type of communications should receive the highest protection, she would likely say that religious communications trump all others.

Nevertheless, religious communications must meet the Wigmore test on a case-by-case basis. Although some have argued that the disclosure of religious communications infringes an individual's right to protection of his freedom of religion as guaranteed by the Charter, the courts have ruled that disclosure can be justified and is dependent on the particular circumstances that come before the court (see *R v. Gruenke*). The courts have also ruled that the approach must be a "non-denominational" one. The religious leader or adviser need not be ordained and the communications need not be in the context of a formal confession. Thus, in considering the circumstances of the communication, the courts give great deference to the multicultural nature of Canadian society.

3. Relationship Between Complainant and Another Party in Criminal Matters

A matter of considerable controversy of late has been whether privilege should attach to private communications of complainants where an accused person seeks to have them disclosed as part of his defence. The *R v. O'Connor* case brought this simmering issue to a head. Bishop O'Connor was charged with a number of counts of sexual assault that dated back about 30 years. The defence sought production of psychiatric records dealing with the treatment received by the complainants over the intervening period since the alleged assaults. There are two arguments to be made for the defence in this respect. First, the records may shed light on the incidents and support defences available to the accused, such as the defence of consent. Second, where the complainant has been injured and the accused has been found guilty, the records may assist the defence in qualifying the degree of injury caused by the accused, and thus bring a lighter sentence.

In *O'Connor*, the trial judge was satisfied that the records sought by Bishop O'Connor were relevant and ordered them disclosed by the Crown, who had them in her possession. This ruling was appealed through to the Supreme Court of Canada, where the Crown urged the court to consider three criterion for keeping the records private:

1. Societal interest in encouraging the reporting of sexual offences.

2. Societal interest in encouraging complainants to seek out treatment.

3. Impact of the decision on the integrity of the trial process.

In rejecting the criteria, the Supreme Court provided specific guidelines for when such records would be discoverable by the defence, setting out a two-stage process, set out below.

FIRST STAGE

- The accused must establish that the information he seeks is "likely to be relevant" to his defence.

- There is no balancing of interests, just relevancy as a test.

- If this test is met, the information is produced for the judge to review; if the test is not met, the information is not disclosed.

SECOND STAGE

- If the test in the first stage is met, the trial judge reviews the records and determines whether and to what extent the records will be produced.

- The judge must balance the interests of the accused in obtaining a fair trial against the societal and privacy interests of the complainant.

- The reviewing court must consider

  a. the necessity of the records for the accused to defend himself,

  b. the probative value of the records,

  c. the complainant's privacy expectation,

  d. whether production of the record is based on a discriminatory belief or bias, and

  e. the impact on the dignity or right to privacy of the complainant.

In the end, the Supreme Court rejected the appeal and the records were disclosed. The decision caused a considerable backlash as victim's support groups rallied against a determination that would make it more likely that complainants would see their most personal thoughts and confidences made public and made available to their abusers. In reaction to the *O'Connor* case, Parliament enacted ss. 278.1 to 278.91 of the *Criminal Code* in 1997. These sections set out a multi-staged procedure for an accused to seek production of records where there is a privacy interest of another person. The process may include a written application, a subpoena served on the person who holds the record, an in camera hearing, a judge's review of the actual records, and a decision by a judge as to whether any, part, or all of the record should be disclosed. An accused can potentially be stopped even prior to the judge's reviewing the records, should the judge feel that the exercise is akin to a fishing expedition. Under the legislated provisions, the two-stage process is maintained. In fact, the first stage is essentially the same: the accused must convince the trial judge that the information is likely to be relevant. What the legislation does, however, is specifically indicate 11 assertions that are out of bounds to an argument of relevance. These include the three criteria noted above that the Supreme Court of Canada rejected in *O'Connor*. In other words, those three assertions that the Supreme Court of Canada said were not relevant to the issue, Parliament determined to be relevant.

There has since been indication that the courts are not as zealous as Parliament in cutting off opportunities for an accused to establish the relevancy of third-party records. In a few cases that have dealt with the new provisions, the courts have opened the door a crack to give an accused some hope of convincing a trial judge that some relevant evidence likely exists. In a broad interpretation of the 11 assertions, this window of opportunity would be closed off. It is very likely that the limits imposed by the very restrictive application of the criteria will be subject to further litigation and clarification by the Supreme Court of Canada. What must be remembered is that restricting the availability of third-party records from disclosure will mean that in some instances relevant information will not be available to the trier of fact. This increases the likelihood of wrongful convictions—of innocent persons being jailed.

If an accused somehow manages to come up with a novel assertion that is not specifically proscribed by the legislation, he still must overcome the criteria in stage two in order to access the third-party records. Parliament adopted the criteria listed above for the second-stage test in *O'Connor* but they listened to the concerns of victim's groups and included the three criteria specifically excluded by the Supreme Court. By putting these criteria in and substantially tightening up the first-stage test, Parliament has made it much more unlikely that an accused will see or be able to use third-party information in his defence.

4. Other Confidential Relationships

There are many other relationships that could potentially be covered by Wigmore's four criteria and granted privilege. Consider again the relationship between an accountant and his client. If one is skirting the line between tax avoidance and tax evasion, the information communicated to an accountant is definitely intended to be confidential. One tax lawyer has advertised that he may be able to reach an agreement with Canada Revenue Agency on an anonymous basis, to pay tax on undeclared income. This advertisement goes on to mention that both tax consultants and accountants can be forced to disclose information about their clients while a lawyer cannot be required to do so. Is this advertisement accurate or does it mislead the public? The advertisement suggests that communications between accountants and their clients are not privileged. This may not be entirely accurate because privilege is determined on a case-by-case basis in these instances. It is difficult to envision how a court would justify not upholding the claim for privilege by an accountant who is essentially providing the same service as a lawyer.

In other relationships, such as that between a reporter and her source, the courts have not granted privilege. Some reporters have been jailed for contempt of court for refusing to divulge the source of their information during court proceedings. For example, in 2005, *New York Times* reporter Judith Miller was jailed because she refused to identify her confidential source in the case where someone in the Bush administration had leaked the identity of CIA operative Valerie Plame. Although Ms. Miller was not the one to publish the identity of the CIA operative, a grand jury investigating this leak wanted her to testify and identify her source in the administration. Ms. Miller spent 85 days in jail in defence of journalistic freedom and it was not until White House official Lewis "Scooter" Libby confirmed her release of the confidentiality of their communications that she agreed to testify, thus being released from jail. Many other relationships are of the sort where one or more of the parties would like to keep the information confidential. However, if the information becomes relevant, whether the information will stay confidential will depend on the court's interpretation of the criteria outlined by Wigmore.

CHAPTER SUMMARY

In determining whether a communication is privileged, the court first looks at whether the communication arose within a class of protected relationships. If the court finds that the communication does not attract privilege by class, the court applies Wigmore's four criteria to determine whether the communication is protected on a case-by-case basis. If privilege does not attach and the communication is otherwise admissible, the court will allow the evidence. If the communication is privileged, the court will exclude the evidence unless it falls within one of the exceptions to the privilege rule, such as the public safety exception.

KEY TERMS

privilege

privilege by class

privilege by case

public safety exception

solicitor–client privilege

innocence at stake exception

litigation privilege

without prejudice

spousal privilege

judges' privilege

Wigmore test

REFERENCES

A. (L.L.) v. B. (A.) (1995), 130 DLR (4th) 422 (SCC).

Canada Evidence Act, RSC 1985, c. C-5.

Canadian Charter of Rights and Freedoms, part I of the *Constitution Act, 1982*, RSC 1985, app. II, no. 44.

General Accident Assurance Company v. Chrusz (1999), 45 OR (3d) 321.

Griffin, R v. (1853), 6 Cox CC 219.

Gruenke, R v. (1991), 8 CR (4th) 368 (SCC).

Hay, R v. (1860), 175 ER 933.

McClure, R v., [2001] 1 SCR 445.

O'Connor, R v., [1995] 4 SCR 411.

Pritchard v. Ontario (Human Rights Commission), [2004] 1 SCR 809.

R.J.S., R v. (1985), 45 CR (3d) 161 (Ont. CA).

Rules of Civil Procedure, RRO 1990, reg. 194.

Smith v. Jones, [1999] 1 SCR 455.

Tarasoff v. Regents of the University of California, 17 Cal. 3d 425, 551 P. 2d 334, 131 Cal. Rptr. 14 (1976).

REVIEW QUESTIONS

1. Briefly describe Wigmore's four criteria for assessing claims of privilege.

2. What features distinguish spousal privilege from other kinds of privilege?

3. When might a lawyer be required to divulge communications with a client?

4. What are the differences between solicitor–client privilege and litigation privilege?

5. What protections for psychiatric records did the Supreme Court of Canada put in place in the *R v. O'Connor* decision?

DISCUSSION QUESTIONS

1. Discuss public interest immunity including in matters of national security.

2. Brad is charged with threatening to kill his estranged wife, Janet. His lawyer, Frank Fruter, has objected to the admission of the threat on the basis of spousal privilege under the *Canada Evidence Act*. Is this evidence admissible? Why or why not?

3. Jim and Brock are a married same-sex couple. Jim confided in Brock that while honeymooning in Niagara Falls with Brock, he accidentally ran over a pedestrian while driving his SUV. The Crown has subpoenaed Brock, hoping that he has incriminating evidence against Jim. Is Brock's statement admissible? Why or why not?

4. Sir Oswald Osborne, an eccentric English gentleman, has recently been ordained a Catholic priest. During confession, Deborah Boone confides that she once downloaded a song from the Internet and played it backwards to look for hidden messages. Oswald is offended by what he considers theft of protected material and goes to the police. Is the information conveyed by Deborah during the confession privileged? Why or why not?

5. Tommy Chang is charged with the murder of Dennis Yeung. Tommy is having drinks with his lawyer, Edward Nugent, when, in a drunken stupor, he blurts out, "I killed Dennis because he always got the glory." Lori, the bartender (and a number of other patrons), overhears this conversation. Is Lori's evidence as to what she heard admissible? Is Edward's? Why or why not?

6. Patrick Ramos coaches high school hockey. He has forged a reputation as a firm but caring person who can be trusted. It is widely known that he has been a father figure for hundreds of troubled youths and is credited with saving dozens from a life of drug abuse. A star player has turned to Patrick for help with his drug problem and confided that he sold drugs to teammates. Is this evidence admissible? Why or why not?

7. Ed consults lawyer Michael Oliverio. Ed tells Michael that he murdered a young girl. Is this evidence admissible? Why or why not?

8. Ed consults lawyer Michael Oliverio. Ed has a severe speech impediment and writes Michael a note indicating that he murdered a young girl. Is this note admissible? Why or why not?

9. Ed consults lawyer Michael Oliverio. Ed has a severe speech impediment and brings in a page from his diary indicating that he murdered a young girl. Is this page admissible? Why or why not?

10. Ed consults lawyer Michael Oliverio. Ed has a severe speech impediment and brings in a short video showing that he murdered a young girl. Is this video admissible? Why or why not?

PART III

Evidence and the Charter

CHAPTER 11

Self-Incrimination

CHAPTER OBJECTIVES

After completing this chapter you should be able to:

- Understand the scope of the right against self-incrimination.
- Define conscriptive evidence and understand its dangers.
- Define derivative evidence and understand when it is prohibited.
- Understand the dimensions of the right against self-incrimination, including the right to remain silent, the right not to be compelled to be a witness against oneself, the right to testify freely without fear that the testimony will be used in a subsequent proceeding, and the right to be free from oppressive or unfair police questioning.

INTRODUCTION

The **right against self-incrimination** can be generally described as a person's right not to be compelled to be a witness against himself in criminal or quasi-criminal proceedings. When looking at the issue of self-incrimination, we must be mindful of the context within which the right is claimed. In this chapter, we examine a number of questions relating to the issue of self-incrimination. When we speak of the right against self-incrimination, we are talking about a suspect's right to refuse to speak to police investigating a crime. But what if a suspect confesses to committing a crime to the police? What if the confession is made to a teacher or other private citizen? What happens to the right against self-incrimination after a person has been charged with an offence? What happens if the right is breached?

In the past, persons accused of crimes did not always enjoy the right to silence. In fact, an accused person could be subjected to extreme forms of persuasion, including violence or threats of violence, to induce a statement. However, the information that derived from coerced statements was often unreliable. The authorities who were subjecting the accused to coercion obviously believed that the accused committed the offence, and were unlikely to stop if the accused simply professed his innocence. Often, the accused realized this and would confess to end his pain. In fact, the torturers would often write out the confessions for the accused to sign.

right against self-incrimination
a person's right not to be compelled to be a witness against himself in criminal or quasi-criminal proceedings

In such circumstances, accused persons were known to confess to crimes they could not have committed, simply to avoid the brutality being inflicted upon them. Present-day protection against self-incrimination during the investigative stages of a crime derives from those times when authorities were likely to extract a confession from an accused through violence or threats of violence.

A good way to approach the subject of self-incrimination is to first look at the kind of evidence that is at issue—is it something that the accused said or did, or is it something that the authorities were able to locate as a result of information obtained from the accused? The distinction is historically significant because courts have used it in deciding whether to admit evidence or not. The distinction continues to be important because, before a court will even consider applying a remedy, the accused must first establish a connection between the violation of a right and the impugned evidence.

CONSCRIPTIVE EVIDENCE

conscriptive evidence
evidence obtained as a result of the accused's being compelled to participate in the creation or location of evidence

testimonial evidence
evidence provided by a person in the form of words

non-testimonial evidence
evidence that is not in the form of words from a witness; typically an object

Evidence obtained from a suspect or an accused person by the authorities is often referred to as **conscriptive evidence**. There are two types of conscriptive evidence, testimonial and non-testimonial. **Testimonial evidence** is what it sounds like—the words of an accused person introduced in evidence against him. **Non-testimonial evidence** is evidence provided by a person that is not in the form of words. In this case, the person is required by the authorities to provide evidence against himself, but not by words. An example of this is where a person is required to perform sobriety tests or provide a breath sample.

In Canada, the courts have turned away from forced interrogations by authorities as a means of obtaining incriminating evidence because of a number of problems that have been identified with conscriptive evidence. Among those problems are the following:

1. *Conscriptive evidence tends to be unreliable.* Under physical or emotional duress, a person tends to say whatever he thinks the torturer or interrogator wants to hear, regardless of whether it is true.

2. *Conscriptive evidence compels a person to reveal his innermost thoughts.* Freedom of thought is a principle that we have elevated to the highest level. It is one of the fundamental freedoms outlined in s. 2 of the *Canadian Charter of Rights and Freedoms.*

3. *Conscriptive evidence shifts the responsibility to prove a case against an accused from the state to the accused himself.* The presumption of innocence is an important principle that protects individuals from abuse by the more powerful state. An accused can do nothing and still be acquitted where the state does not have sufficient proof. In the past, there have been circumstances where the accusation alone required that individuals take immediate action to prove their innocence, as in the case of an individual accused of saying treasonous things against the king.

The common-law protections against conscriptive evidence before the enactment of the Charter were narrower in some ways than the protections that currently exist.

For example, the protection against self-incrimination applied to the words of a suspect or an accused person, but not to any tangible items that were taken from him or were located as a result of clues contained in the words that were conscripted from him. So, if the police beat a confession out of a suspect who, in the process, told them where he hid the bloody knife, the words would not have been admitted but the knife would. With the advent of the Charter, the courts began to extend the prohibition against conscriptive evidence to non-testimonial evidence such as breath and bodily samples.

The courts have ruled that non-testimonial evidence may be in violation of s. 7 of the Charter, which provides:

> Everyone has the right to life, liberty and security of the person and the right not to be deprived thereof except in accordance with the principles of fundamental justice.

The case of *R v. Stillman* provides an example. *Stillman* concerned the murder of 14-year-old Pamela Bischoff, who was last seen with 17-year-old William Stillman. Her body was found in the Oromocto River in New Brunswick, six days after she disappeared. Stillman arrived home the night she disappeared with a cut above one eye and mud and grass on his pants. Witnesses who saw him said he was cold, shaking, and wet from the upper thighs down. He said that he had been in a fight with "five Indians." Ms. Bischoff had been sexually assaulted: Semen was found in her vagina and a human bite mark was found on her abdomen. Stillman was arrested and taken to the police detachment, where he was met by his lawyers. The police requested hair samples and teeth impressions and said they wished to question Stillman about the murder. The lawyers told the police that Stillman refused to consent to any of the above and gave the following letter to the police:

> This is to confirm that Bryan Whittaker and I are representing the above young person who we understand has been arrested for murder.
>
> This is to confirm that we have advised this young person that he is not to consent to provide any bodily samples whatsoever including hair and or teeth imprints to you or anybody else.

In spite of this, once the lawyers had left, the police took hair and bite samples on threat of violence against Stillman. In reviewing whether the non-testimonial evidence obtained by the police should be admitted against Stillman, the Supreme Court of Canada stated that s. 7 of the Charter would be breached if the search conducted by the authorities

- was without consent or legal authorization, and
- intruded on the person's body in more than a minimal fashion.

What then of a search where the police pluck hairs from a person's head, nostrils, or even pubic area? What if the police wanted to take a blood sample or decide that they want the accused to perform some physical tasks so they can gather some useful measurements? What if the accused has a religious prohibition regarding the letting of blood? Would taking a blood sample still be a minimal intrusion? These are the sorts of questions that courts have to look at in balancing interests, as in the *Stillman* case above. However, courts usually find that such searches violate the Charter and, as more fully discussed in chapter 12, may not permit the Crown to rely on any evidence that is derived from these kinds of searches.

DERIVATIVE EVIDENCE

derivative evidence
evidence that derives from
a breach of an accused's
rights

Derivative evidence is any evidence that derives from a breach of an accused's rights. Recall the example from the previous section where the police beat a confession out of a suspect who tells them where he hid the bloody knife. Clearly, the knife is derivative evidence.

Before the advent of the Charter, the words extracted from a suspect through a breach of his rights might not be admissible but the tangible product of the interrogation—for example, a murder weapon—would be. This evidence was sometimes referred to as "the fruit of the poisoned tree." The Charter prompted the courts to ask: if the tree is poisoned, why should the Crown be permitted to feed that fruit to the trier of fact? In answering this question, the Charter changed the way the fruit was dealt with. If the words were obtained in breach of an individual's right not to be conscripted in gathering evidence against himself, then any product of that breach was also excluded. However, an exception is made in the following situation. If the police would not have located the evidence without having breached the suspect's right to silence, then the evidence is excluded, but if the Crown can show that the evidence would have been discovered regardless of the breach, the evidence may be admitted. The example that is sometimes used is where the police conduct a search warrant on a home, looking for drugs. In this example, the police fail to inform the accused that he has the right not to speak to the police, and he blurts out, "You're probably looking for the cocaine on the kitchen table." Indeed, the police locate the drugs there. At trial, the defence tries to get the cocaine excluded because the accused was not read his rights. But because the search warrant was valid and because the drugs would certainly have been discovered by the police even if the accused had not described their location, the court rules that the accused's statement did not assist the police in wrongfully obtaining evidence. In this situation, it is likely that the cocaine will be admissible on the basis of "inevitable discovery."

Another approach for the police to take in attempting to admit evidence even where there has been a breach of the accused's rights is where there was an independent source for the evidence. Consider the following example. An accused gives a coerced statement telling the police he stashed his cocaine in his neighbour's garage. Meanwhile, the little old lady who lives next door to the accused, and who seldom uses her garage, decides to retrieve some mementoes she has stored there and notices some unusual packages in the corner. She calls the police and they get the message at about the time they are heading out the door with their search warrant for her garage. Because the little old lady was an independent source for the evidence, the evidence may be admitted. In essence, the rule is designed to ensure that if "perfectly good" evidence would have been discovered even without the breach, it is not inadmissible because of a coincidental breach.

THE RIGHT TO SILENCE

Many people find it surprising that the *Canadian Charter of Rights and Freedoms* does not expressly provide the right for an accused to remain silent when dealing with authorities during the investigation of a crime or prior to trial. The Supreme

Court of Canada, in *Rothman v. The Queen*, described the source of the right to silence in the following terms (at 683):

> In Canada the right of a suspect not to say anything to the police is not the result of a right of no self-crimination but is merely the exercise by him of the general right enjoyed in this country by anyone to do whatever one pleases, saying what one pleases or choosing not to say certain things, unless obliged to do otherwise by law.

In other words, the right to silence is really the absence (in most cases) of an obligation to provide any information to the police. We have all seen television shows where the arresting officer informs the arrested person of his rights, including the right to remain silent. This means that an individual does not have any obligation to assist the authorities who are trying to build a case against him.

Section 7 of the Charter has been interpreted as reinforcing the pre-trial right to silence. In *R v. Hebert*, the accused spoke to his lawyer and advised the police that he wished to remain silent. The police placed an undercover officer in the accused's cell and tricked the accused into providing an incriminating statement. The Supreme Court of Canada ruled that this evidence should be excluded because of the interaction of s. 7 of the Charter with the general right to remain silent. The court stated:

> *Charter* provisions related to the right to silence of a detained person under s. 7 suggest that the right must be interpreted in a manner which secures to the detained person the right to make a free and meaningful choice as to whether to speak to the authorities or to remain silent.

The court went on to add:

> In keeping with the approach inaugurated by the *Charter*, our courts must adopt an approach to pre-trial interrogation which emphasizes the right of the detained person to make a meaningful choice and permits the rejection of statements which have been obtained unfairly in circumstances that violate that right of choice.

In spite of this interpretation of s. 7, we still see the use of jailhouse informants as a method of extracting information from an accused person. Generally, the courts have not treated jailhouse informants as police agents and thus have not subjected them to the same restrictions as police officers. Accordingly, the courts have generally allowed statements made to these informants. However, where such informants are essentially "professionals" who use their ability to gain the confidence of a suspect in order to obtain some information that they can trade for a lesser sentence or parole eligibility, the line between them and a police agent blurs. In addition, the use of jailhouse informants has been strongly criticized as being dangerous and unreliable, in various wrongful-conviction reviews including the Sophonow inquiry conducted by Supreme Court of Canada Justice Peter Cory.

The right to silence remains with a person charged with an offence as she goes through the court system. The basic right is found in both the *Canada Evidence Act* and the *Canadian Charter of Rights and Freedoms*. Section 11 of the Charter provides:

> Any person charged with an offence has the right ...
>
> c) not to be compelled to be a witness in proceedings against that person in respect of the offence.

This Charter right applies not just to criminal offences but to all offences, including provincial offences. If either the police or the Crown required the accused to provide information over her objections, this would be grounds for excluding the evidence at a trial.

It should be noted that s. 11 does not prevent an accused person from testifying in her own defence; it only prevents the Crown from calling the accused as a witness. However, once the accused has decided to testify, s. 11 has no further application and the Crown can freely cross-examine the accused. In other words, an accused person cannot testify selectively, providing only information that helps her defence while avoiding harmful details.

The Charter right to silence is reinforced by s. 10, which provides:

> Everyone has the right on arrest or detention …
>
> b) to retain and instruct counsel without delay and to be informed of that right.

This basically ensures that all persons will have access to legal advice if arrested or detained. Even a law student or a properly trained paralegal will have enough legal knowledge to tell an accused that she enjoys a right to silence and suggest that the accused exercise that right.

The Accused's Choice Not to Testify

An accused's right to silence would be meaningless if her choice not to speak to the police could be used against her at trial. If the Crown were permitted to suggest that the accused could have explained her actions to the police but chose not to, the trier of fact might reason, "If she doesn't have anything to hide, why didn't she talk to the police?" To a trier of fact who draws this conclusion, remaining silent would be tantamount to acknowledging guilt.

Because of this potential, a rule has developed that neither the Crown nor the judge can comment on the accused's choice not to testify. This is often referred to as adverse comment on the accused's *failure* to testify. Note, however, that the language contains a bias that testifying is expected. Testifying or not is a tactical choice, usually arrived at through consultation with counsel, not a "failure." Similarly problematic is what appears to be an exception to the "no comment" rule, which is that if there is already enough evidence before the trier of fact to find the accused guilty beyond a reasonable doubt, it is permissible to comment on her choice not to testify. In a case where the jurors are already convinced of the accused's guilt beyond a reasonable doubt, they can be told that the accused had no innocent explanation to counter the Crown's case (*R v. Noble*). This raises several troubling questions. If the jorors already know he is guilty, why consider his choice not to testify in their deliberations? And why would the judge or Crown even think of commenting on the accused's decision not to testify, unless they thought that the evidence did not prove his guilt beyond a reasonable doubt? This sort of circular logic only serves to confuse a relatively simple concept—nobody, Crown, judge, or trier of fact, should consider the accused's choice not to testify for any purpose at all.

The rationale for the exception is that this is what is sometimes referred to in civil matters as the "slip rule": the Appeal Court does not want to throw out an entire trial if, at the very end, someone slips up and mentions "the elephant in the room"—the fact that the accused has not testified. The exception is created to address circumstances where mentioning the lack of testimony would not make any difference to the outcome.

As mentioned above, although an accused person is under no obligation to testify, once a decision has been made that the accused will tell her side of the story to the court, the Crown is free to cross-examine the accused extensively on her evidence. In that respect, anything that the accused does tell the court can be used against her in the same proceeding. The Charter does, however, protect all witnesses from having incriminating evidence used against them in any other proceeding. Section 13 provides:

> A witness who testifies in any proceedings has the right not to have any incriminating evidence so given used to incriminate that witness in any other proceedings, except in a prosecution for perjury or for the giving of contradictory evidence.

Section 13 has two implications. First, the Crown cannot use in the present proceeding any incriminating evidence that was given by the accused in a prior proceeding. Second, an accused can testify freely without having to worry that her testimony will be used against her in a subsequent proceeding. For example, a person who has been charged with murder can freely testify that it was impossible for her to have committed the offence because she was robbing a bank across town at the same time the victim was shot. The Crown would not be permitted to introduce this testimony if the accused was later charged and tried for robbing the bank.

It is now clear that s. 13 applies not only to different offences, but also to the same offence. In *R v. Dubois*, the accused was tried twice for the same murder as a result of a successful appeal of the first trial. The accused had testified at the first trial but not at his second. As part of its case, the Crown used the accused's testimony from the first trial. This evidence was admitted by the trial judge but the Supreme Court of Canada later ruled the evidence inadmissible.

However, the accused is not free to lie to the court without fear of repercussions. There is a stipulation with the s. 13 protection that the witness must tell the truth. Her words can be used against her in a prosecution for perjury or to contradict the witness at a subsequent proceeding. Section 13 states that it does not apply if the accused is facing perjury-related charges as a result of providing false evidence in an earlier proceeding. The accused's prior testimony may be introduced notwithstanding the provisions of s. 13 when the accused is being tried for lying in the previous proceeding.

We have seen that persons accused of crimes have a right to remain silent while being investigated and being tried for a crime. They also have a right not to have their own testimony used against them in subsequent proceedings. However, what if an accused does not stand on her rights and confesses to the police? Does the right against self-incrimination extend in any way to confessions made by the accused?

CONFESSIONS

We have already seen that there are significant dangers associated with admitting conscriptive evidence that is testimonial in nature. Apart from various societal issues that we may have, this evidence can be extremely unreliable if made under physical or emotional threat. Similarly, if the authorities offer promises of favour or offer other inducements, an arrested person may be much more likely to tell the authorities what he believes they want to hear. After all, if the police tell a suspect that they will release him if he simply admits to the crime, there is no real way of knowing whether any confession was made truthfully, or made simply to gain freedom. As a result, the common law developed a rule that essentially deemed a confession to be inadmissible unless the Crown could prove it to be voluntary. In order to be voluntary, the statement had to be free from threats or promises. Statements not made voluntarily can thus be viewed like privileged communications—they are not admissible before the trier of fact. A judge sitting alone may hear a confession to determine whether it was made voluntarily, but once she rules it was made involuntarily, she is then required to "disabuse" her mind of it. If the other evidence falls short of a conviction on its own, the judge would then be required to acquit a person she knew had confessed to the offence he is charged with.

The Confession Rule

confession rule
rule that a statement made to a person in authority is not admissible unless it was made voluntarily

The **confession rule**, also called the *Ibrahim* rule, can be stated in the following terms:

> A statement made by an accused to a person in authority is a confession and is not admissible against the accused unless the Crown proves beyond a reasonable doubt that the confession was made voluntarily.

This rule was first established at common law in the 1914 *Ibrahim* case. *Ibrahim* remained the leading case on the confession rule for three-quarters of a century. In essence, it stated that the Crown was obliged to prove that a statement made to a person in authority was voluntary "in the sense that it has not been obtained from the accused either by fear of prejudice or hope of advantage exercised or held out by a person in authority."

The *Ibrahim* rule has been refined over time and the Charter raised the standard that needed to be met by the state in proving voluntariness. The case of *R v. Oickle* set a new standard for admission of statements from an accused to persons in authority. In *Oickle*, the accused was charged with setting a series of eight fires in the Waterville, Nova Scotia area. He was a volunteer fireman and attended each fire. The police questioned Oickle extensively over a period of about eight hours. He had agreed to take a polygraph test along with four or five other individuals to help the police narrow down suspects. Of note is the finding that the police exaggerated the reliability of the polygraph when informing Oickle that he had failed the test. Over a series of interrogations from a number of officers, Oickle progressively incriminated himself to the point where he took the police on a videotaped tour of the scenes, describing how he set each fire. The police gave him "official warnings" at a number of key points in the interview process and informed him that he could leave at any time, but there was some "unfortunate" use of language implying that "it would be better" for him to confess his involvement in setting these fires and the making of offers of psychiatric help to overcome his pyromania. The Supreme Court of Canada examined the traditional confession rule and whether it continued to be appropriate in the present context. The court felt that the *Ibrahim* rule (which had undergone some modifications at common law) required further modification and clarification and extended the rule to provide a thorough template for assessing the voluntariness of a statement by an accused to a person in authority. The extended rule is known as the ***Oickle* rule**. What underlies the majority reasoning in *Oickle* is the provision that any choice by a suspect to speak to the authorities must be a meaningful one. The *Oickle* rule may be summarized as follows:

1. The rule applies to statements made to persons in authority.

2. The Crown has the obligation to establish beyond a reasonable doubt that any statement to a person in authority is voluntary in the circumstances by showing that the will of the accused has not been overborne by

   a. threats or promises,

   b. oppressive circumstances, or

   c. lack of an operating mind.

3. The Crown has the obligation to establish beyond a reasonable doubt that there has not been any police trickery that *unfairly* takes away the accused's right to silence.

(An abridged version of the case is available on the Emond Montgomery website at www.emp.ca/evidence.)

***Oickle* rule**
rule requiring that the will of the accused has not been overborne by inducements, oppressive circumstances, or lack of an operating mind and that police trickery has not unfairly denied the accused his right to silence

The Test for Voluntariness

The obligation on the Crown to prove, beyond a reasonable doubt, that a statement was made voluntarily has been maintained from the *Ibrahim* approach. This means that the prosecution must show that the confession was made freely without threats or promises to the accused. Before the advent of the Charter, those parts of a confession that were proven to be true could be admitted as evidence even if the confession was made involuntarily. This makes sense if the purpose of the confession rule is only to exclude unreliable evidence. If the evidence was collaterally proven to be reliable, what possible reason can there be for throwing it out of court? There are, of course, other societal reasons for the confession rule. Do we want to sanction police beatings even if an accused confesses the truth? What about the right to remain silent? The Charter has now changed the situation so that involuntary statements are always excluded, whether they are proven to be true or not.

The test for voluntariness is subjective—is the person making the statement voluntarily?—because what would be "oppressive circumstances" to one person would not faze another. For example, a person who is claustrophobic and locked in a tiny interrogation room may do almost anything if she believes that it will get her some more space. Similarly, what would constitute an inducement to a nicotine addict, such as withholding cigarettes until a confession is offered, would not significantly affect a non-smoker. The use of the expression "in the circumstances" assures that the interpretation must be individualized.

What this means is that there cannot be a list of objective factors that can be used to determine voluntariness. In *Oickle*, the Supreme Court of Canada found that "hard and fast rules simply cannot account for the variety of circumstances that vitiate [spoil or invalidate] the voluntariness of a confession." The court recognized that while certain factors such as "imminent threats of torture" will obviously make a confession involuntary, most cases will not be so clear. For example, the use of veiled threats may require close scrutiny, but will not always result in the inadmissibility of a confession. The court also recognized that the police will often offer some inducement to obtain a confession and not every inducement will invalidate a confession. This is only a problem if, after looking at all of the factors, the inducements are strong enough to raise a reasonable doubt about the voluntariness of the confession. One especially important consideration is whether there was a *quid pro quo* offer made. A confession may not be invalidated simply because a cigarette was offered during the interrogation. However, the court may take a dimmer view if the accused was told that he would get a cigarette after telling the police what had occurred.

To ensure that the statement truly is voluntary, the rule requires a "free" operating mind. That is, the accused must know two things: he must know what he is saying, and he must know that it may be used against him. Thus, a suspect who is mentally ill, intoxicated, high on drugs, or hypnotized might not pass the *Oickle* test. Significantly, the court does not need to determine whether the accused made a wise choice in speaking to the authorities or whether the choice was in the accused's best interest, simply whether the accused had the "limited degree of cognitive ability to understand what he or she is saying and to comprehend that the evidence may be used in proceedings against him" (*R v. Whittle*).

Police trickery is not outlawed; indeed, some of the best work that police departments do is by tricking the "bad guys." But such trickery cannot be of the unfair kind. In addition to a sense of fair play, the courts have a vested interest in ensuring that the administration of justice not be sullied by the endorsement of unfair police practices. Police trickery is not acceptable where it violates the right to silence, undermines voluntariness as such, or is so appalling as to shock the community. If a police officer pretended to be a justice of the peace setting bail for an accused, this would be not only an unfair trick, but one that would cast the justice system in a negative light.

Sometimes during a trial, an accused person or his lawyer will admit that a confession was made voluntarily because it may be exculpatory or simply because there may not be any chance of it being excluded. Normally, however, if the prosecution wishes to introduce a confession into evidence, it must prove voluntariness on a voir dire. As you may recall from chapter 1, a voir dire is a trial within a trial to determine the admissibility of a piece of evidence. The evidence on a voir dire does not form part of the case against the accused in the trial. The evidence is used solely to determine whether a confession is admissible. The accused may testify on the voir dire if he wishes, offering his side of the story. However, it is fairly well established in Canada that the Crown can ask the accused whether the confession is true or not because this relates directly to the issue of voluntariness.

Person in Authority

Not all statements are confessions. Only statements made to a person in authority are confessions, and subject to the confession rule. The court system is designed to regulate state action and not individual initiatives. Thus, a private vigilante who acquires evidence of child pornography by coercing a confession would not run afoul of these provisions, although the evidence would still fall within a judge's residual discretion to exclude.

The test for determining whether someone is a **person in authority** is whether the accused reasonably believed that the person was in a position to influence the prosecution against him. Clearly, police officers are persons in authority. But so too are prosecutors, jailers, security guards, fire marshals, and even owners of property that has been stolen. However, an undercover police officer (who is not recognized as such by the accused) is not a person in authority because the accused has no reason to believe that the officer can have any impact in the prosecutorial process.

The accused's belief must not only be honest, but also be reasonable. In other words, the test is partly subjective—what did this person believe?—and partly objective—what would a reasonable person believe? Both parts must be satisfied before someone qualifies as a person in authority.

person in authority
a person in a position to influence the prosecution against an accused

COMPELLABILITY IN "RELATED PROCEEDINGS"

Because the world that we live in is layered and complex, it often occurs that one legal matter influences or interconnects with another. While an accused has a right to remain silent and not testify in a criminal proceeding, what happens where a "related" civil proceeding requires his evidence in order to proceed? This sort of situation arises where one unfortunate circumstance leads to both a criminal process and a civil one, such as where a mine collapse results in a public inquiry as well as criminal negligence charges, or where a death results in a coroner's inquest as well as murder charges. Even something like a securities hearing can arise from facts that also lead to fraud charges. While the jeopardy that a person faces in these civil proceedings can include fines, public humiliation, and loss of vocation, in criminal matters an accused faces imprisonment. It is because of this serious potential consequence that our system of justice ensures that the accused is afforded the greatest possible protection. However, procedures such as public inquiries are often used to try to address causes of tragedies that affect scores of people, so it is equally important that they not be frustrated.

Take the example of the Walkerton inquiry and the criminal charges arising from the same incident. Clearly, the people of Ontario and, to a lesser extent, the people of Canada had a lot at stake in determining what caused seven people to die and 2,300 to become seriously ill. The inquiry commenced and two primary witnesses were Stan Koebel, the manager of the Walkerton Public Utilities Commission, and his brother Frank, who was a foreman during the relevant time. During the inquiry, the police were in the process of an investigation that could and in fact did result in charges against the brothers. In April 2003, both were charged with endangering the public and various forgery and breach of trust offences. The brothers would have been well advised to be concerned that the information that they provided to the inquiry would aid the investigators in their job of determining whether any criminal acts led to the disaster. Of course, s. 13 of the Charter ensured that their words in the Walkerton inquiry could not used in evidence against them in a criminal proceeding. However, even though the actual words could not be used, they would be helpful to police investigators.

What determines whether a person can decline to participate in a civil proceeding on the basis that criminal charges are pending? In order to balance an accused's right to silence with the protection of the public and administration of the overall justice system, the courts apply the following principles in determining whether an accused or suspect may be compelled to testify in related civil proceedings.

1. The judge must determine the purpose of the civil proceeding.

2. If the sole purpose is to obtain information from a suspect or accused to aid in prosecuting him, the subpoena for the civil matter will be quashed.

3. If the purpose includes resolution of a legitimate public interest concern, then, unless the predominant purpose is to conscript the accused's testimony against him, the suspect or accused will be required to testify.

Balancing the right of an accused to remain silent and the importance of the inquiry to the state can be difficult. If the state were to call a public inquiry into the increase in marijuana grow operations and call as a witness someone the police suspect of being a kingpin in the drug trade, the right of the accused might well outweigh the interests of society, particularly were there are less intrusive means of obtaining information on grow ops. When considering the administration of justice, if the police were to routinely use a public inquiry process to aid their investigations of suspected criminals whom they could not catch through conventional investigative means, then the public's perception of the administration of justice and respect for public inquiries would diminish, causing damage to this legal process.

CHAPTER SUMMARY

The right against self-incrimination is broad and protects a person during the investigative stage right through to trial. It includes the right to remain silent, the right not to be compelled to be a witness against oneself, the right to testify freely without having to worry about authorities using the testimony in a subsequent proceeding, and the right to be free from oppressive or unfair police questioning. The courts are willing to grant relief when a person's rights have been violated to obtain conscriptive evidence or derivative evidence.

KEY TERMS

right against self-incrimination

conscriptive evidence

testimonial evidence

non-testimonial evidence

derivative evidence

confession rule

Oickle rule

person in authority

REFERENCES

Canada Evidence Act, RSC 1985, c. C-5.

Canadian Charter of Rights and Freedoms, part I of the *Constitution Act, 1982*, RSC 1985, app. II, no. 44.

Dubois, R v., [1985] 2 SCR 350.

Hebert, R v., [1990] 2 SCR 151.

Ibrahim, The King v., [1914] AC 599 (PC).

Noble, R v., [1997] 1 SCR 874.

Oickle, R v. (2000), 147 CCC (3d) 321 (SCC).

Rothman v. The Queen, [1981] 1 SCR 640.

Stillman, R v. (1997), 5 CR (5th) 1 (SCC).

Thomas Sophonow Inquiry Report. Final report released November 4, 2001. Available online at http://www.gov.mb.ca/justice/publications/sophonow.

Whittle, R v., [1994] 2 SCR 914.

REVIEW QUESTIONS

1. What is conscriptive evidence?

2. What is derivative evidence?

3. Summarize the Supreme Court of Canada's extension of the confession rule.

4. How is an individual's "right to silence" protected in Canada?

5. What three principles do the courts consider in deciding whether to compel a suspect or an accused to testify in a related civil proceeding such as a public inquiry?

DISCUSSION QUESTIONS

1. Patrick MacNamara teaches at a local high school and coaches the school hockey team. He suspects that certain members of his team are smoking marijuana. Patrick calls them into his office individually for a "friendly chat." All of the players initially deny drug use but Patrick assures them that it is in their best interests to "come clean" and further states that if he finds out that any of his players lied to him, he will kick them off the team. The team captain readily admits to using drugs as well as providing drugs to some of his teammates. Patrick goes to the police with this information and the player is charged with both possession and trafficking offences. Is the statement made by the player a confession? Is it admissible? Why?

2. The police go door to door after a six-year-old girl is brutally assaulted and murdered. They ask all males who live within two blocks of the girl's home for samples of their DNA. Most comply but several refuse. The police subsequently follow those who refused, hoping to find some evidence linking them to the deceased. The police remove a pop can from the trash after it is discarded by one of the suspects and recover a sample of the suspect's DNA. The police match the suspect's DNA with samples found on the body of the girl. Is the evidence admissible? Why? Do you think that the police have a right to ask all adult males in a certain geographical area to provide samples of their DNA? Is this any different from maintaining a DNA data bank of the entire population, as England's Prime Minister Tony Blair proposed in 2006?

3. A police officer investigates a minor traffic accident and asks both drivers to provide the usual documentation and their version of events. One complies but the other refuses to provide any information, including his driver's licence and evidence of insurance, claiming a "right to silence." Do you think that the second driver was justified in his actions? Why?

4. Ravi Singh is a former police officer. As a cop, he was as tough as they come. He is being questioned about $5 million in drug money that has disappeared from the police station. The investigating officers tell Ravi that they have a video of him removing the money. No such video exists. They also tell him that they are sick of bad cops and will put him in a holding cell with other criminals unless he talks. Police officers are known to have short life spans when placed in the general population. Ravi, however, has no fear of being put in a holding cell and relishes the opportunity to knock a few heads. However, he decides that there is ample evidence to convict him based on the video so he admits to taking the counterfeit money. Is Ravi's statement a confession? Is it admissible? Why?

CHAPTER 12

Wrongfully Obtained Evidence

CHAPTER OBJECTIVES

After completing this chapter you should be able to:

- Understand when a right under the *Canadian Charter of Rights and Freedoms* may be limited.

- Identify the two criteria set out in the *Oakes* test that must be met before a Charter right can be limited.

- Describe the remedies a court may prescribe when evidence is obtained through a breach of a person's Charter rights.

- Understand the five components of an exclusionary remedy.

INTRODUCTION

Wrongfully obtained evidence is often referred to as "improperly obtained evidence." The authors have chosen to use the word "wrongfully" because it has a stronger connotation than "improperly." This is another area of evidence law where the principle that all valuable evidence should be put before the trier of fact may give way to another, more important principle—that the courts cannot be seen to support illegitimate methods of acquiring evidence. The court must balance the interests of putting all relevant evidence before the trier of fact against the importance of preserving individual rights and the reputation of the justice system.

The fact that evidence was obtained through illegitimate avenues does not mean that the evidence is less trustworthy; indeed, evidence that has been wrongfully acquired may, in many respects, be more reliable. For example, if the police break into a private home or a dwelling to surreptitiously place a listening device, the occupants, having no fear of repercussion, will likely speak openly and honestly. Similarly, the police would likely put a large dent into the marijuana grow op industry if they were permitted to search all private dwellings on mere suspicion. The problem is that illegally obtained evidence infringes the rights of individuals and harms the reputation of the justice system.

Before the *Canadian Charter of Rights and Freedoms* existed, individuals had little recourse when the police obtained evidence against them through illegitimate means. The prevalent view in the court system was that it was appropriate to "set a thief to catch a thief." In other words, the courts believed that individuals who resorted to criminal means should have no expectation that the state would treat them in anything but a like manner. Evidence that was illegally obtained was not usually excluded and the police were not usually disciplined. However, it was always open to a judge to exclude evidence on the basis that to admit it would undermine the public's faith in the justice system. But judges seldom did, choosing instead to save this remedy for the most extreme abuses.

OVERVIEW OF THE CHARTER

The Charter sets out a number of legal rights. Some Charter rights serve to confirm and reinforce existing common-law rights but others are entirely new. The rights and freedoms contained in the Charter, however, are not absolute. Section 33 permits governments in Canada to expressly declare any statute valid, notwithstanding the guarantees contained in s. 2 and ss. 7 to 15 of the Charter. By invoking the notwithstanding clause, the government can trump the rights set out in these sections of the Charter.

Another important factor to keep in mind is that, by virtue of s. 32, the Charter only applies to interactions between governments in Canada and an individual. That is, the Charter does not apply to interactions between individuals and foreign governments. A case that dealt with this issue was *R v. Harrer*. In that case, the accused's boyfriend escaped custody in Vancouver, BC while in the process of being extradited for trial in the United States on drug charges. The accused was detained by US immigration authorities after they learned that she was staying with her mother in Cleveland. Immigration authorities turned her over to US Marshals officers, who questioned her about her boyfriend. During that interrogation, the officers changed their focus from the boyfriend to possible criminal activity by her in Canada. They did not re-warn her of her rights, as would be required under Canadian law, when the focus of their investigation shifted to her activities. The question before the Supreme Court of Canada was whether the subsequent statements made by her were admissible in her trial in Canada, in light of the fact that the actions of the US authorities would have breached her Charter rights if they had taken place in Canada. The court found that Canadian authorities have no right to control the US investigative process and the US authorities were not acting as agents of the Canadian authorities. In his analysis, La Forest J, writing for the majority, stated (at para. 12):

> What I think is determinative against the argument that the *Charter* applied to the interrogation in the present case is the simple fact that the United States immigration officials and the Marshals were not acting on behalf of any of the governments of Canada, the provinces or the territories, the state actors to which, by virtue of s. 32(1) the application of the *Charter* is confined .... It follows that the *Charter* simply has no direct application to the interrogations in the United States because the governments mentioned in s. 32(1) were not implicated in these activities. The United States authorities involved in the present case can in

no way be considered as acting on behalf of those governments, and this was not really contested at the hearing.

Although this chapter deals mainly with the interaction between the Charter and evidence that has been wrongfully obtained, it is noteworthy that the Charter can have other implications to the law of evidence. Section 52(1) of the *Constitution Act, 1982* can be used to strike down or modify laws that are inconsistent with the provisions of the Charter. Section 52(1) provides:

> The Constitution of Canada is the supreme law of Canada, and any law that is inconsistent with the provisions of the Constitution is, to the extent of the inconsistency, of no force or effect.

Because the Charter is part of the constitution, any law that violates or infringes a Charter right is, to the extent of the inconsistency, of no force or effect. The courts have taken a very broad approach to s. 52(1); not only will the offending parts of any law be removed, but in appropriate cases, courts may, in effect, amend the impugned law by **reading into** or adding provisions that would make the law consistent with the provisions of the Charter. Clearly, this can have implications in evidence law. Any law that offends a Charter right is open to a Charter challenge. For example, the statutory provisions dealing with spousal privilege require spouses to be married to each other in order for their communications to be privileged. This law discriminates against common-law spouses on the basis of their marital status and may be contrary to the equality provisions of s. 15 of the Charter. As a result, it is possible that a future court will extend this form of privilege to unmarried common-law spouses.

However, as mentioned above, the rights and freedoms set out in the Charter are not absolute. The drafters of the Charter recognized that in a democracy a friction exists between the rights of the individual and the will of the majority, and attempted to balance these competing interests by including s. 1, which provides:

> The *Canadian Charter of Rights and Freedoms* guarantees the rights and freedoms set out in it subject only to such reasonable limits prescribed by law as can be demonstrably justified in a free and democratic society.

This provision does two things: it guarantees the rights that follow it and, at the same time, it sets out certain limitations on those rights. What this means is that s. 1 permits governments to enact legislation that infringes a Charter right where the criteria of s. 1 are met.

Once the courts establish that a Charter right has been infringed, the onus shifts to the state to justify the law on a balance of probabilities. As a threshold consideration, the limit must be prescribed by law. In *R v. Therens*, the Supreme Court of Canada found that the prosecution could not rely on the provisions of s. 1 to remedy a breach of the accused's s. 10(b) right to retain and instruct counsel because the limit on the accused's right to consult counsel was imposed by the conduct of the police officers and not by Parliament.

The Supreme Court of Canada in *R v. Oakes* found that two criteria must be satisfied before s. 1 can apply. This is known as the ***Oakes* test**. First, the objective of the measures limiting the Charter right must be "of sufficient importance to warrant overriding a constitutionally protected right or freedom." Second, the means chosen must be reasonable and demonstrably justified. This second criterion

read into
a court's adding of language into legislation in order to make it comply with Charter provisions

***Oakes* test**
test used by the courts to determine whether a Charter right or freedom can be limited by s. 1; the measure limiting the right or freedom must be sufficiently important and the means chosen must be reasonable and demonstrably justified

involves a "proportionality test," which consists of three parts. The first part requires that the measures limiting the Charter right be rationally connected to the objective in question. They must not be arbitrary, unfair, or based on irrational considerations. The second part examines to what degree the measures impair the Charter right. The measures should impair "as little as possible" the right or freedom in question. The third part compares the effects of the measures and their objective. There must be a proportionality between the effects of the measures that are responsible for limiting the Charter right or freedom, and the objective that has been identified as being of "sufficient importance." What this means is that the more severe the effects of a measure, the more important the objective must be if the measure is to be saved by s. 1.

THE OAKES TEST

1. Sufficient Importance
The Crown must show that the objective of the statute is sufficiently important to override a Charter right.

2. Proportionality Test

a. Rational Connection
The measures limiting the Charter right must be rationally connected to the objective sought.

b. Minimal Impairment
The measures must impair the Charter right as little as possible.

c. Proportionality
There must be a proportionality between the effects of the measures limiting the Charter right and the objective referred to in the threshold requirement.

The Charter contains a number of basic rights that everyone enjoys, and state interference with many of these rights has direct evidentiary implications. We have already looked at some of the rights enshrined in the Charter when we dealt with self-incrimination in chapter 11. We saw that the Supreme Court of Canada has interpreted the s. 7 right to life, liberty, and security of the person as including a general right to silence (*R v. Hebert*) as well as offering protection from non-testimonial conscription (*R v. Stillman*). Other rights that we looked at were the right under s. 11(c) not to be compelled to be a witness against oneself, the right under s. 10(b) to retain and instruct counsel and to be advised of that right, and the right under s. 13 not to have incriminating evidence given in one proceeding used against the person in another proceeding.

There are several provisions of the Charter that we have not yet discussed that significantly affect how evidence is gathered and presented in court. These are discussed in the sections below.

BREACH OF A CHARTER RIGHT

Unreasonable Search or Seizure

Section 8 of the Charter expressly protects individuals against unreasonable search or seizure, as follows:

> Everyone has the right to be secure against unreasonable search or seizure.

Any protection against unreasonable searches by the state must balance the competing interests of a person's right to privacy against the state's interest in crime prevention. Otherwise, we would have a rule that either outlawed all searches or permitted all searches. In order to reconcile these competing interests, the courts have adopted the concept of a reasonable expectation of privacy. It is only where there is a reasonable expectation of privacy that a search must be conducted in a reasonable manner. In other words, s. 8 of the Charter does not apply to those situations where there is no reasonable expectation of privacy. For example, a person who openly consumes alcohol in a car or walks down the street waving a gun cannot have any reasonable expectation of privacy. In fact, the converse is true: that person can be expected to be apprehended by the authorities because of the public manner in which he displayed his actions. On the other hand, a person who consumes marijuana at home may be breaking the law, but is doing so privately and has a reasonable expectation of privacy.

The Supreme Court of Canada, quoting from Abella JA in her dissent in *R v. Edwards*, summarized the principles applicable to s. 8 in *R v. Belnavis* as follows:

> [1] As a general rule, two distinct inquiries must be made in relation to s. 8. First, has the accused a reasonable expectation of privacy. Second, if he has such an expectation, was the search by the police conducted reasonably.
>
> [2] A reasonable expectation of privacy is to be determined on the basis of the totality of the circumstances.
>
> [3] The factors to be considered in assessing the totality of the circumstances may include, but are not restricted to, the following:
>
> > [a] presence at the time of the search;
> >
> > [b] possession or control of the property or place searched;
> >
> > [c] ownership of the property or place;
> >
> > [d] historical use of the property or item;
> >
> > [e] the ability to regulate access, including the right to admit or exclude others from the place;
> >
> > [f] the existence of a subjective expectation of privacy; and
> >
> > [g] the objective reasonableness of the expectation.
>
> [4] If an accused person establishes a reasonable expectation of privacy, the inquiry must proceed to the second stage to determine whether the search was conducted in a reasonable manner.

We see that the Supreme Court is vague when assessing the circumstances where a reasonable expectation of privacy arises. This is because there really is no way to predetermine the circumstances where such an expectation exists. Ownership and possession, while important, are not the sole considerations. For example, just because a person happens to own and be in possession of a car does not mean that he has a reasonable expectation of privacy if a gun is openly displayed on the dash. Courts refer to this as the **plain view doctrine**. On the other hand, a person may reasonably expect privacy if he places something in the trunk.

The **reasonable expectation of privacy test** as set out in *Belnavis* contains both a subjective and an objective element. The question the court must ask is whether the accused had an actual expectation of privacy that was reasonably held. So, even if a suspect expected to be free from intrusion by the state, s. 8 would not apply if that expectation was unreasonably held. For example, in *R v. Lauda*, a trespasser growing marijuana in a private field was found to have no reasonable expectation of privacy even though the accused may have been actively avoiding detection.

Once it has been determined that there is a reasonable expectation of privacy, the inquiry then focuses on whether the search was reasonable. The first point to recognize is that s. 8 of the Charter places a limit on state powers to conduct searches or to seize evidence of a crime. It does not confer any additional powers on the state to conduct "reasonable" searches. The Supreme Court of Canada held in *Hunter v. Southam Inc.* that the purpose of s. 8 is to prevent unreasonable searches from happening, rather than to determine after the fact whether a search should have been conducted in the first instance. This can only be achieved by a system of "prior authorization" rather than "subsequent validation." The court went on to say that there is a presumption that all searches conducted without the express authority of a search warrant are presumed unreasonable.

This does not mean that the police must always have a search warrant for a search to be reasonable. There are strict technical and procedural requirements for obtaining a search warrant. An officer must usually first appear before a justice and swear a legal document called an information. The justice must be satisfied that there are reasonable and probable grounds to believe that there is physical evidence related to an offence at the place to be searched before issuing a search warrant. As a practical matter, it is simply not possible for the police to obtain a search warrant every time they wish to conduct a search for evidence. For example, suppose the police have good reason to believe that a suspect has narcotics in his car. By the time the officer has prepared the necessary documentation and obtained a search warrant from a justice, there is a real risk of the vehicle and evidence disappearing, especially if the suspect knows that the police are interested in what is in the trunk or under the seat.

The *Criminal Code* authorizes searches without a warrant in exigent or urgent circumstances where it is either impossible or impractical to obtain a search warrant. So, if the police are chasing a suspect with a gun or some other piece of evidence, they would be permitted to follow the fleeing suspect into a house because there is simply not enough time to obtain a search warrant.

The common law also permits the police to conduct a search without a warrant in those circumstances where the search is incidental to the arrest of a suspect. What this means is that if the police have arrested a person, they are permitted to search the suspect for weapons or for evidence.

The Supreme Court of Canada refined the law as set out in the *Hunter* decision in *R v. Collins*. In that case, the court stated that although a person accused of a crime has the burden to demonstrate that his Charter rights have been violated, once it is shown that a search was conducted without benefit of a warrant, the onus shifts to the Crown to show that the search was, on a balance of probabilities, reasonable. According to the ***Collins* test**, a search is reasonable if

1. it is authorized by law (either common law or statute),

2. the law that authorizes the search is itself reasonable, and

3. the search is conducted in a reasonable manner.

As a result of the second and third parts of the *Collins* test, even searches authorized by law must be reasonable and conducted in a reasonable manner. What is reasonable depends largely on the circumstances. The standard of reasonableness varies depending on the facts in any given situation. One factor that a court considers is the nature of the charge—is it criminal or regulatory? For regulatory offences, which do not carry criminal sanctions, the court usually applies a less rigorous standard than that used for criminal charges. Some other factors are whether it was necessary to infringe on the accused's privacy and whether other, less intrusive, alternatives existed. Thus, a border search may be reasonable but the same search conducted four hours later on a motor vehicle stopped at a service station may be unreasonable. Bodily searches that use more force than required would also be unreasonable since there are less intrusive searching methods available.

Arbitrary Detention or Imprisonment

Section 9 offers broad protection from arbitrary detention or imprisonment. Section 9 provides:

> Everyone has the right not to be arbitrarily detained or imprisoned.

We all know that imprisonment means taking a person's liberty away by putting them in jail. The meaning of detention is not as clear but acts that fall short of imprisonment can qualify as a detention. The courts have interpreted "detention" in both ss. 9 and 10 as meaning a restraint of liberty. Obviously, a physical act of restraint would qualify as a detention, but so too would control over the movement of a person by a police officer by demand or direction.

Not all detentions or arrests result in a breach of s. 9 of the Charter. Otherwise, the police would not be able to detain or arrest any suspect. In order for a detention or arrest to offend s. 9, it must be arbitrary. The courts have found that a detention is arbitrary if is "capricious, despotic or unjustified." Clearly, an arrest or detention under the authority of a warrant or summons is not arbitrary. Similarly, the police may arrest without a warrant anyone found committing an offence or, in some situations, a person whom the officer has reasonable grounds to believe has committed or will commit an indictable offence. The police also have the power to detain suspects in the course of an investigation to determine whether the person is involved in a criminal activity, provided that there is "articulable cause" for the detention. Articulable cause means that there must be objective facts sufficient to provide the officer with reasonable cause to suspect that the person has done something criminal. Officers have to be able to articulate an objective basis for detaining an accused. A mere hunch is not sufficient.

In assessing whether a detention is arbitrary it is sometimes helpful, although not necessarily determinative, to look at whether the detention was authorized by law. In *Brown v. Durham Regional Police Force*, an Ontario police force set up checkpoints to stop all members of a motorcycle gang travelling to a weekend retreat, believing that the club was involved in illegal activities. The Ontario Court of

Appeal found that the stops were lawful under certain provisions of the *Highway Traffic Act* that gave police broad powers to stop motor vehicles. The court went on to examine whether the stops were arbitrary. In finding that the stops were not arbitrary, the court looked at the purpose of the stops (at para. 31):

> In addition to ensuring that the driver is properly licensed, the police may wish to identify the driver for other purposes. It may be, as in this case, that the police are interested in knowing the identity of all those who are connected with what they believe to be organized criminal activity. The gathering of police intelligence is well within the ongoing police duty to investigate criminal activity. As long as the additional police purpose is not improper and does not entail an infringement on the liberty or security of the detained person beyond that contemplated by the purpose animating s. 216(1) of the *HTA*, I see no reason for declaring that a legitimate police interest beyond highway safety concerns should taint the lawfulness of the stop and detention.

The court later added (at para. 34):

> If, however, one of the purposes motivating a stop and detention is improper, then in my view the stop is unlawful even if highway safety concerns also factor into the decision to make the stop and detention.

In this particular case, the court found that the stops were justified on the basis of valid highway safety concerns, maintenance of the public peace, investigation of other criminal activity, and intelligence gathering, and concluded that the stops were not arbitrary. The court did state, however (at para. 39):

> Officers who stop persons intending to conduct unauthorized searches, or who select persons to be stopped based on their sex or colour, or who stop someone to vent their personal animosity toward that person, all act for an improper purpose. They cannot rely on s. 216(1) of the *HTA* even if they also have highway safety concerns when making the stop.

The key point is that the police had valid reasons for stopping members of the motorcycle gang. On the other hand, stopping motorists entirely at random under statutory authority will result in an arbitrary detention. The Supreme Court of Canada dealt with this issue in *R v. Hufsky* (at para. 13):

> Although authorized by statute and carried out for lawful purposes, the random stop for the purposes of the spot check procedure nevertheless resulted, in my opinion, in an arbitrary detention because there were no criteria for the selection of the drivers to be stopped and subjected to the spot check procedure. The selection was in the absolute discretion of the police officer. A discretion is arbitrary if there are no criteria, express or implied, which govern its exercise. The appellant was therefore arbitrarily detained, within the meaning of s. 9 of the *Charter*.

REMEDIES FOR BREACH OF A CHARTER RIGHT

The next issue to look at is what happens once it has been established that there has been a breach of a person's rights by the police. There must be some mechanism to give effect to Charter rights. In other words, there must be a remedy available to anyone whose rights have been infringed. Section 24 of the Charter provides:

> 24(1) Anyone whose rights or freedoms, as guaranteed by this Charter, have been infringed or denied may apply to a court of competent jurisdiction to obtain such remedy as the court considers appropriate and just in the circumstances.
>
> (2) Where, in proceedings under subsection (1), a court concludes that evidence was obtained in a manner that infringed or denied any rights or freedoms guaranteed by this Charter, the evidence shall be excluded if it is established that, having regard to all the circumstances, the admission of it in the proceedings would bring the administration of justice into disrepute.

The first thing to note about s. 24 is that s. 24(1) provides a remedy that is "appropriate and just" to anyone whose rights or freedoms, as guaranteed by the Charter, have been infringed or denied, while s. 24(2) provides a remedy where evidence was obtained in a manner that infringed or denied any rights or freedoms guaranteed by the Charter. Clearly, there are two separate remedies contained in s. 24, a general remedy under s. 24(1) and a remedy for evidence that was obtained in a manner that infringed on a person's rights.

Section 24(1) provides a broad remedy of what is "appropriate and just" in the circumstances. Although "appropriate and just" remedies might include damages and injunctions, the usual remedy in a criminal or quasi-criminal context is a stay of proceedings, where the accused is not acquitted but where the Crown is prevented from continuing the tainted prosecution. This may be an appropriate remedy where there has been a breach of an accused's right to be tried within a reasonable period of time pursuant to s. 11(b) (see *R v. Askov*) or where the Crown has failed to provide complete disclosure to the accused (see *R v. Stinchcombe*).

The words "appropriate and just" provide a wide range of other possible remedies. Clearly, there can be no exhaustive list and the possibility exists for novel approaches in appropriate cases. For example, s. 24(1) has been used to return property seized in violation of s. 8 of the Charter to the lawful owner (*Lagiorgia v. Canada*).

Although s. 24(1) of the Charter is best known in a criminal context, this section has been applied extensively in a civil context to provide civil relief where an individual's Charter rights have been breached. For example, in *Eldridge v. BC*, the applicant was successful in obtaining a declaration that the government must provide public funding for medical interpreters. In *Little Sisters v. Canada*, the Supreme Court of Canada determined that customs officers had breached the store's freedom of expression and equality rights through their seizures of materials destined for the store. Although the court declined to provide injunctive relief, it did note that there was a place for carefully structured relief in the right circumstances. So, from a civil-law perspective, s. 24(1) relief will usually be in the form of an injunction or declaration, which might provide a limited period of time for the government to rectify the offending practice or legislation before it would be deemed invalid.

The primary Charter provisions with regard to wrongfully obtained evidence are contained in s. 24(2). When the provisions of s. 24 are combined with Charter protections such as s. 7 (life, liberty, and security of the person), s. 8 (unreasonable search or seizure), s. 9 (arbitrary detention or imprisonment), s. 10 (rights on arrest or detention) and s. 12 (cruel and unusual treatment or punishment), any evidence that is obtained in breach of those rights is subject to exclusion by the court.

Section 24(2) of the Charter provides the exclusionary remedy that allows the court to take away the fruits of the authorities' wrongful acts. Thus, it removes the incentive for committing those wrongful acts and discourages the police from conducting themselves in this manner. So, if the courts rule that strip searching a person in public is contrary to the individual's rights to be secure from unreasonable search or seizure and they exclude the cocaine found in the attendant body cavity search, the police will very quickly stop that practice and conduct such searches in private. The process of excluding evidence is not so much punitive as an attempt to reform substandard practices and educate or retrain law enforcement personnel regarding the proper Charter standard that applies to their dealings with the public.

The courts have identified a number of purposes for excluding evidence that is wrongfully obtained. These include:

- to restore the parties to the position they were in before the Charter breach;

- to stop the police from engaging in an improper practice;

- to educate the police and the public;

- to ensure that the courts continue to be held in high regard; and

- to recognize and protect a core group of basic human rights.

The question whether s. 24(2) is the only available remedy for excluding evidence was first dealt with by the Supreme Court of Canada in *R v. Therens*. In that case, Le Dain J, who dissented in the result, made the following comments, which the majority of the court appeared to approve (at para. 64):

> I am satisfied from the words of s. 24 that s. 24(2) was intended to be the sole basis for the exclusion of evidence because of an infringement or a denial of a right or freedom guaranteed by the *Charter*. It is clear, in my opinion, that in making explicit provision for the remedy of exclusion of evidence in s. 24(2), following the general terms of s. 24(1), the framers of the *Charter* intended that this particular remedy should be governed entirely by the terms of s. 24(2).

The first indication from the Supreme Court of Canada that evidence may also be excluded under s. 24(1) came in *R v. Harrer*, where McLachlin J stated for the minority (at para. 42) that although evidence obtained in breach of the Charter may only be excluded under s. 24(2),

> [e]vidence not obtained in breach of the *Charter* but the admission of which may undermine the right to a fair trial may be excluded under s. 24(1), which provides for "such remedy as the court considers appropriate and just in the circumstances" for *Charter* breaches.

The law is now clear that s. 24(1) can be used to exclude evidence in certain circumstances. The Supreme Court of Canada held in *R v. White* that s. 24(1) "may serve as the mechanism for the exclusion of evidence whose admission at trial would violate the *Charter*" (at para. 88). In that case, the issue was whether the admission of a statement would contravene the principle against self-incrimination. The court found that s. 24(1) "may appropriately be employed as a discrete source of a court's power" to exclude evidence whose admission would render a trial unfair. The key point is that s. 24(1) would only apply when the admission of evidence creates a breach of the Charter or an unfair trial, not where the evidence has been obtained in a manner that has violated a Charter right. In the latter case, s. 24(2) would apply.

The Requirements for an Exclusionary Remedy

It is clear from the wording of the Charter that there is a relationship between the exclusionary remedy contained in s. 24(2) and the wording of s. 24(1). Before there is even a consideration of whether or not the evidence should be excluded, there has to be a "proceeding" under s. 24(1) to determine whether there in fact has been an infringement of an individual's right or freedom. For this reason, it is not possible to ignore the provisions of s. 24(1) when looking at the exclusionary remedy under s. 24(2).

The components of the exclusionary remedy are therefore as follows:

1. Anyone

2. Whose rights or freedoms, as guaranteed by this Charter, have been infringed or denied

3. May apply to a court of competent jurisdiction ... .

4. Where, in proceedings under subsection (1), a court concludes that evidence was obtained in a manner that infringed or denied any rights or freedoms guaranteed by this Charter,

5. The evidence shall be excluded if it is established that, having regard to all the circumstances, the admission of it in the proceedings would bring the administration of justice into disrepute.

The individual components of the remedy are discussed below.

1. Anyone

   It is the person whose rights or freedoms have been infringed who has a remedy.

It is only the individual who has been subjected to an infringement of his rights that has a remedy. So, if the police enter your friend's home without a warrant (which they are required to obtain in searching a "dwelling house") and they find you in possession of cocaine, you have no remedy under the Charter to have the cocaine excluded as a result of the warrantless search. However, your friend would have such a remedy if he were charged. At trial, your friend, who was trafficking in cocaine and from whom the police seized three kilograms of cocaine, might go free because the evidence against him could be excluded under s. 24 of the Charter while you are convicted of possession of cocaine for having the poor judgment to be caught in the apartment when the unlawful raid happened.

It should be noted that the word "anyone" sets out a remedy for all individuals, whether natural persons or artificial persons such as corporations. Accordingly, a corporation charged with an offence would have the same Charter protection as any natural person.

In the civil-law context, the courts have determined that an estate cannot pursue Charter remedies for a breach of the deceased's rights (*Stinson Estate v. British Columbia*), and a union cannot rely on the Charter where members' rights have been breached. Only the member can do so on her own behalf (*CLAC v. BC Transportation Financing Authority*).

> 2. Whose rights or freedoms, as guaranteed by this Charter, have been infringed or denied
>
> A *Charter right* must have been breached by the authorities in dealing with an accused.

In considering an exclusionary remedy, the court must determine whether a Charter right has been breached. Note that not all poor behaviour on the part of the authorities constitutes a Charter breach. For example, if an accused complains, "The officers were very impolite to me and made me feel like a criminal when they stopped me for impaired driving," he would not have a remedy, barring some more scandalous behaviour by the police.

This is the part of the analysis where the court considers the Charter rights that we dealt with earlier in this chapter—for example, the right to be secure against unreasonable search or seizure and the right not to be arbitrarily detained. The court reviews the conduct of the police to determine whether any of the accused's Charter rights have been breached, what the impact of the breach was, and what would be the appropriate remedy.

Of some interest is the fact that the Supreme Court has determined that, in spite of the retrospective language in s. 24(1), courts can grant remedies in anticipation of a Charter breach (*New Brunswick (Minister of Health and Community Services) v. G. (J.)*). In that case, the Supreme Court of Canada dealt with the issue of whether indigent parents have a constitutional right to be provided with a state-funded lawyer in situations where the state is seeking an order suspending the parents' custody of their children. By the time the case reached the Supreme Court, the constitutional issue was moot because the substantive elements had already been decided and the appellant had pro bono legal representation. Nonetheless, the court decided to approach the constitutional question as though a prospective breach of the Charter was at issue.

> 3. May apply to a court of competent jurisdiction
>
> The application must be made to a court of competent jurisdiction.

This provision has been interpreted by the courts as giving authority to the trial judge to deal with applications to exclude evidence. However, judges presiding over preliminary hearings do not have the discretion to exclude evidence using the Charter. (Note that in Canada we have not followed the American example of constitutional "suppression" hearings, where applications are made prior to trial for determinations that evidence will be excluded.) The leading case on this point is *Mills v. The Queen*, where the court found that a preliminary-hearing judge is not a court of competent jurisdiction within the meaning of s. 24. According to McIntyre J (at para. 264), who wrote the majority decision, a preliminary-hearing judge

> is given no jurisdiction which would permit him to hear and determine the question of whether or not a *Charter* right has been infringed or denied. He is, therefore, not a court of competent jurisdiction under s. 24(1) of the *Charter*.

The Supreme Court of Canada followed the *Mills* approach in considering whether an administrative tribunal is a court of competent jurisdiction. In *Cuddy Chicks v. Ontario*, the court stated that such jurisdiction "must have expressly or impliedly been conferred on the tribunal by its enabling statute or otherwise." An administrative tribunal will be a court of competent jurisdiction within the meaning of s. 24 of the Charter where it has been granted this function. This would occur, for example, if the enabling statute provided the tribunal with the power to decide questions of law. However, this is not necessarily determinative of the issue because jurisdiction can also be conferred impliedly on the tribunal in order for it to have the power to carry out its functions. The court concluded that

> a tribunal prepared to address a *Charter* issue must already have jurisdiction over the whole of the matter before it, namely, the parties, subject matter and remedy sought.

> 4. Where, in proceedings under subsection (1), a court concludes that evidence was obtained in a manner that infringed or denied any rights or freedoms guaranteed by this Charter,
>
> The evidence was obtained in a way that infringed a Charter right.

The threshold requirement of s. 24(2) is that the evidence was obtained in a manner that infringed or denied a right or freedom. What this means is that there must be a connection or relationship between the breach and the obtaining of the evidence. If there is a direct causal connection between the infringement of the right or freedom and the evidence, the threshold will be met. So, if an accused is denied his right to speak to a lawyer and makes a confession or has his dwelling house searched for stolen property without a warrant, the connection between any evidence obtained as a result of these breaches will satisfy the threshold requirement. In these cases, the obtaining of the evidence flows directly from the Charter breach.

However, there will be many cases where the connection is not as direct or obvious. For example, assume that a motorist was arrested for impaired driving and read his rights, but the police failed to mention that free and immediate legal advice was available from duty counsel. The accused then indicated that he did not want to call a lawyer and the police administered a breathalyzer test that the accused failed. Is there any causal connection between the failure to advise the accused of his right to duty counsel and the failed test? Most people would think not, because a lawyer would probably have advised the accused that he would be charged if he failed to take the breathalyzer test. In other words, the accused would have been charged with either operating a motor vehicle with an excess of alcohol in the blood or failing to comply with an officer's demand, both of which carry the same penalty, regardless of whether any legal advice was received by him.

There really is no direct causal connection in the above example between the Charter breach and the impugned evidence. However, the Supreme Court of Canada dealt with these precise facts in *R v. Bartle* and found that:

> Under the first threshold requirement, there must be some connection or relationship between the infringement of the right or freedom in question and the obtaining of the evidence which is sought to be excluded. However, a strict causal link between the *Charter* infringement and the discovery of the evidence is not required. ... Generally speaking, so long as it is not too remotely connected with the violation, all the evidence obtained as part of the "chain of events" involving the *Charter* breach will fall within the scope of s. 24(2). ... This means that in the initial inquiry under s. 24(2) as to whether evidence has been "obtained in a manner that infringed or denied" *Charter* rights, courts should take a generous approach.

The "chain of events" test is far broader and easier to meet than the "causal connection" test. Critics charge that the approach the Supreme Court has adopted represents a kind of judicial activism and extends the reach of the court beyond what the Charter envisioned. Defenders of this approach argue that in the era of the Charter, the courts have a supervisory role to ensure that police action in obtaining evidence for use in courts meets a high standard of propriety and does not trample on anyone's rights.

> 5. The evidence shall be excluded if it is established that, having regard to all the circumstances, the admission of it in the proceedings would bring the administration of justice into disrepute.
>
> The evidence is excluded if the admission of the evidence would harm the reputation of the justice system.

Evidence that meets all of the other components of the exclusionary remedy will still be admissible unless its admission would bring the administration of justice into disrepute. Another way of saying this is that the public would lose respect for the justice system if such evidence were admitted. For example, a confession that was obtained by torture or evidence that was obtained by police officers who searched people because of their skin colour or the way they dressed would cause the public to have less respect for the justice system.

R v. Collins was an early Charter case to consider this particular phrase. Ruby Collins was the girlfriend of a known drug dealer and both were together at a pub. She was subjected to a flying tackle and choke hold in the course of a police "take down" of suspected drug dealers. At trial, no evidence was led that the police had reasonable grounds to believe that Ms. Collins was carrying drugs. An important factor in this case is the fact that the choke-hold procedure is inherently dangerous, and has resulted in a number of deaths of people being arrested.

The *Collins* decision served to clarify a number of points. First, the Supreme Court made it clear that the burden is on the party seeking to have the evidence excluded to demonstrate on a balance of probabilities that its admission would bring the administration of justice into disrepute. Second, the court noted that the English and French versions of the Charter are very different, with the French version of "would bring the administration of justice into disrepute" translating as "could bring the administration of justice in disrepute." The Supreme Court therefore found that the test to be applied is whether the admission of the evidence could (not would) bring the administration of justice into disrepute.

The court also clarified the meaning of disrepute, making the following observation:

> The concept of disrepute necessarily involves some element of community views, and the determination of disrepute thus requires the judge to refer to what he conceives to be the views of the community at large.

Finally, the Supreme Court analyzed the factors that a court should consider in determining whether the administration of justice was brought into disrepute. The court identified three factors to consider:

1. Would the admission of the evidence affect the fairness of the trial?

2. Is the breach serious or merely technical in nature?

3. What would be the impact on the reputation of the justice system if the evidence were excluded?

We take a closer look at these three factors below.

1. Would the admission of the evidence affect the fairness of the trial?

If admission of the evidence would render the trial unfair, the evidence would tend to bring the administration of justice into disrepute and generally, be excluded. That is because having a system of justice that is fair is essential to a democracy and cannot be compromised in the rush to obtain a conviction. Section 11(d) of the Charter guarantees individuals a "fair and public hearing" and mandates this outcome. Most people accept this principle when a minor offence is being considered but have greater difficulty where an accused person stands trial for a very serious offence, particularly a violent one. The courts have determined that fairness of a trial is a fundamental principle that cannot be compromised, no matter how serious the offence.

How does the court resolve whether admitting the evidence affects the fairness of the trial? First, the court considers whether the evidence is conscriptive. Where an accused person is forced to assist in his own prosecution and the Crown cannot establish that the police would have discovered the evidence without conscripting the accused, the evidence would render the trial unfair and therefore be excluded.

Conscriptive evidence includes requiring the accused to make a statement, provide a bodily sample, or assist the prosecution with the use of his body—for example, by standing in a police lineup or re-enacting an alleged crime. Any evidence that flows from or is derived from the above conscription is also considered a Charter breach and treated as the "fruit of the poisoned tree." However, if the Crown is able to establish on a balance of probabilities that the evidence would inevitably have been discovered or that there was an independent source for this evidence, the conscription becomes irrelevant because the evidence would have been available to the Crown without the Charter breach.

For an example of the inevitable discovery consideration we can look to *R v. Black*. In that case, the accused was charged with murder. During the investigation, the police breached the accused's s. 10(b) rights, which led her to make an inculpatory statement. She was later taken to her apartment, where she produced a knife and acknowledged that it was the murder weapon. The knife was derivative evidence because it was obtained as a result of the conscripted statement. However, the court concluded that the police would have searched the accused's apartment and discovered the knife in any event, and therefore determined that the admission of the knife would not render the trial unfair. As the Supreme Court stated in *R v. Stillman* (at para. 107):

> In summary, where it is established that either a non-conscriptive means existed through which the evidence would have been discovered or that its discovery was inevitable, then the evidence was discoverable; it would have been discovered in the absence of the unlawful conscription of the accused. The Crown must bear the onus of establishing discoverability on a balance of probabilities. Where the evidence was "discoverable," even though it may be conscriptive, its admission will *not*, as a general rule, render the trial unfair. The Court should therefore proceed to consider the seriousness of the violation.

2. Is the breach serious or merely technical in nature?

In *R v. Silveira*, the Supreme Court of Canada dealt with the issue of the seriousness of the Charter violation. In this case, the police violated the accused's right to be secure against unreasonable search or seizure during an investigation of drug trafficking. An undercover police operation determined that there was trafficking of cocaine in and around a community centre in Toronto. They connected the trafficking with a particular residence belonging to Silveira and were in the process of applying for a search warrant when they arrested three of the suspects. They were concerned that word of the arrests would get back to the residents of the house before the warrant was issued, so in order to preserve evidence that might be there, they entered the house without permission and "stood by" for about an hour until the warrant arrived. They then commenced their search, where they located a duffel bag containing cocaine and a large amount of cash that included some of the marked money from the undercover operation. The court considered the following factors in determining the seriousness of the Charter violation:

- Was the violation inadvertent or committed in good faith or was it willful, deliberate, and flagrant?

- Was the violation serious or merely technical in nature?

- Was the violation motivated by a situation of urgency or necessity?

- Were there other investigative means available to the police that would not have infringed the Charter?

The court gave considerable weight to the "exigent circumstances" in determining that the evidence ought to be admitted in spite of the fact that the entry of the dwelling house was not authorized by law. The court did state, however (at paras. 166–167):

> As the trial judge and the majority of the Court of Appeal found, *the Charter violation was rendered less serious in light of the particular facts of this case.*
>
> If the urgent emergency circumstances are such that the police are required to enter a dwelling without a warrant to preserve evidence, the question as to whether or not the serious nature of the breach would render the evidence obtained in a subsequent search inadmissible will have to be carefully considered on a case-by-case basis. *I reiterate, however, that it would be only in rare cases that such evidence could be admitted in the future.* It would be preferable for the police to obtain a search warrant prior to the arrest even if it was on the basis of more limited information than that which could be advanced after the arrest. [Italics added.]

In ruling that the evidence should nonetheless be admitted, the court took into account the serious societal damage done by drug trafficking. The court also pursued its role as educator of the police and public by making it clear that only in rare cases would it tolerate this practice. (An edited version of *R v. Silveira* is available on the Emond Montgomery website at www.emp.ca/evidence.)

In evaluating the seriousness of the Charter breach, courts will place substantial emphasis on the mental state of the authority who took the action. So, if a police officer knew that she was breaching the individual's Charter right and went ahead regardless, the court will view her actions as a much more serious violation than the actions of an officer who thought she was acting under legal authority. For example, where a police officer complies with a statute that is later determined to be unconstitutional, the officer's "good faith" efforts to respect an accused's Charter rights will go a long way toward a determination that the evidence ought to be admitted notwithstanding the Charter breach. This is not to say, however, that the police can claim ignorance of the law as an excuse for breaching an accused's Charter rights. In *R v. Kokesch*, the court found that the police should have known that their perimeter search of the accused's residence was unconstitutional even though they indicated that they thought the search was legal. Conversely, where police officers have gone to the trouble of obtaining legal advice that incorrectly indicated that their actions were legal, the courts have been more willing to admit the evidence.

3. What would be the impact on the reputation of the justice system if the evidence were excluded?

This is the *weighing* part of the process where the court looks at the impact on the reputation of the justice system if the evidence were admitted or if it were excluded. In exercising its role in weighing evidence, the court considers how a "reasonable person" would view the situation. Would a reasonable person, in viewing the value of the evidence to the prosecution and the seriousness of the crime compared to the seriousness of the breach, feel that the justice system is brought into disrepute by admitting the evidence or rejecting it? Although the court must refer to the views of the community in answering this question, this does not mean that public perception is determinative of the issue. It is this balancing act, as first outlined in *Collins*, that will ultimately determine the admissibility of evidence obtained as a result of a Charter breach.

NON-STATEMENT CONSCRIPTION: BODILY SAMPLES AND USE OF THE BODY

With the widespread acceptance of DNA evidence by the courts and improved reliability of DNA testing, the police practice of obtaining bodily samples as an investigative tool has increased explosively. Bodily samples include blood, hair, and skin samples, mouth swabs, and breath samples—virtually anything that a body can produce. Where a perpetrator has left DNA at the scene in the form of saliva, semen, hair, or skin, comparison of the crime scene DNA to a suspect's can significantly shorten an investigation and narrow the suspect list to one. However, unless an individual consents to participate in bodily sample testing, taking such samples with or without a warrant is considered obtaining evidence through conscription.

Similarly, where an individual is required to assist an investigation with the use of his body, this may be viewed as conscriptive. As mentioned above, when a suspect is required to stand in a police lineup or participate in a re-enactment, perform sobriety tests, or use his body to assist the police in any other way, the evidence is considered conscriptive. The issue is less clear if the police merely require the accused to aid them in obtaining evidence—for example, if the police ask an accused to open up a bag and remove its contents. While enlisting a suspect's "co-operation" cannot be used to "sanitize" an unconstitutional search, merely having an accused perform some mundane act, which technically aids the police, may not be enough to cause the court to conclude that the evidence was obtained by conscription. The key seems to be whether the evidence is created by the use of the body, such as in a lineup, or whether the body simply makes the job of the police easier, such as opening the trunk of a car. In the latter situation, the evidence pre-exists the use of the body—the suspect's body is just enlisted to reveal it—whereas without the use of the body in the former situation, the evidence would not exist.

CHAPTER SUMMARY

The *Canadian Charter of Rights and Freedoms* has brought about significant changes in how the police deal with suspects and accused persons. Evidence that is wrongfully obtained is often excluded by the courts when police actions have resulted in violations of the Charter. The exclusion of evidence applies equally to the original evidence and to any evidence derived from it unless the Crown can establish on a balance of probabilities that the derived evidence would inevitably have been found or that there was an independent source for the derived evidence. Section 24 of the Charter has been carefully analyzed and applied to maintain a high level of respect for the administration of justice in Canada. Where evidence is obtained as a result of a breach of a suspect's or accused's Charter rights, a court may exclude the evidence if the admission of the evidence would bring the administration of justice into disrepute.

KEY TERMS

read into   reasonable expectation of privacy test

Oakes test   *Collins* test

plain view doctrine

REFERENCES

Askov, R v., [1990] 2 SCR 1199.

Bartle, R v., [1994] 3 SCR 173.

Belnavis, R v., [1997] 3 SCR 341.

Black, R v., [1989] 2 SCR 138.

Brown v. Regional Municipality of Durham Police Service Board (1998), 43 OR (3d) 223 (CA).

Canadian Charter of Rights and Freedoms, part I of the *Constitution Act, 1982*, RSC 1985, app. II, no. 44.

Christian Labour Association v. B.C. Transportation Financing Authority (2000), 187 DLR (4th) 565 (BCSC).

Collins, R v., [1987] 1 SCR 265.

Constitution Act, 1982, RSC 1985, app. II, no. 44.

Cuddy Chicks Ltd. v. Ontario (Labour Relations Board), [1991] 2 SCR 5.

Edwards, R v., [1996] 1 SCR 128.

Eldridge v. British Columbia (Attorney General), [1997] 3 SCR 624.

Harrer, R v., [1995] 3 SCR 562.

Hebert, R v., [1990] 2 SCR 151.

Highway Traffic Act, RSO 1990, c. H.8.

Hufsky, R v., [1988] 1 SCR 621.

Hunter v. Southam Inc., [1984] 2 SCR 145.

Kokesch, R v., [1990] 3 SCR 3.

Lagiorgia v. Canada, [1987] 3 FC 28 (CA); leave to appeal to Supreme Court of Canada refused (1988), 43 CCC (3d) vi (note).

Lauda, R v., [1998] 2 SCR 683.

Little Sisters Book and Art Emporium v. Canada (Minister of Justice), [2000] 2 SCR 1120.

Mills, The Queen v., [1986] 1 SCR 863.

New Brunswick (Minister of Health and Community Services) v. G. (J.), [1999] 3 SCR 46.

Oakes, R v., [1986] 1 SCR 103.

Silveira, R v., [1995] 2 SCR 297.

Stillman, R v., [1997] 1 SCR 607.

Stinchcombe, R v., [1991] 3 SCR 326.

Stinson (Estate of) v. British Columbia (1999), 182 DLR (4th) 407 (BCCA).

Therens, R v., [1985] 1 SCR 613.

White, R v., [1999] 2 SCR 417.

REVIEW QUESTIONS

1. What section of the Charter does the court rely on to exclude evidence that is unconstitutionally obtained?

2. What are the five components of the exclusionary remedy under s. 24?

3. What factors do the courts take into account when determining whether the admission of evidence could bring the administration of justice into disrepute?

4. Can unfair evidence be excluded even where there is no Charter breach?

DISCUSSION QUESTIONS

For each of the following scenarios, identify whether there have been any Charter breaches and the appropriate remedy or remedies.

1. James Horton, a 19-year-old black male, was driving his parents' 2007 Lexus when he was stopped by police, who indicated that they were investigating a rash of auto thefts in the area. During the stop, the police smelled marijuana and asked James where the smell was coming from. James freely admitted that he was smoking marijuana and turned over a small quantity to the police. James was charged with possession of a narcotic.

2. Derek Malley, a 19-year-old white male, was driving his parents' 2006 Acura. He was stopped by police, who indicated that they were investigating the kidnapping of a six-year old girl. During the stop, the police heard a muffled noise from the trunk. Upon further investigation, the missing girl was discovered unharmed in the trunk. Derek was charged with the abduction of the girl.

3. Sally Quick was stopped for speeding at 145 kilometres an hour in a 100 kilometre an hour zone. After she stopped her vehicle, the police officer came over and asked her if she knew why she was being pulled over. Sally responded by telling the officer that he should be more concerned about apprehending real criminals. Sally was charged with speeding.

4. Margaret Evans was stopped by police at a roadside checkpoint designed to reduce impaired driving. Sally had not consumed any alcohol but police detected the odour of marijuana and asked Margaret to open her glove compartment. Margaret complied and a quantity of marijuana was discovered. Margaret was charged with possession of a narcotic.

5. Scott Kwan was going to a rock concert downtown. Before entering the stadium, he was asked by arena security to empty his pockets and Scott turned over a marijuana cigarette. The security officer in turn handed the marijuana over to police and Scott was charged with possession of a narcotic.

PART IV

Methods of Presenting Evidence

CHAPTER 13

Forms of Evidence

CHAPTER OBJECTIVES

After completing this chapter you should be able to:

- Identify the three forms of evidence.

- Understand when a view may be used.

- Define the best evidence rule and understand how it has evolved.

- Identify the three criteria that judges use in determining whether to admit photographs and videos.

- Understand the role of computers in documentary evidence.

- Understand how the spoliation of evidence undermines the justice system in Canada.

INTRODUCTION

Evidence constitutes the building blocks of any party's case in any hearing. Judges and juries are not entitled to make decisions based on emotions or a "gut feeling" about the matter at hand. They are charged with the responsibility for making decisions based on the facts in evidence before them. Evidence can take three forms:

1. oral evidence,

2. real evidence, and

3. documentary evidence.

This chapter provides an overview of these three forms of evidence. The following chapter discusses oral evidence in detail.

ORAL EVIDENCE

By far the most common form of evidence in any hearing is **oral evidence**. Witnesses come to the hearing or trial and are questioned, according to various rules, by the lawyers representing the parties in the case.

oral evidence
evidence given verbally
by witnesses

The common law at one time required that all evidence be taken under oath. This meant that the witness had to swear on a Bible to tell the truth. The idea behind testimony under oath was to emphasize to the person testifying the solemnity of the occasion and the importance of telling the truth. When the practice of testifying under oath arose, the belief that there were religious consequences for lying was common, so it was quite natural to look at swearing an oath as the means to encourage truth telling in court. For many years, the process of testifying under oath continued as the proper form for witnesses to testify, but the oath itself was clearly not very meaningful for those persons who did not believe in God or who were not Christians.

More recently, given both the cultural and religious diversity in Canada, and the diminishing influence of religion in the lives of many, both statute law and the common law have evolved to the point where giving evidence under oath no longer plays the same role in determining truth telling. Although **oaths** are still regularly used in courtrooms, now a person may instead give a **solemn affirmation** to tell the truth. A solemn affirmation, often referred to as simply an affirmation, is a promise to tell the truth. Evidence given under oath and evidence given under affirmation both carry the same weight, and no legal differentiation is made between the two methods.

oath
promise made on the Bible or other holy book to tell the truth in court

solemn affirmation
promise to tell the truth in court that has the same value as an oath

REAL EVIDENCE

real evidence
tangible evidence that is put before the trier of fact

Real evidence is any tangible evidence put before the trier of fact. Tangible evidence is evidence that can be touched. (This category of evidence technically includes documents but because there are some issues that pertain specifically to documentary evidence, we deal with documents as a separate category under the heading "Documentary Evidence.") Real evidence is unique because the trier of fact experiences it first-hand rather than having it interpreted by a witness. The trier of fact is entitled to draw its own conclusions about the evidence, even to draw from it information unnoticed by those presenting the evidence.

Real evidence is usually evidence that was created in the course of the events that gave rise to the charge or dispute—for example, a knife stained with the blood of the victim or a defective product that has caused injury and is brought into the courtroom in a manufacturer's liability case. Real evidence may also take the form of demonstration devices such as diagrams, maps, models of body parts, and PowerPoint presentations that aid the trier of fact in understanding evidence. Forensic evidence, such as blood, fingerprints, or hair samples, is a specific type of real evidence that courts are currently relying on a great deal.

For real evidence to be admissible, the judge must determine that the evidence does not distort the facts or create a biased perspective. Real evidence may be excluded if the court determines that its potential for prejudice outweighs its probative value.

Views

Usually, real evidence is brought into the courtroom and entered into evidence as an exhibit, but this is not always possible. The tangible object may simply be too large, or there may be a valid reason for the trier of fact to see the scene of the alleged offence. In such cases, the court may order a **view**, whereby the courtroom is relocated to a particular place so that the jury will have the opportunity to see the real evidence first-hand. The judge, court staff, jury, accused, and sheriffs all attend the view and one of the parties, or perhaps both, makes a presentation at the site. The presentation could be in the form of expert explanation in relation to the scene or object being viewed by the fact finder, or simply a request by counsel to have the fact finder personally examine the scene or object so that this personal observation will aid their understanding when they hear evidence at a later date. Views are an interesting aspect of evidence law but are rarely used because they usually involve substantial arrangements and considerable expense. However, in the following two examples, views were deemed necessary by the court.

In the Air India trial, which concerned the bombing of Air India Flight 182 on June 22, 1985, the jury was taken to view the location where the wreckage was stored and where experts had viewed it to develop their theories about the site of the explosion on the plane. The Crown expert testified that the luggage that exploded was in a location on the plane indicating that it was loaded in Vancouver, whereas the defence expert testified that the location of the explosion confirmed that it was loaded in Toronto. Presumably, by viewing the wreckage laid out in a giant warehouse, the jury would be better able to determine which of these theories deserved more merit.

Another example of a view took place years ago when an accused struck a pedestrian who was walking alone at night on a dark road. The driver continued home, switched cars, and returned to the scene of the accident. When he noticed police there, he left again, but ultimately turned himself in to the police with the assistance of his lawyer. The driver, charged with dangerous driving and leaving the scene of an accident, stated that he did not know he had hit anyone until he got home. He claimed that while he was fiddling with something in the car, the wheels left the road and moved onto the soft shoulder. The bump that he felt, he initially concluded, was the wheels bumping up onto the road again. By attending the scene, the jurors were in a position to weigh this evidence more effectively and compare it with the Crown's theory. They convicted the accused, likely based on Crown evidence that showed that the body bounced up onto the hood of the car and struck the windshield, as well as other evidence from the damage to the vehicle that undermined the accused's claim that he did not realize he had hit a person.

view
relocation of the court to the site of the alleged offence; a judge may order a view when the evidence is too large to bring into the courtroom or when there is a valid reason for the trier of fact to see the site

DOCUMENTARY EVIDENCE

Most people, if asked to define a document, would describe some sort of text, written or printed on a piece of paper. Certainly, that is a document, but **documentary evidence** includes many more types of evidence. For instance, the Ontario *Rules of Civil Procedure* for the Ontario Superior Court of Justice provide that the word "document" includes a sound recording, videotape, film, photograph, chart, graph, map, plan, survey, book of account, and data and information in electronic form. In British Columbia, the *Supreme Court Rules* of that province provide that "document" includes a photograph, film, recording of sound, any record of a permanent or semi-permanent character, and any information recorded or stored by means of any device.

documentary evidence
any document, including writing, video, film, tapes, and photographs, presented in court for reference by the trier of fact

In criminal law, the definition of document is also fairly broad. For example, s. 321 of the *Criminal Code* defines "document" for the purposes of part IX as "any paper, parchment or other material on which is recorded or marked anything that is capable of being read or understood by a person, computer system or other device, and includes a credit card."

Documents are regularly relied on as evidence in both civil and criminal cases, as well as in hearings before administrative tribunals. In order to be admitted into evidence, a document of any type must first be authenticated, or validated. This process has become particularly important with the advent of sophisticated copying techniques and computer records, which can be used to doctor documents. Authentication requires establishing that the document is truly what it purports to be. Very often, the opposing party does not challenge the validity of the document and agrees to have it admitted on consent. For example, in a contract dispute, both parties may agree that the document presented is in fact the contract on which the case is focused.

Another method of validating a document is through calling a witness to identify it. The witness may have written or created the document, or may have been present when the document was created or signed. If the document is a photograph, the photographer is usually called to identify it and to provide some evidence of how and when it was taken. Sometimes, an expert witness is called to help verify a document. In some cases, a document may be presumed to be authentic if there is no indication of fraud and the document has been properly preserved, or if there are a series of documents—for example, a set of e-mail messages in which a message could only be a response to an earlier message.

Best Evidence Rule

best evidence rule
a largely outdated rule that the original document must be presented in evidence if it is available

The **best evidence rule** was designed to ensure that only original documents would be presented in evidence. With present-day technology, it is frequently almost impossible to tell an original from a copy. In order to combat potential adulteration of documents, the rule developed that the original, or "best evidence," must be provided to the court, the point being that any careful inspection of an original document is much more likely to uncover a forgery whereas it would be much harder to uncover alterations by examining a photocopy.

An example of how close examination may reveal a forgery is the alleged memo from the supervising colonel of the Texas Air National Guard that called into question George W. Bush's military service during the war in Vietnam. The problem with this particular forgery is that the type font used in this memo was not available or at least not in common use in the 1970s, but rather was a product of computers and Microsoft word processing.

The best evidence rule has historically been used to stop a party from entering a copy of a document as evidence. Where the original could not be located or produced, the party might not be able to prove the contents of the document, which might contain information crucial to his position. Today, this approach is much more relaxed. An original is preferred—in fact, if the original is available, the court likely would require the party to actually produce it—but if it is not available because it is lost, has been destroyed, or is out of the reach of the court (in another jurisdiction), a copy can be admitted. The trier of fact gives the copy whatever weight it would deserve in the circumstances. For example, if there is not good reason why the original is not available and one party provides two witnesses who insist that some wording on a contract was scratched out and initialled on the original, the trier of fact could conclude that the copy was of no assistance to them as evidence of the wording of the contract. But in many other instances, copies are admitted. In fact, the *Canada Evidence Act* has substantially modified the best evidence rule to facilitate the entry into evidence of copies with respect to business matters.

Photographs and Videos as Documentary Evidence

It is not unusual in a criminal case for the Crown to attempt to introduce photographs of the crime scene or, in a murder case, photographs of the autopsy. Often, the evidence is admitted, even when the evidence is graphic, as in photos of a dismembered body. Critics have charged that such graphic documentary evidence has little evidentiary value and has a high potential to prejudice a jury.

Photographs of crime scenes can also present problems. Consider the following scenario. A prostitute takes a john to her room for sex. After having sex, the john insists that she have sex with him a second time without charge and grabs her to force her to comply. She reaches over to the counter, grabs a butcher knife, and stabs him. The prostitute is charged with attempted murder and pleads self-defence. The Crown wants to enter into evidence photos of the room where the stabbing took place. The photos show the bed and the counter where the knife was. The problem is that in the pictures the counter looks like it is a considerable distance from the bed. The photos therefore imply that the accused got up, walked a number of steps back to the bed, and stabbed the victim. In reality, the counter is within arm's reach of the bed, making it possible that the accused was still in the john's grasp when she reached over for the knife and stabbed him with it. The photographer acknowledges that the photos make the distance between the counter and the bed appear greater than it is because of the type of lens that he used. The court decides to admit these pictures, but their impact is lessened by the photographer's testimony about the distorting effect of the photos.

Judges assess the admissibility of photographs and videos using the following criteria:

1. their accuracy,

2. their fairness and absence of potential to mislead, and

3. verification on the oath of a witness that they are what they purport to be.

In *R v. Maloney*, the court rejected videotaped footage of a hockey assault because of the distorting effect of slow motion taping. Periodically, particularly gruesome photos of corpses are not admitted because, although they obviously relate to the issues to be decided, they have no value in determining the issues before the trier of fact. However, videotape evidence has even been used by the court to identify a person charged with robbing a convenience store where the witnesses at the scene could not identify the accused. In *R v. Nikolovski*, the judge was prepared to make that identification using the surveillance video from the store.

RODNEY KING: TV JUSTICE

Rodney King, a black taxi driver, was stopped by the Los Angeles Police Department (LAPD) after a high-speed chase on March 3, 1991. The police jolted him with high-powered electric batons twice and when that did not sufficiently subdue King, they delivered over 50 baton blows and six kicks to him, resulting in 11 skull fractures, and brain and kidney damage. If it were not for George Holliday, who filmed the beating from his balcony with his camcorder, the false reports filed by the police might have been the end of the incident. When the videotape was handed over to the media and aired the next day, Los Angeles residents saw the beating first-hand. Four of the almost 20 officers at the scene were charged with assault with a deadly weapon and using excessive force. The defence was successful in getting a change in venue from Los Angeles to the much more police officer–friendly Simi Valley. The four officers were acquitted on April 29, 1992.

In the wake of the acquittals, a riot ensued in which thousands of people in South Central Los Angeles took to the streets, hauling innocent motorists from their cars and viciously beating them, looting stores, and setting vehicles on fire. The riot lasted for six days, resulted in over 50 deaths, 2,000 injuries, and thousands of arrests. It took the combined forces of the LAPD, the National Guard, and federal troops to restore order. The estimates of property damage were in the order of $700 million. Even though the jury acquitted the officers after viewing the video, this does not change the fact that this evidence was of great value; indeed, without such clear evidence Rodney King might not have been able to obtain a $3.8 million award in a later civil trial where another jury determined that his civil rights had been violated by the beating.

Computer-Generated Records

Computer-generated records is an area of evidence law that will likely see increased attention in the future. Where the evidence was input by humans, the rules dealing with hearsay exceptions can determine admissibility. But with some computer-generated evidence, the work is done by the computer. For example, where a computer stores and retrieves data automatically in creating telephone usage records, approving credit card transactions, or tracking websites visited, no person has input the information and yet it will be invaluable in answering many questions that arise in both civil and criminal trials. This sort of evidence is not real hearsay but more like a snapshot in time and should be treated like a photograph. In other words, it should be authenticated and based on the authentication given weight by the trier of fact.

Another area where computers will be valuable, although potentially dangerous, is re-creations or models that are created to assist a party in visually demonstrating a fact. Triers of fact will have a much clearer understanding, particularly of complex matters, when they can be led through it watching an animated program. The dangerous aspect is that the animation will show whatever it is programmed to. What the triers of fact are viewing is not "reality" or a historical replay, but just what the party presenting it wants them to see. Like evidence from any novel science, computer-generated information should be treated with caution and scrutinized for reliability and bias.

Spoliation of Evidence

Spoliation refers to the destruction, mutilation, alteration or concealment of evidence. We see this where e-mails are deleted and documents shredded. Deleted e-mails, in particular, are a common source of spoliation because they can be retrieved by skilled computer technicians. When deleted e-mails are recovered, they can form even more damning evidence in light of the effort that was put into hiding the information. Lawyers are warned that when they forward correspondence to the opposing counsel electronically, the communication will contain metadata, which includes electronic instructions contained in the document and not visible unless one has the expertise to display it. This means that earlier versions of the same document that contain drafts that have been rejected will be recoverable in an electronic communication. This can have implications in a civil suit if sensitive information such as a less favourable offer or position was considered in the earlier version—for example, "I'd take $100,000 but let's try for $150,000 first."

The concern with the spoliation of evidence is that courts are left with a harder job if relevant evidence is destroyed and may be forced to render decisions based on even more imperfect evidence. Various jurisdictions in Canada are currently working on how to remedy the problem presented by after-the-fact coverups and we can expect that this will be an active area for pro-active responses to a problem that undermines our system of justice.

spoliation
the destruction, mutilation, alteration, or concealment of evidence

CHAPTER SUMMARY

There are three forms for presenting evidence: oral evidence, real evidence, and documentary evidence. Oral evidence is presented by witnesses who are called to give testimony under oath or solemn affirmation. Real evidence is tangible evidence that can be put before the trier of fact by physically bringing the item into court or by taking the trier of fact to the location of the evidence for a view. Documentary evidence is evidence in a recorded form, and includes written words, film, video, audio recordings, photographs, charts, graphs, maps, plans, books of account, and information recorded in electronic form.

The best evidence rule is a largely outdated rule that requires the original document to be presented into evidence if it is available. Today, this approach is far more relaxed. An original is preferred, but if it is not available, a copy can be admitted by the court.

Judges assess the admissibility of photographs and videos using three criteria: their accuracy; their fairness and absence of potential to mislead; and their verification by a witness under oath. Computer-generated records may be of great value to the trier of fact, but also carry the potential to mislead and must be scrutinized for reliability and bias.

The spoliation of evidence refers to the destruction, mutilation, alteration, or concealment of evidence.

KEY TERMS

oral evidence   view

oath   documentary evidence

solemn affirmation   best evidence rule

real evidence   spoliation

REFERENCES

Canada Evidence Act, RSC 1985, c. C-5.

Canadian Charter of Rights and Freedoms, part I of the *Constitution Act, 1982*, RSC
    1985, app. II, no. 44.

Maloney (No. 2), R v. (1976), 29 CCC (2d) 431 (Ont. Co. Ct.).

Nikolovski, R v. (1996), 3 CR (5th) 362 (SCC).

Oickle, R v. (2000), 147 CCC (3d) 321 (SCC).

Rules of Civil Procedure, RRO 1990, reg. 194, rule 30.01(1)(a).

Supreme Court Rules, BC reg. 221/90, rule 1(8).

REVIEW QUESTIONS

1. Name the three forms in which evidence may be presented and admitted.

2. What is the difference between an oath and a solemn affirmation?

3. What is a "view"? Give an example of when it might be used.

4. What types of information can be grouped under the heading of
   "documentary evidence"?

5. What is the best evidence rule? How is it applied by the courts today?

6. What criteria will the judge use in determining the admissibility of videos
   and photographs?

DISCUSSION QUESTIONS

1. Discuss how the development of information stored on computers has
   affected the manner in which evidence is recorded and presented. What
   are the benefits of computers in gathering and presenting evidence? What
   are some of the concerns that this type of evidence gathering and
   presentation has generated?

2. It is often said that "seeing is believing." Discuss this saying in relation to
   video and photographic evidence. Is seeing always believing? What are some
   of the benefits of and problems with video and photographic evidence?

CHAPTER 14

Oral Evidence

CHAPTER OBJECTIVES

After completing this chapter you should be able to:

- Describe the two facets of the test for competence of a witness.

- Understand the provincial rules governing the testimony of child witnesses.

- Understand who can be compelled to testify and who cannot.

- Understand the purpose of examination-in-chief; cross-examination, including the limits on cross-examination; and re-examination.

- Describe the ways in which the testimony of witnesses can be undermined by opposing counsel.

- Understand when a judge may issue a discretionary warning regarding corroborating evidence.

CALLING WITNESSES

We say that a witness is "called" to testify. This may be done by simply arranging with a willing witness for her to testify, but the best practice is to subpoena or summon a witness even if the witness is a good friend or a family member of the party who is relying on her testimony. A **subpoena** or a **summons** is a formal, legal document requiring the witness to appear or to suffer legal consequences for failing to do so. Generally speaking, "subpoena" is the term used for the document calling a witness in a criminal case, and "summons" is the term used in civil or non-criminal matters. If a witness has been formally called to give evidence and she does not appear, it is much more likely that the court will grant an adjournment. Should a subpoenaed or summoned witness fail to appear at the hearing, a warrant may be issued for her arrest.

However, not all witnesses who attend a hearing are permitted to testify. In order to give testimony at a hearing, a witness must be both competent and compellable.

subpoena
formal, legal document requiring a witness to appear at a hearing in a criminal case

summons
formal, legal document requiring a witness to appear at a hearing in a civil case

COMPETENCY AND COMPELLABILITY

Competence

competence
the legal ability to give oral evidence in a hearing

capacity
an acceptable ability to observe and then correctly recall observations or experiences, and an acceptable ability to communicate these observations to the trier of fact

responsibility
the ability to comprehend the necessity of being truthful and the consequences for not telling the truth

incompetent
not permitted to give evidence

Competence is the legal ability to give oral evidence in a hearing. Whether or not a witness is competent is a matter to be determined by the judge. The test for competence of a witness has two facets. The first facet is **capacity**. The witness must have an acceptable capacity to observe, then to correctly recall his observations or experiences, and an acceptable ability to communicate these observations or experiences to the trier of fact.

The second facet requires that the witness be able to comprehend the necessity of being truthful and the consequences should he not tell the truth. This facet of the test for competency is referred to as **responsibility**.

Historically, at common law, the parties to the proceedings were regarded as incompetent to testify in their own case. The courts believed that the parties' personal interest in the outcome of the case severely compromised their ability to give an objective account of their experiences or observations. It was thought that, at best, they would tend to slant their testimony and, at worst, they would lie outright.

In addition to the parties historically being **incompetent**, or not permitted to give evidence in matters they are litigating, the spouses of the parties were also considered incompetent. The assumption was that spouses are just as likely to slant their observations or to lie as the parties themselves. Because the courts believed that the potential evidence was tainted by this close association, the evidence was avoided entirely. This approach certainly avoided the possibility of the fact-finder's abusing potentially unreliable evidence but it also had the effect of reducing the amount of information that the fact finder could rely on in coming to a conclusion.

Other persons historically considered to be legally incompetent were persons disqualified due to infamy—that is, persons with a criminal history. The courts believed that persons who had shown disregard for society's rules could provide no credible information. Today, a criminal history does not make a witness incompetent but it may lessen the impact of that witness's testimony. Being a child was another basis for disqualification as a witness. Vestiges of this approach remain today in the qualification of child witnesses, discussed below under the heading "Competency of Child Witnesses." Mental incapacity was another disqualification, and one that persists to this day, although it has been criticized for contributing to the vulnerability of a group that is already the target of physical, sexual, and economic abuse. Critics charge that the abuse of mentally incompetent persons is more likely to occur if abusers feel that they can abuse members of this group without fear that their victims will testify against them.

One aspect of incompetence that has fallen by the wayside is the exclusion of persons who do not profess a belief in a supreme being. Taking an oath in order to testify was initially based on the belief that persons would be loath to lie if they had promised in God's name to tell the truth and feared divine punishment for breaking their oath. With the increasingly secular nature of our society, one would be hard pressed to find persons who truly believe that they will be struck by lightning for lying under oath and it is exceedingly rare for anyone with an interest in litigation to "tell the whole truth and nothing but the truth." The fact-finder's job is more often sorting through the evidence to find the version of the truth that is the most reliable version or likely the most accurate.

COMPETENCY OF CHILD WITNESSES

Historically, at common law, there was a rebuttable presumption that children over the age of 14 were competent to give evidence. This means that children under 14 had to be qualified to testify. The judge would question the witness to determine whether the child understood the nature of an oath and to verify that the child comprehended the religious aspects of taking an oath. If the judge determined that the witness did not understand an oath, the child would be found incompetent and would be unable to testify.

Statute has changed the common law, largely in an attempt to discourage those who believe they can abuse children without fear that the children will testify against them. The first legislative changes permitted child witnesses to give unsworn evidence if the judge determined that the child could understand the necessity of telling the truth. However, no one could be convicted of an offence or found liable in a civil court on the uncorroborated evidence of the child. This meant that there had to be other evidence that supported the child's testimony—for example, forensic evidence or evidence from an adult witness.

The corroboration requirement has been removed from the *Canada Evidence Act.* In addition, recent changes to the Act in ss. 16 and 16.1 provide that a child under 14 years of age is presumed to have the capacity to testify. Section 16.1 requires that the test to be applied by the judge to determine the admissibility of a child's testimony is that the child is capable of understanding and responding to questions. No child under the age of 14 will be permitted to take an oath or make a solemn declaration, but the evidence given by the child shall have the same effect as if it were taken under oath or affirmation. Instead of taking an oath or affirmation, a child will be required to promise to tell the truth.

There is no uniformity on this issue among the evidence statutes of the common-law provinces. We find a number of different approaches. British Columbia, Saskatchewan, and Manitoba use the previous wording of the *Canada Evidence Act* in their evidence acts.

Under the evidence acts of Alberta and Nova Scotia, a child of tender years may give unsworn evidence at the discretion of the judge if the child does not understand the nature of an oath; however, the unsworn testimony must be corroborated by other material evidence.

Under the evidence acts of New Brunswick and Ontario, the court must determine whether or not a child understands the nature of an oath (or solemn affirmation in Ontario). If the court determines that the child does not, the child may give unsworn evidence without the need for corroboration. The evidence act for Newfoundland and Labrador does not require that a child comprehend the nature of an oath; rather, the child must demonstrate that he understands what it means to tell the truth and is capable of communicating the evidence. Even if the child does not promise to tell the truth or is unable to understand what it means to tell the truth, the court may still admit the evidence if it is thought to be reliable. There is no requirement for corroboration in either event.

Finally, Prince Edward Island has no statute dealing with child evidence and therefore the common law applies. A child must understand the nature of an oath or he will be found incompetent and will be unable to give evidence.

Most of the evidence statutes either directly require or imply that the court must conduct any inquiry into a child's competence. That said, in some jurisdictions, judges may leave this task to the lawyers for the parties, who will question the child. The ability to perceive and recollect is a general one and not tied to the specific facts before the court, and the test for competency of a child witness is not a very high hurdle for the child to clear. If he or she can string together coherent sentences, that is usually enough to satisfy the court.

COMPETENCY OF SPOUSES

As we noted earlier, historically at common law, neither a party to the litigation or their spouse could give evidence in the proceeding. They were regarded as incompetent to testify in either a criminal or a civil proceeding on the basis that it was unlikely that they would tell the truth given their interest in the outcome of the case.

This common-law rule no longer applies in civil matters, and parties and their spouses are regarded as competent witnesses. They can be called to give testimony by any party, including the opposing litigant.

In criminal matters, the competency of accused persons and their spouses is no longer determined by common law, but by s. 4(1) of the *Canada Evidence Act*, which provides:

> Every person charged with an offence, and, except as otherwise provided in this section, the wife or husband, as the case may be, of the person so charged, is a competent witness for the defence, whether the person so charged is charged solely or jointly with any other person.

Both the accused and his or her spouse are competent to give evidence for the defence but the prosecution may not ever call the accused to testify. In some circumstances, outlined in ss. 4(2) and 4(4) of the statute, the prosecution may call a spouse of an accused person when the accused is charged with one of the offences listed in the subsections. These offences are primarily sexual offences or, in the case of s. 4(4), offences involving injury to or violence toward children under the age of 14. In addition, s. 4(5) preserves the common-law right of a spouse to give evidence against the accused, without the accused's consent, when the spouse's own safety is at risk. This rule offers some protection to spouses who have been victims of violence by the accused.

Both the statutory provisions and the common-law rule apply only to persons who are legally married and not to couples who are living together. The marriage must also be a functioning marriage at the time of the proceeding. If the marriage has broken down, the spouse may be called to give evidence.

Compellability

compellable
legally required to give
evidence at a hearing

In addition to being competent to testify in a proceeding, a witness must also be **compellable**. The general rule is that a witness who is competent is also compellable. This means that the witness can be compelled, or forced, to give evidence and her failure or refusal to do so will result in legal consequences. A witness's refusal to testify in the face of a court order to do so will result in a finding of contempt of court, which can easily lead to incarceration.

There are some exceptions and limitations to the rule that a competent witness is compellable. Under the *Canadian Charter of Rights and Freedoms*, a person charged with an offence cannot be compelled to give evidence against himself in a criminal or quasi-criminal proceeding. Therefore, an accused person cannot be forced to give evidence for the prosecution.

Accused persons did not always enjoy the right to silence. Indeed, in the 15th and 16th centuries, the Court of Star Chamber in England used various methods to compel accused persons to provide evidence in the proceedings against them. Torture was a common interrogation technique, and failure to take an oath in the Star Chamber was tantamount to a confession of guilt.

The current approach to an accused's right to silence owes its existence in part to the excesses of the Star Chamber, which ultimately led to sweeping changes to protect the rights of an accused. By the 18th century, an accused could, by right, refuse to answer any question put to him at trial where the answer would tend to incriminate him. Initially, this privilege only applied to statements made by an accused at trial and did not preclude the questioning of a witness prior to trial. This approach was extended to pretrial questioning by the *Jervis's Act* of 1848.

Ultimately, a common-law right developed for the accused not to cooperate with the authorities in their efforts to obtain a conviction as well as a right not to take the stand and subject himself to cross-examination. So, the accused is protected from answering questions either before the trial or during the trial. However, if an accused decides to take the stand, he becomes a witness, almost like any other, and he can be cross-examined thoroughly about the events leading to the charge.

In Canada, the tradition of being able to compel testimony from a witness who is not an accused continues and shows a distinct difference from the approach in the United States. Section 5 of the *Canada Evidence Act* requires a reluctant witness to testify. Prior to the Charter, where an objection was made, the witness was protected from having that specific evidence used against him in a subsequent proceeding. The Charter extended the protection to all testimony.

The right against self-incrimination as set out in the Charter applies to all dealings with authorities both pretrial and during a trial and places a heavy onus on the authorities to play by the book. In *R v. Hebert*, the Supreme Court of Canada determined that a statement made by Hebert to his cellmate (who was an undercover officer) after he had expressly refused to give a statement to the authorities breached his right to silence. In excluding the statement, the court effectively put an end to police trickery. (For more on this topic, see chapter 10, "Self-Incrimination.")

As noted above, the spouse of an accused is not compellable by the prosecution in most criminal matters. However, if the marriage has broken down or it is found to be a sham, even if the spouses are still legally married, one spouse can be compelled by the prosecution to give evidence against the other. In addition, a spouse may voluntarily give evidence against an accused. The thinking behind this is that if a spouse is willing to give evidence against the accused, the marriage is already likely in significant difficulty.

EXAMINATION-IN-CHIEF

Typically, in a civil trial, the lawyer for the party who calls the witness asks the witness a series of questions aimed at bringing out information that will help to establish facts that this litigant must prove to win the case. This questioning is known as **examination-in-chief**, or direct examination.

examination-in-chief
questioning of a witness
by the party who called
the witness; its object is to
bring out information that
will establish facts that the
litigant must prove to win
the case

The questions during examination-in-chief must not be leading questions. Instead, they must allow the witness to tell her story for the trier of fact. A general guideline provided by the courts is that a question that requires a yes or no answer, without elaboration, is a leading question. However, a question such as, "Did you kill her?" is a yes or no question, but it is not leading because it doesn't imply that a certain answer is sought or preferred. Perhaps the best guide is that a question that contains the answer without elaboration is a leading question. Thus, "You didn't want to hurt her, did you?" is leading because we can expect the answer to be "No, I didn't want to hurt her." The court requires that the witness give her evidence with the least amount of direction from counsel as is possible. If counsel seems to be "putting words into the witness's mouth," the evidence from the witness is much diminished in value, even worthless, to the trier of fact.

Another example of the use of leading questions is obtaining information from a witness by asking questions that contain the answer being sought:

> "So, you live in the British Properties, I take it?"
>
> "You always travel down Georgia Street when you visit your sister, don't you?"
>
> "You hadn't consumed any alcohol that night, had you?"
>
> "When you struck Mr. Jones, you thought that he had a weapon, didn't you?"

In examination-in-chief, asking leading questions can give the witness a clue as to what the "right" answer or what the expected answer is. It is much like a marionette show, where the questioner pulls the strings and the puppet-witness responds accordingly. Thus, with the question, "You hadn't consumed any alcohol that night, had you?" the witness easily gets the point that it would be a good thing if he had not and will be strongly tempted to answer accordingly. Similarly, with the question, "When you struck Mr. Jones, you thought that he had a weapon, didn't you?" the witness is likely to give the anticipated answer designed to shore up a self-defence strategy. The answers to these questions should not be given much weight, if any, by the trier of fact. On the other hand, a question such as, "What was going through your mind when you struck Mr. Jones?" is much more instructive and valuable to the trier of fact.

Leading questions also include questions that presume a fact that has not been proved, thus tricking the unwary witness into agreeing with a proposition that she might not accept:

> "What speed were you going when you ran into my client's car?"
>
> "So, you made the decision because you are the head of your household?"
>
> "You felt sorry that Mr. Jones was injured in your attack, didn't you?"

In the first question, if the witness answers, "The speed limit," he has been tricked into acknowledging that he ran into the other driver. In the second question, if the witness answers yes, it is unclear whether he is agreeing to the fact that he is the head of the household or that he made the decision, or both. In the third question, if the witness answers yes, he has expressed his regret but also admitted to the attack on poor Mr. Jones.

Not all leading questions asked in examination-in-chief are objectionable. In fact, it would be very awkward indeed to conduct a trial without permitting counsel to ask some leading questions of its own witness. There are guidelines for when leading questions are permissible, and in some instances the judge will allow opposing counsel to alert the examiner to avoid leading the witness.

The most frequent use of leading questions in examination-in-chief is in relation to introductory or uncontentious matters, as in the following exchange between counsel and witness:

> "Your name is Frank Olson?"
> "Yes."
> "And you live at 132 West 19th Avenue?"
> "Yes, that's correct."
> "You were at home on the night of March 12, 2004?"
> "I was."

At this point, opposing counsel would likely interject:

> "Your honour, my friend appears to be about to get into the actual incident that took place. I would like to remind him to avoid leading the witness on disputed matters."

There is nothing objectionable about this sort of introductory questioning as long as it does not tread upon matters that the parties are disputing. Probably nobody questions that the witness's name is Frank Olson, or that he lives next door to the plaintiff, or that he was at home on the evening the incident in dispute took place. But it may be very crucial to hear from the witness exactly what he saw and did on that occasion. His credibility and reliability as a witness may be in dispute and the opposing party may want to make sure he gets no help from the plaintiff's counsel in "remembering" the events as they unfolded.

The court may also allow leading questions for the following purposes:

- to jog the memory of a witness, or give a witness a "jump start";

- to aid the witness in communicating complex, scientific, or technical matters;

- to question a witness about statements made by other witnesses for the purpose of contradicting those statements;

- to allow the witness to identify objects in evidence or related persons; and

- to facilitate the testimony of nervous, confused, young, or old witnesses.

The main concept here is that, in many instances, leading will aid in the flow of the litigation and will not have any contaminating effect on the information that results. Leading questions may also be permitted where a witness has been declared hostile or adverse, discussed more fully under the heading "Cross-Examining Your Own Witness," below. This is a special provision designed to help counsel get at the truth even where a witness has no intention of helping that lawyer's client.

CROSS-EXAMINATION

Cross-examination is mostly reserved for questioning an opponent's witness. After the lawyer who called the witness has questioned the witness in examination-in-chief, it is the opposing party's turn to ask questions. The method of questioning will usually differ from that used in examination-in-chief. Unlike examination-in-chief, **cross-examination** affords an opportunity for opposing counsel to ask leading questions and to suggest answers to the witness. It is thought that by permitting the examiner to test the evidence that the witness has brought in the crucible of cross-examination, the truth will emerge.

cross-examination
the questioning of a witness by opposing counsel after examination-in-chief

Cross-examination is generally considered the most effective method of challenging or diminishing the impact of an opponent's testimony. Remember that most witnesses are very inexperienced in the art of giving evidence. It will usually be the one and only time that a witness testifies in court, whereas examining counsel will have examined witnesses numerous times.

One danger of cross-examination is that the witness may contradict herself in spite of her efforts to be honest and forthcoming with the trier of fact. The only safeguard in that situation is the trier of fact's ability to discern willful dishonesty from honest mistake. For example, when cross-examining a witness, lawyers look for contradictions between what the witness says and previous statements by that person. The prior statements can be in an earlier hearing such as a preliminary inquiry or in statements to the police or other entities. They can even be in earlier statements in the very trial that is ongoing. Jurors tend to think of the truth as immutable and therefore expect the statements by a witness to be consistent over time. When counsel uncovers a contradiction in the statements of a witness, this can be very effective in undermining that witness's credibility or, at the very least, the witness's reliability.

Judges, being experienced triers of fact, know that not all contradictions imply dishonesty or even unreliability in a witness. A witness who tells the police that an event took place at about 6:00 p.m. but later in court places the time at closer to 7:00 p.m. is not necessarily dishonest. She may have had the opportunity to think through her day more carefully and be more precise in her time estimate. Similarly, a witness who initially indicates that a fight she witnessed took place on December 19, 2003 may correct herself and say it was December 18, 2003 without calling into question her credibility. Usually, there is no dispute that the fight in dispute in the litigation is the same fight the witness observed. The trier of fact must look at the contradiction and determine whether it is significant given the issues in dispute in the litigation or whether it is simply an indication of the witness's nervousness. If the key issue is who the aggressor was, the witness may have given excellent evidence describing the way in which each of the parties conducted themselves. Being uncertain of the exact date is of no consequence to the value of that evidence and should not impact on it. Nevertheless, opposing counsel may try to trap witnesses in silly contradictions and it is important for the trier of fact to assess whether the contradiction is significant before determining what impact those contradictions will have. It is also within the purview of the trial judge to stop counsel from pursuing picayune or irrelevant contradictions because of the potential to confuse the jury.

Typically, leading questions are used extensively in cross-examination. Lawyers sometimes refer to this as "leading the witness down the garden path." The questioning is not hostile or threatening to the witness, which would only tend to make the witness more wary and careful with her responses, but gradually works the witness into a corner, forcing her to divulge the desired information. The examiner begins by asking the witness a series of inoffensive questions, which cause the witness to increasingly relax. She lets her defences down, developing a false confidence in her ability to deal with what she anticipated would be an onslaught from opposing counsel. Consider the following exchange between defence counsel and a witness who has testified he saw the accused strike the victim at a house party:

"Now, you were at the party on Halloween night last year?"

"Yes, I was."

"And you had been to Bert's Halloween parties before, right?"

"That's correct."

"And Bert throws a good party, doesn't he?"

"Yes, he does."

"So you were looking forward to having a good time that night?"

"I was."

"And there were a lot of your friends there having a good time, weren't there?"

"Quite a few, yes."

"People were drinking alcohol at the party, your friends were consuming alcohol, weren't they?"

"Yes, most people were drinking."

"Well, it's quite natural, quite expected to drink at a Halloween party, I take it?"

"Yes, it's common."

"And you were drinking too, weren't you?"

"Well, I guess so, yes."

"You arrived at the party at 9:00 p.m. or so?"

"Yes."

"Had you had anything to drink before going to Bert's?"

"A few beers, I guess."

"A few beers, would that be more than two?"

"Well, a bit more, I guess."

"So, four or five beers?"

"Probably, I wasn't counting."

"Okay, and you had your first drink at the party around 9:00 p.m.?"

"I suppose."

"People were drinking shooters, at the party, kind of a loosen up and get to know ya thing?"

"Yeah, Bert had shooters lined up at the door to welcome us."

"And you had a few of those when you arrived?"

"I expect that I did."

"And a few being four or five?"

"Could be."

"And the fight in question took place at 4:30 the next morning?"

"About that time, yes."

"So you'd been drinking and partying that whole time, I take it?"

"Pretty much so, I guess."

As you can see, counsel has slowly worked the witness into a corner where he acknowledges that he consumed a huge quantity of alcohol that night. At the very least, the trier of fact will have to give his testimony less weight, if not discount the testimony entirely, because of his level of impairment.

Cross-examination has another role to play in relation to evidence matters: to gain information that is helpful to your case from the opponent's witness. This can be as valuable to a party as attacking credibility. However, the witness usually does not want to give helpful information. In such cases, examining counsel may use very specific leading questions that force the witness to give very short answers. Consider the following exchange between defence counsel and a crime scene investigator who has testified against the accused:

> "You examined the body at the scene?"
> "I did."
> "And you saw my client, Frank Getty, there?"
> "I did."
> "Did you observe any blood on his hands, clothing, or any other part of his body?"
> "I did not."
> "Yet there was blood all over the room where the victim was found, wasn't there?"
> "There was."

Through this tightly scripted questioning, the examiner has controlled a non-supportive witness and obtained valuable concessions and information. Note that the last question is meant to imply that if the accused had killed the victim, he would have gotten blood on his clothes, given that there was blood all over the room. The examiner might have asked this question outright: "So, can you explain how my client could have killed the victim and gotten no blood on himself?" However, this strategy carries a risk: if the witness replies, "No," the gamble has paid off, but if the witness offers a credible explanation, it can be devastating to the examiner's case. For example, the witness may well say:

> "Yes counsel, I can. I noticed that your client's hair was wet, as if he had recently showered. I then examined the downstairs shower, which was also wet, and in the drain we recovered traces of blood, which we matched to the victim. If you want my opinion, I think your client killed the victim, then went downstairs and showered before calling the police."

As long as this answer is responsive to the question, counsel is powerless to stop it. It is like letting a genie out of a bottle.

Limitations on Cross-Examination

We sometimes get the impression from watching television shows that cross-examination is a matter of shouting at and badgering a witness to the point that they emotionally break down and admit everything. This is not the sort of cross-examination that will be permitted in Canadian courts of law. Yes, counsel is entitled to "test" the witness, to challenge her and point out discrepancies and logical gaps, but the witness is entitled to a certain degree of respect. This means that lawyers, when questioning a witness, must not be insulting, aggressive, or hostile in either tone or manner. The judge has the right and obligation to restrict cross-examination that is irrelevant, prolix, or insulting. Prolix cross-examination occurs when the examiner is unnecessarily lengthy in questioning or pursues a topic in excessively minute detail. The point is that counsel must avoid wearing the witness down to the point where she will say anything just to get off the stand. In addition, counsel is not permitted to suggest or imply facts that are not in evidence or that counsel is not in a position to prove, or the judge may order that the conversation be struck from the record, as in the following example:

> Examining counsel: "Witness, how often do you get stoned?"
>
> Witness: "I don't do drugs."
>
> Examining counsel: "Come, come, witness, you're a teenager. You expect the jury to believe that you don't do any drugs?"
>
> Witness: "No, I don't."
>
> Examining counsel: "So, you are really trying to assert that you have never smoked marijuana?"
>
> Witness: "No, I haven't."
>
> Examining counsel: "How about on the May long weekend when you went to Long Beach with your friends?"
>
> Witness: "None of them smoke marijuana."
>
> Examining counsel: "So a bunch of teenagers go to Long Beach for a wild weekend and sit around playing Monopoly?"
>
> Witness: "Trivial Pursuit, actually."
>
> Opposing counsel: "I object to this line of questioning."
>
> Judge: "Finally. What about it, counsel, do you have any evidence to support these allegations?"
>
> Examining counsel: "Well no, Your Lordship. I was sort of hoping that he might just admit to it. I thought all young kids did drugs."
>
> Judge: "Well, you're way out of line, counsel. You can't go around making negative allegations without any evidence to back it up. I'm going to strike that entire conversation and you had better be a lot more careful in the future or I'll cite you for contempt."

A related issue arose in *R v. Ellard*, in which a young woman in British Columbia was charged, and eventually convicted, of the bullying murder of a female classmate, Reena Virk. Crown counsel cross-examined Ms. Ellard and repeatedly asked her to explain why the Crown witnesses would lie in their testimony. The Court of Appeal, in reviewing the Crown's questioning, stated (at para. 22):

> The potential prejudice arising from this form of questioning is that it tends to shift the burden of proof from the Crown to the accused. It could induce a jury to analyze the case on the reasoning that if an accused cannot say why a witness would give false evidence against her, the witness's testimony may be true. The risk of such a course of reasoning undermines the presumption of innocence and the doctrine of reasonable doubt. The mind of the trier of fact must remain firmly fixed on whether the Crown proved its case on the requisite standard and not be diverted by the question whether the accused provided a motive for a witness to lie.

A condensed version of the *Ellard* decision, in which portions of the improper questioning are reproduced, is available on the Emond Montgomery website at www.emp.ca/evidence.

The courts impose these limits on cross-examination, not only in the interest of a fair trial, but because the behaviour of counsel affects the public's perception of the justice system. If the judicial process is seen as unfair and witnesses are permitted to be bullied, the public may view the justice system as hostile and avoid the courts, leading to greater lawlessness in society.

Cross-Examining Your Own Witness

By calling a witness to testify, counsel is taken to be "vouching" for the witness's credibility. It stands to reason that counsel would not usually call someone to testify whom it thinks is unreliable or untruthful. Therefore, counsel is not usually permitted to cross-examine its own witness. To do so would be to attack the very witness being offered up to the court as trustworthy. However, sometimes witnesses turn out to be neither trustworthy nor cooperative. In such cases, counsel may want to cross-examine the witness. If counsel wishes to engage in cross-examination of its own witness, it must seek the court's permission to do so.

There are two ways that counsel can get permission from a judge to challenge its own witness's. The first is to ask that the witness be declared hostile. A **hostile witness** is just what it sounds like—a witness who responds with hostility to the lawyer's questioning. The exchange might go something like this:

hostile witness
a witness who has been called by a party to give evidence but is uncooperative and responds with hostility to the questions posed by counsel during cross-examination

> "Do you know the accused person, Randolph Small?"
> "What if I do?"
> "Can you tell me how long you have known Mr. Small?"
> "Long enough."
> "I'm not very clear about how long 'long enough' is."
> "Well, that's your problem then, isn't it?"
> "Your Honour, I'd ask that the witness be declared hostile."

If the judge declares the witness hostile, counsel can shift into cross-examination to more closely control the witness and to attempt to corner the witness into being truthful.

The second approach is to ask the court to declare the witness to be "adverse." Unlike a hostile witness, an **adverse witness** may be polite and forthcoming in her evidence, yet it is simply clear that the witness's interests are aligned with the opponent and that she is likely to colour her evidence in favour of the opponent. This may be the case where one party is suing another and calls the opposing party's spouse to testify because she is uniquely positioned to provide the information required to win the case. The spouse may be honest and of good character yet the information she provides can be expected to be unfavourable because she is biased in favour of her spouse. In practice, counsel would likely only call such a witness where counsel has in hand a statement from the witness confirming the information that counsel wishes to get before the trier of fact. Because the statement would be considered hearsay and be inadmissible, counsel must have the person testify if the information is to get before the trier of fact. When the spouse reluctantly testifies and "disappoints" by testifying differently about the events she had described in the earlier statement, counsel can apply to the court under s. 9 of the *Canada Evidence Act* to have the witness declared adverse:

adverse witness
a witness whose testimony shows her interests to be aligned with the opponent and who is therefore likely to colour her evidence in favour of the opponent

9(1) A party producing a witness shall not be allowed to impeach his credit by general evidence of bad character, but if the witness, in the opinion of the court, proves adverse, the party may contradict him by other evidence, or, by leave of the court, may prove that the witness made at other times a statement inconsistent with his present testimony, but before the last mentioned proof can be given the circumstances of the supposed statement, sufficient to designate the particular occasion, shall be mentioned to the witness, and he shall be asked whether or not he did make the statement.

9(2) Where the party producing a witness alleges that the witness made at other times a statement in writing, reduced to writing, or recorded on audio tape or video tape or otherwise, inconsistent with the witness' present testimony, the court may, without proof that the witness is adverse, grant leave to that party to cross-examine the witness as to the statement and the court may consider the cross-examination in determining whether in the opinion of the court the witness is adverse.

It may be possible to establish this adversity by showing an inconsistency between what the witness says on the stand and an earlier statement made by that witness. However, the cross-examination must be restricted to the inconsistencies evident in the witness's testimony and cannot expand to a general attack on the character of the witness, because the party calling the witness still imparts an aura of credibility to the witness by presenting this witness to the court. At the same time, the cross-examination can extend beyond "impeaching" the specific testimony of the witness and can permit an exploration of the underlying circumstances to attempt to ascertain other relevant information.

What use can the evidence derived from this cross-examination be put to? If the witness acknowledges that the earlier statement given by her is in fact correct, then the trier of fact may adopt that evidence as a proven fact in the case. If, however, the witness sticks to her guns and denies making the earlier statement or says that it must have been wrong, the trier of fact cannot rely on that earlier statement to prove the fact in issue. The statement, can, however, be used to establish that the witness cannot be relied on in relation to the "new" evidence. Thus, a witness who says he saw Alex stab the deceased and later says Alex wasn't even there is a less believable witness. While the trier of fact may not be able to rely on the earlier evidence of stabbing to convict Alex, they can disregard the part about Alex not being there as equally unreliable. In some circumstances, the earlier, recanted version of the evidence may be admissible if it was taken in circumstances that make it particularly reliable. Taking this approach one step further, the Supreme Court of Canada in *R v. B. (K.G.)* determined that a prior inconsistent statement that has **particularized indicia of reliability** can be admitted as proof of the truth of the assertions in the statement. This is not due to the provisions of the *Canada Evidence Act* but more properly as a result of a hearsay exception as outlined in *R v. B. (K.G.)*, which is discussed in more detail in chapter 6, "Traditional Exceptions to the Hearsay Rule."

particularized indicia of reliability
specific details of the circumstances that make the evidence more likely to be true

AIR AMNESIA

A high-profile example of how ss. 9(1) and 9(2) of the *Canada Evidence Act* provisions may come into effect arose in the Air India case concerning the bombing of Air India Flight 182 in which 329 people were killed. As seen in this example, a hostile witness may be nothing more than a frightened witness who succumbs to threats or anticipated reprisals and develops circumstantial amnesia about the issues before the court. We will refer to the witness as Ms. X because she is in the witness protection program and cannot be named. Although the accused clearly know who she is, she has some concerns that publication of her identity will put her in danger from militant Babbar Khalsa members.

When called to testify, Ms. X claimed to have no memory of statements she made to the RCMP where she stated that Ajaib Singh Bagri confessed his involvement in the Air India bombing to her and subsequently threatened her life if she revealed this to anyone. She made the statements over a considerable period of time in a series of 17 interviews.

Crown counsel sought to have Ms. X declared hostile to permit cross-examination of her in relation to her earlier statements, pointing out to the court how unlikely it was that she would forget these conversations given her discussions with the police, the fact that her life had been threatened, and the fact that she lost relatives on the Air India flight. Ms. X had always told the police that she would never testify against Bagri and her "forgetfulness" appears to be the embodiment of this promise.

The judge rejected the Crown argument in a ruling where he stated that although he did not believe that the witness did not remember these events, he was not convinced that the inconsistencies in her testimony about Bagri were enough to have her declared hostile.

The court had earlier ruled against the Crown request to have their witness Inderjit Singh Reyat declared hostile. After pleading guilty to his role in the bombing and receiving a five-year sentence, he also developed significant memory loss, which limited any usefulness to his testimony.

FAILURE TO CROSS-EXAMINE A WITNESS

When cross-examining an opponent's witness, counsel must give the witness a chance to explain any contradictions or inconsistencies that it intends to later rely on. This rule ensures fairness in the proceeding and prevents the confusion that could result if this approach were not taken. Failure to cross-examine a witness on a point that counsel wishes to later contradict the witness on could result in the judge's directing that the earlier witness be recalled so that she can comment on the discrepancy between her testimony and the later evidence. Not only can this process be confusing and disruptive, the witness may be unavailable. If the witness cannot be recalled, the judge may reject the contradictory evidence entirely or the contradiction may be minimized to the point where it loses its impact.

The judge is charged with ensuring that the trier of fact has helpful and reliable evidence before it. If counsel pursues evidence late in a trial that contradicts earlier testimony that was not cross-examined, the trier of fact is left with an evidentiary imbalance. It unfairly advantages one party by denying the earlier witness the opportunity to explain the apparent contradiction, which has the effect of misleading the trier of fact.

Fairness mandates that when counsel contradicts the witness with a prior inconsistent statement, counsel must alert the witness to the inconsistency and give her an opportunity to explain it. Alerting the witness to a contradiction in an earlier statement is referred to as "laying the foundation" for this particular attack on credibility.

Counsel can even be held to the requirement to cross-examine a witness on a particular fact or else be seen to have accepted this evidence without challenging its veracity. This could be a fatal decision. It sometimes seems pointless to cross-examine because counsel will expect to hear a series of denials but the trier of fact can be aided by hearing those denials in order to assess the demeanour of the witness and weigh that evidence against the opponent's.

RE-EXAMINATION

Once a witness has gone through examination-in-chief and cross-examination, the original examining counsel will often wish to ask some more questions. This can be problematic if the re-examination raises issues that opposing counsel wants to re-cross–examine on, which could lead to a potentially endless cycle. To avoid this, the courts have developed rules governing re-examination.

Re-examination is restricted to asking questions on topics that were not dealt with in examination-in-chief and that the examiner could not have anticipated would be dealt with in cross-examination. In other words, re-examination cannot be used to get the last word in and re-emphasize the key points brought out in direct examination. It is also not appropriate to "split your case" by bringing out some of your key points in examination-in-chief, saving some additional ones until after the cross-examination.

If something new and unanticipated arises in cross-examination, counsel can, with leave of the court, ask a few additional questions in that area. Opposing counsel may even be permitted to ask a few questions arising from the re-examination. It is entirely a factor of the patience and flexibility of the judge.

One instance where re-examination will generally be permitted is where the witness's credibility has been attacked in cross-examination. The court usually permits some questions designed to "rehabilitate" the credibility of the witness. If the attack has been with regard to the witness's general credibility, counsel may even be permitted to call additional witnesses, including possibly expert witnesses, to provide evidence to reinforce the general credibility of the witness or undermine this attack on general credibility.

CREDIBILITY AND RELIABILITY

By calling a witness, a party vouches for that witness's credibility, in effect saying to the court, this is a person worthy of being believed. Typically, that witness dutifully recites the expected evidence that supports the party who called her to testify. The opponent, in cross-examination, tries to limit or minimize the harmful impact of this witness's evidence. This can be done by attacking the credibility of the witness or by undermining the witness's reliability. These concepts differ because attacks on credibility imply that the witness is trying to deceive the trier of fact, whereas attacks on reliability suggest only that the witness got it wrong, and apply equally to deceitful and honest witnesses.

Credibility

Typically, counsel attacks the credibility of a witness by attempting to show that the witness is biased and therefore has a motive for lying. The relationship that the witness has with the party they have testified on behalf of will imply motive or lack of motive. For example, it is presumed that a spouse, child, parent, or other close relative will shade her evidence to support her relative. "Blood is thicker than water" is an expression that will resonate with most triers of fact. Another way to reveal bias is to show that the witness and the party have a common interest, such as where the two are business partners or the witness stands to benefit from a successful verdict by the party. In some cases, counsel may attempt to prove that the witness has been induced to change or fabricate her story, such as where counsel had evidence of an exchange of cash or benefits such as a promotion that could be linked to their testimony.

Bias can be more general. The witness may think all young people are trouble-makers or have religious or racial views that favour the party she is testifying on behalf of and discriminate against the opponent. Where bias can be shown, the trier of fact is entitled to discount the evidence of that witness on the basis that the witness's bias may colour her perspective and cause her to either intentionally or unintentionally make misleading statements.

Counsel may also attack the witness's credibility by attempting to show that the witness has a history of dishonesty and is of poor character. Thus, a witness (excluding a criminal accused) may be subject to broad-ranging questions about her criminal past, reputation in the community, and general character.

The following techniques, then, are commonly used to challenge a witness in cross-examination:

- showing that the witness has a bias that would taint her evidence;

- showing that the witness has interests that are aligned with the opponent;

- establishing that the witness may have succumbed to inducements to alter or fabricate a story;

- showing that the witness is prejudiced against a party, either because of personal beliefs or just because of who the party is;

- attacking the character of the witness by showing a criminal record or other bad acts; and

- attacking the witness's reputation.

Reliability

Counsel attempts to undermine the confidence that the trier of fact has in the witness's reliability so that the evidence will not compare well with the opponent's evidence in the final analysis. Attacks on the reliability of the witness are primarily focused on the witness's capacity to observe, remember, and communicate.

For example, counsel may attempt to discredit the testimony of a witness who claims to have seen the accused stab the victim by establishing that the incident was at night and the witness was 20 metres away, behind some bushes, and not wearing her prescription glasses. Counsel may also try to reduce the impact of testimony given in examination-in-chief by testing the witness's ability to recall details of the event. If the witness does not recall whether the accident happened at night or during the day, whether it was raining or sunny, whether the accused's car was white or black, or whether anyone else was at the scene, her claim to have a complete memory of other specific points may be called into question by the trier of fact. Finally, counsel may attempt to show that the witness's testimony is imprecise or misleading and therefore unreliable. For example, a witness who describes the accused as "completely blotto," and then concedes under cross-examination that she really meant she smelled alcohol on his breath, is unreliable. Or if she says that the assailant was a "giant, hulking man," but later agrees that he was about the same build as the prosecutor, who is 1.7 metres tall (5 foot, 8 inches) and 63 kilograms (140 pounds), she shows her testimony to be unreliable.

IMPEACHING TESTIMONY

There are several methods that may be used to "impeach" the evidence of a witness—that is, limit the impact of the evidence on the trier of fact or convince the trier of fact to ignore the evidence entirely. The most common method is cross-examination, where the statements of the witness are challenged directly. Internal consistency, or pointing out where the witness has said different things during the course of her testimony, is another mechanism of impeachment. In addition, a witness can be challenged with regard to previous statements that are inconsistent with what she has stated under oath on the witness stand. Additionally, other witnesses, including on occasion expert witnesses, can be called to contradict what a witness has said, thus eliminating or reducing the impact of the witness's statements.

Prior Inconsistent Statements

Impeachment through prior inconsistent statements involves, as a first step, confirming the evidence that counsel wishes to establish a prior contradictory statement regarding. Next, the witness is alerted that there is a prior statement that counsel believes is contradictory. The witness is given an opportunity to read the prior statement, and then asked whether the statement was truthful. In so doing, the examiner hopes to trick the witness into saying that two contradictory statements are both true, thus destroying the witness's credibility. Occasionally, the witness will be cooperative enough to adopt the former statements, aiding the examining opponent. If the statement is adopted, it forms part of that person's evidence and may be weighed by the trier of fact. If the prior statement is not adopted, it can only be used to challenge the truthfulness of that witness, but is not evidence of its contents. The exception to this is where there are **circumstantial guarantees of reliability** that allow the statement to fit into the principled approach to hearsay exceptions, such as in *R v. B. (K.G.)*, referred to above.

circumstantial guarantees of reliability
aspects of the circumstances surrounding the formation of the evidence that enhance its reliability

BOLSTERING THE CREDIBILITY OF YOUR OWN WITNESS

Because all witnesses are presumed to be truthful unless shown to be otherwise, a party is prohibited from calling evidence that is designed to enhance or shore up the credibility of one of his witnesses. For example, Robert testifies that he bought a car privately, thinking that it was brand new because the odometer showed only 23 kilometres, but discovered a year later that it had 30,000 kilometres on it and had been in an accident. The defendant claims that he told Robert there were 30,000 kilometres on the car, and explained that the odometer said 23 kilometres because the mechanism had to be repaired after the accident. Robert wishes to call Father Michael, who has known him as a parishioner and choir boy for the past 18 years. Father Michael, the court is told, will testify that Robert is as honest as the day is long, that he handled church monies for years, and that he was very polite and kind to the older parishioners. Is this evidence relevant? Would it help the trier of fact? Should the judge admit it?

The evidence will not be admitted because it is offered simply to enhance the believability of the witness. Father Michael knows nothing of the parties' transaction but is prepared to support his longtime parishioner from a sense of duty. We also recognize that in many instances otherwise honest and reliable people have been known to be untruthful. (See chapter 8, "Character Evidence.")

COLLATERAL FACTS RULE

This is a case management rule for the benefit of the court. In order to conduct a trial that does not spin out of control, judges will restrict the calling of evidence in a number of ways. Sometimes, it is just by limiting the number of witnesses that can be called. Where one witness has testified in relation to a fact, does it add much to have 10, 20, or 30 witnesses say the same thing? Many litigants feel that "more is better" so it is a matter of self-protection for the courts to place a limit on the number of witnesses who will be permitted on one particular issue. In addition, if the courts permit one side to engage in unlimited calling of witnesses, the issues may blur and the trier of fact may lose its focus regarding what it should be determining. In order to provide a protection against the unlimited calling of evidence, courts have developed the **collateral facts rule**. This basically states that where an opponent's witness provides contradictory evidence on matters not in issue, counsel are not permitted to call other evidence in response. Cross-examination on the point is still permitted, but no additional witnesses may be called to disprove the collateral facts.

collateral facts rule
rule that limits the calling of additional evidence to contradict evidence on an issue that is not before the court

Let's say that a witness to a car accident, introduced as a chartered accountant for the past 10 years, testifies that the defendant ran the red light. The defendant happens to know that the witness graduated from high school less than five years ago, so he could not have been a chartered accountant for the last 10 years. He wants to call evidence from the Chartered Accountants of Canada to prove that the witness lied. The collateral facts rule would stop the defendant from calling this witness. He could cross-examine the witness and try to prove him wrong, but if the witness stuck to his guns, the defendant would have no recourse and would be essentially "stuck" with that answer. The trier of fact may choose not to believe the evidence of the witness regarding his vocation, but since it does not relate to an issue between the parties, valuable court time will not be spent in proving this collateral fact. If the witness's vocation evidence is not believed, there will be an absence of evidence on the point, as if nothing were ever said about it.

The rule comes into play often on issues of whether a witness had consumed drugs or was drinking, things that the witness may not wish to share. If the witness denies these allegations, whether counsel will be permitted to call any witnesses to contradict the claims will depend on whether the court feels that the evidence of substance abuse is collateral. Some would argue that matters of credibility or reliability are always substantive while others claim that they are collateral. It seems that in Canada, the courts lean toward finding general credibility matters to be more collateral than substantive. Even there, the courts have shown an inclination to find exceptions, including where the credibility issue goes to showing

1. bias or interest in the litigation,

2. past convictions or untruthfulness, or

3. expert evidence that undermines the reliability of the witness.

Some argue strongly in favour of a more flexible approach to this matter, suggesting that the judge should have considerable discretion to weigh the probative value of the evidence and to admit it when the probative value exceeds the prejudice. In weighing the probative value, the judge could determine, in the context of the matter before her, what significance the contradictory evidence would have and not be bound by a fixed and inflexible rule to reject evidence that would be useful for the trier of fact.

We see some movement in the direction of flexibility in the recent decision of the BC Court of Appeal. In *J.R.I.G. v. Tyhurst* the court dealt with a similar fact issue in a civil context. The collateral facts rule would bar the plaintiff from calling evidence to prove that there had been no "contamination" or cross-fertilization between the two plaintiffs as a result of media reports, contact with the Crown in the criminal trial, and contact with plaintiff's counsel. Because the trier of fact would weigh the value of the similar fact evidence without taking into account the defence's assertion that there was "opportunity for contamination," Huddart J suggested that the plaintiff might therefore be permitted to lead evidence to support the claim of cross-fertilization. The issue was not resolved but left to another day.

REFRESHING MEMORY

With certain witnesses or at certain points in examination-in-chief or cross-examination, a witness's memory may fail him. This is not necessarily an attempt by the witness to lie or distort evidence, but could be merely an indication of nervousness or even forgetfulness with the passage of time since the incident being described. In these circumstances, it is permissible (subject to the judge's discretion) for counsel to jog the witness's memory in various ways. Typically, counsel will show the witness a previous statement. This will often spur a memory and the witness can then continue to testify about the incident from this revived memory. If the witness's previous statement does not revive a memory, the witness may still be permitted to adopt the earlier statement as a truthful statement at the time that it was made. This statement would be hearsay, even though it is that witness's statement but it may be sufficiently reliable to deserve some weight.

Other methods can be used to jog a witness's memory including showing the witness a photograph; playing an audiotape, videotape, or other sound or video recording; taking the witness to the scene of an incident; permitting the witness to examine an exhibit; or using any other strategy that a judge deems is a legitimate effort to access a witness's memory.

Therefore, refreshing a witness's memory can generate evidence in two ways. One is described as **present memory revived**, which implies that the technique of refreshing the memory caused the witness to revive actual memories and details of the incident. Implicit in this is that the revived memories are more complete than the information that was used to jog the memory. On the other hand, if the witness remembers only the words in the statement and not the incident itself, the witness is probably relying on the statement and not having an original memory. In this circumstance, we refer to the process as **past recollection recorded**. With this, the effort at revival does not jog an original memory but the witness acknowledges making the statement and its "truthfulness at the time." The statement may be admitted. Its weight may be less than testimony that derives from an actually memory of the events, particularly where detail is important or effective cross-examination is thwarted by the witness's reliance on the statement for all of her "recollection."

present memory revived
process whereby the witness revives actual memories and details of an incident; cf. past recollection recorded

past recollection recorded
process whereby the witness recalls the words he or she made in a statement but not the incident itself

CORROBORATION

Corroborating evidence has not always worked to support just outcomes in criminal proceedings. The term **corroboration** describes evidence that supports or confirms other evidence. So, if you allege that your neighbour dented your car, another neighbour who also saw it happen would be corroborative of your testimony. As the laws of evidence developed, certain kinds of evidence were thought to be unreliable on their own and so rules requiring there to be independent evidence confirming the substance of the "unsafe" evidence were put in place. The difficulty was that evidence considered to be unsafe included the evidence of children (just because of their age) and in some instances women (because of their sex). It therefore became difficult to obtain a conviction in cases of sexual crimes against children and women where no corroborating evidence existed. Accomplices to a crime were another group where warnings to the jury were required. This is because an accomplice who implicated his partner was almost certainly buying some lesser penalty by cooperating with the authorities. The selfish motive made the allegations against the partner suspect.

In Canada, these rules have changed and, like in many areas of evidence law, the courts have largely moved toward a "principled approach" to the issue of corroboration, moving away from mandatory and arbitrary corroboration warnings to discretionary warnings. With discretionary warnings, the judge only warns the trier of fact about the danger of the evidence if the circumstances warrant such a warning. In adopting the new approach, the courts acknowledged that the rules surrounding corroboration had become extremely rigid and formulistic, often ignoring rather than considering the facts of the case. For corroboration to exist, it was not good enough for it simply to support the allegation; it also had to

- be independent,
- confirm the testimony corroborated in a "material particular" (a particular fact that is specific to the matter before the court), and
- implicate the accused.

Under this formula, a child's evidence that she was sexually assaulted by a neighbour could not proceed based only on the evidence of the child, even with confirmation that there had been injuries from sexual penetration. The medical evidence would be independent and even confirm the material particular of penetration but would not independently implicate the accused. Without DNA, regardless of the clarity and credibility of the child's testimony, no conviction could occur. This approach to the evidence of a child is now considered to be outmoded thinking. Today, a child's evidence may deserve special scrutiny but will not need corroboration for a conviction.

Some evidence still cries out for corroboration because of the inherently "dangerous" circumstances surrounding it. For example, Douglas Martin, a jailhouse informant in the Shannon Murrin murder trial, who shared a cell with Murrin, claimed that Murrin confessed to him that he killed Mindy Tran. His evidence was thoroughly undermined by defence counsel, however, who established that Martin had 109 criminal convictions that included one for perjury. He was known in the cells as "Father Confession" because of the nine times that he claimed to have been

corroboration
evidence that supports or confirms other evidence

the recipient of jailhouse murder confessions. Martin was also involved in the conviction of Thomas Sophonow, who was later released after being exonerated by DNA evidence despite Martin's obtaining his "confession." The experience with Douglas Martin and Thomas Sophonow has gone a long way toward proving just how dangerous evidence from jailhouse informants can be. In addition to jailhouse informants, witnesses of "unsavoury character" will also attract warnings.

Currently, the only situation in which the evidence of a witness attracts a mandatory warning is where the accused has been charged with one of the following historical offences: offences of high treason; perjury; or procuring a feigned marriage. All of these *Criminal Code* offences specify that no person shall be convicted of the offence on the evidence of only one witness, unless the evidence of that witness is corroborated in a material particular by evidence that implicates the accused person. For other classes of precautionary witnesses such as accomplices, jailhouse informants, children and unsavoury characters, warnings are discretionary for the judge. Note that these warnings are now

- no longer mandatory for specific categories of witnesses,
- no longer limited to specific categories of witnesses, and
- not limited to a formulistic warning that includes implication of the accused.

The Supreme Court of Canada case dealing with the discretionary nature of these warnings is *Vetrovec v. The Queen*. In a later Supreme Court decision, the court dealt with the discretion of a judge to provide a **Vetrovec warning** about the testimony of jailhouse informants in the case of *R v. Brooks*. Brooks was charged with murdering his girlfriend's 19-month-old daughter. The disturbing facts of the case are set out below (at paras. 32–36):

Vetrovec warning a warning to the jury given where the judge determines that the evidence of a particular witness is called into question and requires special scrutiny; the jurors are cautioned that they may accept the evidence without corroboration but it is dangerous to do so without independent confirmation of material parts of that evidence

Around 10:30 p.m. on December 13, 1992, 19-month-old Samantha Johnings stirred in her sleep when her aunt checked on her before leaving the apartment. The next day at 11:00 a.m., Samantha's mother Norma Jean Johnings found her dead in her crib. She had been murdered. Rigor mortis was setting in. There was blood and vomit on her face. Her left eye was swollen shut and she had three bruises on her head caused by blunt force trauma. The body was wrapped in a green comforter. Her mother attempted in vain to revive her. She then called 911.

Only two persons had access to Samantha on the night of her murder—her mother and the respondent. The respondent had been living in the apartment with Norma Jean since the previous October. He was not the father of Samantha, nor of her newborn brother, Anthony.

At autopsy, it was noted that Samantha's genital area had a well-demarcated area of bruising and redness, which was inconsistent with a diaper rash but consistent with a rubbing action, or the use of a blunt object. Trace amounts of semen were found on vaginal and anal swabs taken from her body. The cause of death was acute brain injury. The head injuries could have but did not necessarily precede the injuries to the vagina and anus. A healing lesion of one centimetre in diameter was also noted on the right buttock.

DNA testing of the sperm proved inconclusive, likely due to contamination of the sample. No one could be included or excluded as the source.

The respondent's grey track pants were found in the apartment and seized on January 27, 1993. Those pants contained blood stains of the same blood type as Samantha's. An expert witness for the Crown testified that the blood's DNA signature matched Samantha's and that the frequency of that profile in Caucasians is one in 80 million. The track pants had semen on them, as well as a juice substance, similar to what was found in Samantha's bottle.

Although the court was divided on whether the trial judge should have given a *Vetrovec* warning in relation to the evidence of two jailhouse informants, the justices did agree that the decision to give a *Vetrovec* warning is properly at the discretion of the judge:

> In *Vetrovec*, Dickson J (as he then was) held that a trial judge has the discretion, and not the duty, to give a clear and sharp warning to the jury with respect to the testimony of certain "unsavoury" witnesses. Dickson J followed what he referred to as the "common sense" approach, moving away from "blind and empty formalism" and "ritualistic incantations ... ."

The court identified two factors to be considered in determining whether to give the warning, the credibility of the witness and the importance of the witness to the Crown's case (at para. 4):

> In exercising his or her discretion to warn the jury regarding certain evidence, the trial judge may consider, *inter alia*, the credibility of the witness and the importance of the evidence to the Crown's case. These factors affect whether the *Vetrovec* warning is required. In other words, the greater the concern over the credibility of the witness and the more important the evidence, the more likely the *Vetrovec* caution will be mandatory. Where the evidence of so called "unsavoury witnesses" represents the whole of the evidence against the accused, a "clear and sharp" *Vetrovec* warning may be warranted. Where, however, there is strong evidence to support the conviction in the absence of the potentially "unsavoury" evidence, and less reason to doubt the witness's credibility, the *Vetrovec* warning would not be required, and a lesser instruction would be justified.

The majority, in determining that a "clear and sharp" warning was not required in the circumstances, quoted from the Crown's factum in noting that there was substantial corroborating evidence to support the credibility of the informants' information (at para. 10):

> There was a richness of detail concerning the circumstances of the event as opposed to a simple allegation or a bald admission by the accused. King and Balogh's evidence contained details as to the location of the injuries, the prior hitting of Samantha by the Respondent, the detail that the mother had also hit the child on occasion to discipline her, that Samantha was always crying and that she was crying on the night she died and that she choked.
>
> *Many of the facts in the accused's admissions to King and Balogh were confirmed by independent evidence.* The fact that the baby's mother's name was Norma, that she was the Respondent's girlfriend, that they lived in the apartment building near the Centre, and that the mother was going to testify against the Respondent were all accurate. *The evidence that the Respondent told King and Balogh that he had struck ... Samantha repeatedly in the head was consistent with the medical and forensic evidence as to the location of the injuries. The fact that Samantha choked was confirmed by the vomit on ... her face. The fact that the [Respondent] would hit Samantha when she cried was confirmed by the evidence of witnesses at the trial. The fact that Samantha was crying on the night she was killed was confirmed by the mother.*

Judges therefore, are to objectively assess the evidence and to warn where the evidence of the witness is a significant part of the Crown's case and the credibility of the witness is objectively questionable. Now that the rigid formula is gone, judges can give a range of warnings tailor-made to the degree of danger inherent in that witness's testimony.

CHAPTER SUMMARY

In order to testify at a hearing, a witness must be competent and compellable. Children may give evidence if they are deemed competent under the evidence act of the province in which the trial is held.

Witnesses are questioned during examination-in-chief, cross-examination, and re-examination.

Counsel is not permitted to ask leading questions during examination-in-chief unless the questions are in relation to introductory or uncontentious matters, or if counsel is questioning a witness about statements made by other witnesses for the purpose of contradicting those statements.

Counsel may ask an opponent's witness leading questions during cross-examination in an attempt to challenge or diminish the impact of the witness's testimony by showing that the witness is dishonest or unreliable, or to obtain information that is helpful to its case. However, the judge may restrict cross-examination that is irrelevant, prolix, or insulting, or that could prejudice the jury.

Generally, counsel is not allowed to cross-examine its own witness. However, if a judge declares a witness hostile or adverse, counsel may engage in cross-examination to elicit truthful information from the witness for the benefit of the trier of fact.

The court imposes rules to ensure that witnesses are treated fairly and that the information that is put before the trier of fact is reliable and not misleading, including the rule that counsel must give the witness a chance to explain any contradictions or inconsistencies that counsel intends to later rely on.

KEY TERMS

subpoena	hostile witness
summons	adverse witness
competence	particularized indicia of reliability
capacity	circumstantial guarantees of reliability
responsibility	collateral facts rule
incompetent	present memory revived
compellable	past recollection recorded
examination-in-chief	corroboration
cross-examination	*Vetrovec* warning

REFERENCES

Alberta Evidence Act, RSA 2000, c. A-18, s. 19.

B. (K.G.), R v. (1993), 79 CCC (3d) 257 (SCC).

Brooks, R v., [2000] 1 SCR 237.

Canada Evidence Act, RSC 1985, c. C-5.

Canadian Charter of Rights and Freedoms, part I of the *Constitution Act, 1982*, app. II, no. 44, s. 11.

Criminal Code, RSC 1985, c. C-46.

Ellard, R v., 2003 BCCA 68.

Evidence Act, RSBC 1996, c. 124, s. 5.

Evidence Act, RSNB 1973, c. E-11, s. 24.

Evidence Act, RSNL 1990, c. E-16, ss. 18 and 18.1.

Evidence Act, RSNS 1989, c. 154, s. 63.

Evidence Act, RSO 1990, c. E.23, ss. 18.1 and 18.2.

Evidence Act, SS 2006, c. E-11.2, s. 12.

Hebert, R v. (1990), 77 CR (4th) 147.

J.R.I.G. v. Tyhurst (2003), BCCA 224.

Manitoba Evidence Act, CCSM, c. E150, s. 24.

Marquard, R v. (1993), 25 CR (4th) 1.

Vetrovec v. The Queen, [1982] 1 SCR 811.

REVIEW QUESTIONS

1. What do we mean when we say that a witness is "called to give evidence" and how is this accomplished?

2. What are the two facets of the judicial test for competence of a witness?

3. Under the *Canada Evidence Act*, what must the judge determine before a child under the age of 14 is allowed to testify?

4. What is the difference between civil and criminal law in relation to spousal competency?

5. What does s. 5 of the *Canada Evidence Act* state?

6. What is the purpose of examination-in-chief?

7. What is a leading question? Give an example of this type of question.

8. Can a leading question ever be asked during examination-in-chief? Explain your answer.

9. What are the two major roles that cross-examination plays in a hearing?

10. What sorts of limits are placed on the cross-examination of witnesses?

11. In what circumstances is counsel not permitted to cross-examine its own witness?

12. In what circumstances might counsel be able to cross-examine its own witness?

13. What are some of the problems that can arise should counsel fail to cross-examine an opponent's witness?

14. What are the limits placed on re-examination of a witness?

15. What are some of the techniques that may be used to challenge the credibility of a witness?

16. What does it mean to "impeach the evidence of a witness"?

17. How does counsel use prior inconsistent statements to challenge a witness?

18. Why is there a court rule against bolstering the credibility of your own witness?

19. What is the collateral facts rule?

20. What are the two major methods of a refreshing a witness's memory? Explain each method.

21. What is corroboration evidence?

DISCUSSION QUESTIONS

1. Because mentally incompetent persons are not permitted to give evidence, they are more vulnerable to people who feel they can abuse them without fear that they will testify against them. Can you think of any ways that evidence law might deal with this problem?

2. Your client George offers his best friend, Armen, as an alibi witness. Armen is giving this evidence voluntarily. He promises that he will be at court at the date and time you have told him that his evidence is required. You decide not to subpoena him because you want to save George a few bucks and you do not want to antagonize Armen by making him think you find him unreliable. Discuss what problems there may be with this approach.

3. What problems would arise if leading questions were allowed in examination-in-chief? Can you think of any benefits to allowing such questions in examination-in-chief?

4. The rules governing corroborating evidence, such as with the evidence of a child, have changed dramatically in recent times. Discuss these changes. What do you think of this new approach to corroboration?

Glossary

administrative tribunals
decision-making bodies, similar to courts, that rule on regulatory disputes

admissible evidence
evidence that may be considered by the trier of fact

admission by action
meaning or intention conveyed by an act or gesture

admission of a party
anything said by a party by way of word or conduct that the other party wishes to introduce against that party

adversarial system
judicial process in which parties present evidence before an impartial decision-maker, who then makes a decision in the case

adverse witness
a witness whose testimony shows her interests to be aligned with the opponent and who is therefore likely to colour her evidence in favour of the opponent

air of reality test
a test of whether the defence to a charge is reasonable in light of the evidence

balance of probabilities
standard of proof in civil matters, determined on the basis of more likely than not

best evidence rule
a largely outdated rule that the original document must be presented in evidence if it is available

beyond a reasonable doubt
very high standard of proof in criminal matters

burden of proof
a party's obligation to prove certain facts or matters in issue

business record
a record made in the ordinary course of business by an individual performing the duties of employment who has no motive to fabricate

capacity
an acceptable ability to observe and then correctly recall observations or experiences, and an acceptable ability to communicate these observations to the trier of fact

charge to the jury
judge's instructions to the jury, before the jury begins deliberations, regarding the applicable law, the standard of proof, and the available defences

circumstantial evidence
indirect evidence from which the trier of fact can logically infer the existence of a material fact

circumstantial guarantees of reliability
aspects of the circumstances surrounding the formation of the evidence that enhance its reliability

co-conspirator exception
rule allowing evidence against one member of a conspiracy as evidence against all other members

collateral facts rule
rule that limits the calling of additional evidence to contradict evidence on an issue that is not before the court

***Collins* test**
test used by the courts to determine whether a police search is reasonable; the search must be authorized by law, the law that authorizes the search must itself be reasonable, and the search must be conducted in a reasonable manner

compellable
legally required to give evidence at a hearing

compendious mode of expressing facts
testimony in which the witness mixes opinion into his narrative in order to express himself; permitted by the court where it is difficult for the witness to express the information without stating an opinion

competence
the legal ability to give oral evidence in a hearing

conditional relevance
term describing evidence that may not initially appear relevant but is admitted on condition that its relevance will be established

conditionally admissible
term describing evidence that is admitted for a specific purpose but that is not at that stage admissible on the larger issue

confession rule
rule that a statement made to a person in authority is not admissible unless it was made voluntarily

conscriptive evidence
evidence obtained as a result of the accused's being compelled to participate in the creation or location of evidence

conspiracy
a common design or plan by two or more persons to commit a criminal act or omission

corroboration
evidence that supports or confirms other evidence

court martial
formal military justice process in which civilian rules of evidence apply

cross-examination
the questioning of a witness by opposing counsel after examination-in-chief

declaration against interest
a statement made by a party that is against the party's legal interest

derivative evidence
evidence that derives from a breach of an accused's rights

direct evidence
evidence given by a witness about a material fact that the witness experienced

directed verdict
the judge directs that the accused be acquitted because the Crown has not made a *prima facie* case

documentary evidence
any document, including writing, video, film, tapes, and photographs, presented in court for reference by the trier of fact

dying declaration
a statement made by a person who is certain they are about to die

examination-in-chief
questioning of a witness by the party who called the witness; its object is to bring out information that will establish facts that the litigant must prove to win the case

excited utterance
a statement made while the speaker's mind is still dominated by a startling event

excluded evidence
evidence that cannot be considered by the trier of fact

expert opinion
testimony given by a properly qualified person with specific expertise in an area that is in issue before the court; permitted in order to assist the trier of fact in coming to conclusions of fact in that area

hearsay
a statement, originally made out of court, that is repeated in court for the truth of its contents

hearsay evidence
evidence given by a witness that is based on information received from others rather than personal knowledge; generally considered inadmissible

hostile witness
a witness who has been called by a party to give evidence but is uncooperative and responds with hostility to the questions posed by counsel during cross-examination

implied statement
an action, behaviour, or course of conduct that conveys information to observers

incompetent
not permitted to give evidence

innocence at stake exception
an exception to solicitor–client privilege when the otherwise protected communication is necessary to establish the client's innocence

judges' privilege
privilege that protects judges and administrative tribunal members against disclosing information behind their decisions

judicial discretion
a judge's freedom to apply rules or decide issues in the context of a case

judicial notice
a judge's recognition of a fact without requiring a party to prove it

layperson's opinion
opinion given by an ordinary witness on a matter of ordinary experience; permitted where the opinion does not unnecessarily encroach on the trier of fact's role

litigation privilege
privilege that protects communications between a client's lawyer or law firm and third parties

material fact
a fact that relates to any matter in dispute between parties

moral prejudice
prejudice that results from the admission of evidence of bad character showing the accused to be a morally bad person and leading the trier of fact to conclude that he is guilty

natural justice
a fundamental legal principle entitling a person to a fair and unbiased hearing

non-suit
the judge directs the dismissal of the case because the plaintiff has failed to meet a *prima facie* case

non-testimonial evidence
evidence that is not in the form of words from a witness; typically an object

notorious fact
a fact that is so generally known and accepted that it may not reasonably be disputed

***Oakes* test**
test used by the courts to determine whether a Charter right or freedom can be limited by s. 1; the measure limiting the right or freedom must be sufficiently important and the means chosen must be reasonable and demonstrably justified

oath
promise made on the Bible or other holy book to tell the truth in court

oath helping
testimony by a witness in which he approves of, or comments favourably on the credibility of, another witness; generally prohibited because, in the view of the courts, a witness should have her testimony evaluated on its own without the need for another witness bolstering that testimony

***Oickle* rule**
rule requiring that the will of the accused has not been overborne by inducements, oppressive circumstances, or lack of an operating mind and that police trickery has not unfairly denied the accused his right to silence

opinion evidence
evidence given by a witness that is based on conclusions or inferences drawn from facts or observations; generally, the witness is not permitted to state the conclusions or inferences themselves, only the observations

oral evidence
evidence given verbally by witnesses

particularized indicia of reliability
specific details of the circumstances that make the evidence more likely to be true

past recollection recorded
process whereby the witness recalls the words he or she made in a statement but not the incident itself

pecuniary or proprietary interest
concerned with financial or ownership matters

penal interest
a matter that could result in the person's being incarcerated

person in authority
a person in a position to influence the prosecution against an accused

plain view doctrine
rule that a police officer may act without a search warrant if the evidence is in plain view

potential prejudice
the potential for a piece of proposed evidence to be misused (usually, given too much weight) by the trier of fact

prejudice
the potenial for a trier of fact to give evidence more weight than it deserves

present impression
a statement regarding a person's perception of their immediate physical surroundings or actions

present memory revived
process whereby the witness revives actual memories and details of an incident; cf. past recollection recorded

presumption
a fact that is taken to be true without the requirement of formal proof

***prima facie* case**
a case in which there is sufficient proof on its face that no further proof is required for a party to succeed

principled approach
method of applying rules of evidence by reference to the policy underlying the rules

principled exception
exception to the hearsay rule based on the principles of necessity and reliability

privilege
status accorded communicated information that makes the information unavailable to the trier of fact

privilege by case
privilege extended to communication on a case-by-case basis

privilege by class
privilege based on the relationship between the communicator of information and the recipient

probative value
the degree to which a potential piece of evidence helps prove a proposition; the value or strength of a fact in proving what the party seeks to establish

propensity evidence
evidence of an accused's past history or tendency to act in a certain way

public safety exception
an exception to privilege when the otherwise protected communication poses a threat to public safety

rape shield provisions
provisions in the *Criminal Code* that forbid the admission of evidence of a complainant's sexual history to support an inference that she is more likely to have given consent or is less worthy of belief

read into
a court's adding of language into legislation in order to make it comply with Charter provisions

real evidence
tangible evidence that is put before the trier of fact

reasonable expectation of privacy test
test used by the courts to determine whether a police search was lawful; considers whether the accused's expectation of privacy was reasonably held and whether the search was reasonable

reasoning prejudice
applies to evidence that, if admitted, may confuse the trier of fact or distract the trier of fact from the issue it must decide

rebut
to present opposing evidence or arguments

relevant fact
a fact that logically supports a proposition

res gestae or spontaneous statement
a statement made in an excited state or expressing an existing physical, mental, or emotional state

responsibility
the ability to comprehend the necessity of being truthful and the consequences for not telling the truth

reverse onus
situation where the obligation to prove a fact is shifted from the Crown to the accused

right against self-incrimination
a person's right not to be compelled to be a witness against himself in criminal or quasi-criminal proceedings

similar fact evidence
evidence that shows that an accused committed similar offences in the past, which may be admitted provided that it is relevant to establishing an important matter other than the accused's predisposition to commit that type of offence

solemn affirmation
promise to tell the truth in court that has the same value as an oath

solicitor–client privilege
privilege that protects communications between lawyer and client made for the purpose of obtaining legal advice

spoliation
the destruction, mutilation, alteration, or concealment of evidence

spousal privilege
privilege based on the spousal relationship that prevents one spouse from testifying against the other

subpoena
formal, legal document requiring a witness to appear at a hearing in a criminal case

summons
formal, legal document requiring a witness to appear at a hearing in a civil case

testimonial evidence
evidence provided by a person in the form of words

trier of fact
person in a trial who assesses the evidence and renders a verdict; in a jury trial, the jury

trier of law
person in a trial who controls the trial process, determines the admissibility of evidence, and instructs the trier of fact on the applicable law; in a jury trial, the judge

ultimate issue opinion
an opinion on the ultimate issue that is before the trier of fact; generally, witnesses are not permitted to give an ultimate issue opinion because the trier of fact could be swayed by it

Vetrovec warning
a warning to the jury given where the judge determines that the evidence of a particular witness is called into question and requires special scrutiny; the jurors are cautioned that they may accept the evidence without corroboration but it is dangerous to do so without independent confirmation of material parts of that evidence

vicarious admission
an admission made by an authorized speaker for a party

view

relocation of the court to the site of the alleged offence; a judge may order a view when the evidence is too large to bring into the courtroom or when there is a valid reason for the trier of fact to see the site

voir dire

a mini trial, or trial within a trial, that is designed to determine the admissibility of evidence in the absence of the trier of fact

Wigmore test

four criteria for assessing case-by-case claims of privilege

without prejudice

protection claimed for information provided by a party that prevents the information from being used in court

Index